Sex Changes

Psychoanalysis in a New Key Book Series
Volume 10

PSYCHOANALYSIS IN A NEW KEY BOOK SERIES
DONNEL B. STERN
Series Editor

When music is played in a new key, the melody does not change, but the notes that make up the composition do: change in the context of continuity, continuity that perseveres through change. "Psychoanalysis in a New Key" publishes books that share the aims psychoanalysts have always had, but that approach them differently. The books in the series are not expected to advance any particular theoretical agenda, although to this date most have been written by analysts from the Interpersonal and Relational orientations.

The most important contribution of a psychoanalytic book is the communication of something that nudges the reader's grasp of clinical theory and practice in an unexpected direction. "Psychoanalysis in a New Key" creates a deliberate focus on innovative and unsettling clinical thinking. Because that kind of thinking is encouraged by exploration of the sometimes surprising contributions to psychoanalysis of ideas and findings from other fields, "Psychoanalysis in a New Key" particularly encourages interdisciplinary studies. Books in the series have married psychoanalysis with dissociation, trauma theory, sociology, and criminology. The series is open to the consideration of studies examining the relationship between psychoanalysis and any other field – for instance, biology, literary and art criticism, philosophy, systems theory, anthropology, and political theory.

But innovation also takes place within the boundaries of psychoanalysis, and "Psychoanalysis in a New Key" therefore also presents work that reformulates thought and practice without leaving the precincts of the field. Books in the series focus, for example, on the significance of personal values in psychoanalytic practice, on the complex interrelationship between the analyst's clinical work and personal life, on the consequences for the clinical situation when patient and analyst are from different cultures, and on the need for psychoanalysts to accept the degree to which they knowingly satisfy their own wishes during treatment hours, often to the patient's detriment.

PSYCHOANALYSIS IN A NEW KEY BOOK SERIES
DONNEL B. STERN
Series Editor

Sex Changes

Transformations in Society
and Psychoanalysis

MARK J. BLECHNER

Routledge
Taylor & Francis Group

New York   London

Routledge
Taylor & Francis Group
270 Madison Avenue
New York, NY 10016

Routledge
Taylor & Francis Group
27 Church Road
Hove, East Sussex BN3 2FA

© 2009 by Mark J. Blechner

Printed in the United States of America on acid-free paper
10 9 8 7 6 5 4 3 2 1

International Standard Book Number-13: 978-0-415-99435-4 (Softcover) 978-0-415-99434-7 (Hardcover)

Library of Congress Cataloging-in-Publication Data

Blechner, Mark J.
   Sex changes : transformations in society and psychoanalysis / Mark J. Blechner.
      p. cm. -- (Psychoanalysis in a new key; 10)
   Includes bibliographical references and index.
   ISBN 978-0-415-99434-7 -- ISBN 978-0-415-99435-4
   1. Psychoanalysis and homosexuality. 2. Sex (Psychology) 3.
Homosexuality--Psychological aspects. 4. Gender identity--Psychological aspects.. I.
Title.

   RC451.4.G39B54 2008
   616.85'8306--dc22   2008032484

Visit the Taylor & Francis Web site at
http://www.taylorandfrancis.com

and the Routledge Web site at
http://www.routledgementalhealth.com

Dedicated to Christopher Warnke

*I can't understand why people are frightened of
new ideas. I'm frightened of old ones.*

John Cage

Contents

Acknowledgments

My first thanks go to Donnel Stern who, first as editor of the journal *Contemporary Psychonalysis* and then of the book series "Psychoanalysis in a New Key," encouraged and guided my work with discernment and enthusiasm. At Routledge Press, Kristopher Spring and Kate Hawes masterfully moved the book from manuscript into production. The entire manuscript was also read by Richard Gartner, Daniel Kozloff, William Hirst, Jane Bressler, Sandra Buechler, Ellen Cassedy, Jeffrey Blum, and Jennifer McCarroll. They each made unique, substantial suggestions, most of which I have followed, although whatever flaws remain are my responsibility alone. The late Erika Fromm, a tough critic and rigorous thinker, was my first mentor in psychoanalysis and especially sparked my work on the Rorschach with her own ideas. The late Stephen Mitchell, the great psychoanalyst who was more interested in ideas than being right, published my work even when it challenged him. Marylou Lionells, former director of the William Alanson White Institute, also supported me when I challenged her and helped me channel my ideas into real-world changes. I cannot give enough thanks to the Viceroys, a "gang" of colleagues with whom I have met weekly for 25 years and who have enriched my intellectual, personal, and professional life: Robert Watson, John O'Leary, Allison Rosen, Sandra Buechler, and Richard Gartner. Many others have contributed to the ideas in this book or supported my work in other ways: Sue Shapiro, Bertram Schaffner, Naoko Wake, James Marks, Michael Allen, Raul Ludmer, Lawrence Mass, Mark Adams Taylor, Alan Baer, Samuel Beck, Jerome Blake, Susan Casden, Ira Moses, Bertram Cohler, Phillip Cole, Ronald Grossman, Steven Hartman, John Silberman, Philippe Wahba, Jeremy White, Lee Bressler, Irwin Hirsch, Willa Cobert, Jonathan Ned Katz, Robert Benton, Conrad Cummings, Tyler Alpern, John E. Boswell, Alice Leiner, Tony Meola, Jack Morin, Ellis Perlswig, Scott Bressler, Martin Frommer, Ned Rorem, Phillip Blumberg, Adrienne Harris, Muriel Dimen, Sharon Radetsky Hampel, Amy Rubin, Benjamin Wolstein, Jack Drescher,

Cheryl Greenwood, Alan Zwiebel, Barbara Sevde, Carmen Castaneda, and Lucy Ramos. I am enormously grateful to my patients, who must remain anonymous, for giving me the opportunity to understand different ways of experiencing sex, gender, and living. My beloved parents, the late Hannah and Norbert Blechner, nurtured my development since the beginning and enjoined the struggles that needed to be faced. My vibrant partner-in-life, Christopher Warnke, has taught me more than anyone and stood beside me in times of crisis and triumph. It is to him that I dedicate this book.

Introduction

The latter half of the twentieth century and the beginning of the twenty-first have seen an enormous shift in social attitudes toward sex, gender, and sexuality—in society in general and in psychology, psychiatry, and psychoanalysis. Those of us who lived through this tumultuous time have been startled over and over.

In 1950, homosexuals were routinely arrested and publicly humiliated. Who at that time thought that any country or any American state would ratify gay marriage?

In 1950, psychoanalysis was primarily run by conservative men, while ambitious women were routinely told they had penis envy. Who at that time thought that women would come to outnumber men in the psychoanalytic profession, or that a woman, Hillary Clinton, would be a front-runner for president of the United States and that another woman, Sarah Palin, would be the Republican nominee for Vice President?

In 1950, interracial marriage was illegal in 30 states. Who at the time would have thought that the son of an interracial marriage, Barack Obama, would be elected president of the United States?

In 1950, homosexual men and women were routinely excluded from psychoanalytic training. Who at that time thought that organized psychoanalysis would seek out openly gay and lesbian analysts to help them understand sexuality?

On November 11, 1950 (five days after I was born), the pro-homosexual group, the Mattachine Society, was first organized by Harry Hay, and its members dared to declare their sexual orientation openly. Who at that time thought that some young people would think of those gay and lesbian pioneers as out-of-date, that "declaring" one's sexuality as gay or lesbian could be seen as old-fashioned, and that gender itself would become a questionable category? It is thrilling to be alive during a time when so many revolutionary changes have taken place, relatively peacefully.

I have thought and written about these issues for over 35 years. My interest has been scientific and personal. Changes in my life led to changes in my theory, and changes in my theory led to changes in my life. Some people write autobiographies; some publish volumes of their collected papers. In this book, I am going to blend the two forms. I am assembling my papers on sex, gender, sexuality, and prejudice. Before each paper, I describe the facts of my professional and personal life that intersected with the ideas in the paper. It is neither an exhaustive autobiography nor a compilation of all my papers, but rather a selected series of chapters that focus on changing views of sexuality.

I want to chronicle these momentous changes that took place in such a relatively short amount of time. We need to consider: How could so much harm be done to people who pose no real threat to the well-being of others? How could psychoanalysts go so awry in their views? How might other benighted attitudes be affecting psychiatry and psychoanalysis today? Which groups are still suffering under the pathologizing gaze of organized medicine? And could we ever go back? Might we ever again see increased persecution by psychiatry and psychoanalysis of gay, lesbian, bisexual, transgendered, intersex, and other people who differ from society's view of what is "standard and normal"? Might we see a recrudescence of discrimination against women by men? How can we restore the position of psychoanalysis to the cutting edge of progressive thinking on gender and sexuality?

The professional articles in this book span a time period starting in 1972, when the psychoanalytic world was still very homophobic, and extending through nearly four decades of change in psychoanalysis, culture, and society. The first paper is from a time when a man could be arrested for having sex with another man. The most recent paper is from a time when two men or two women can marry in The Netherlands, Spain, Belgium, Canada, South Africa, Massachusetts, California,* and Connecticut.

Beginnings

At the start of my life, in 1950, the worlds of psychoanalysis and homosexuality had a dreadful relationship. Psychoanalysis in America had

---

* On November 4, 2008, Californians voted for a constitutional amendment that defined marriage as between one man and one woman. This effectively stopped further same-sex marriages and put into question the status of same-sex marriages from before the amendment.

decided for the most part to consider homosexuality a disease, one that psychoanalysts claimed to be able to cure. Many homosexuals, for their part, believed psychoanalysts' promise to help them to change their sexual orientation and fit into a conformist society. Most people in those days wanted to fit in. If you wanted to be happy, you had to be normal. Stephen Sondheim captured this ethic, even while he satirized it, in his lyrics for *West Side Story* (which I learned by heart):

> (The group sings):
> Dear Officer Krupke
> You're really a square.
> This boy don't need a job
> He needs an analyst's care.
> Society's played him a terrible trick
> And sociologically he's sick.
> > (One of the group continues):
> > My father is a bastard
> > My ma's an S.O.B.
> > My grandpa's always plastered
> > My grandma pushes tea
> > My sister wears a moustache
> > My brother wears a dress
> > Goodness gracious, that's why I'm a mess.

If you didn't conform to your proper gender role, you were bad, crazy, ridiculous, or all three. I remember being told by one of my friends that I held my schoolbooks like a girl, with my elbow bent and my arm against my chest. Boys, he told me, were supposed to hold their books at their side, balanced in their fingertips at the end of a straight arm. Today, it seems like a silly convention, but in those days it seemed to be one of the keys to happiness. I practiced and practiced, and I learned to carry my books the "right way" from then on.

I first read Freud in 1965. His *Introductory Lectures on Psycho-analysis* (Freud, 1916–1917) were assigned as summer reading in my high school, and I was hooked immediately. I was captured by Freud's idea that the things we do are motivated by drives and wishes that are out of our awareness. It was such an exciting idea then, and it still is. We think we know who we are and what we want, but there is much more going on in our lives than we can imagine. We think we are rational human beings, but much of our thinking is irrational, and we are constantly avoiding and distorting information that threatens us.

In retrospect, I think that Freud's view of human nature had a very personal resonance for me. In those days, I was not conscious of being gay, or at least I never labeled any of my feelings that way, but I probably realized on some level that I was having emotional and maybe sexual attractions whose true nature was unconscious to me. I knew that somehow I was different, but I never gave a name to it. My life was split between what I was feeling and what I thought I was supposed to feel. So while I looked lovingly into my best friend's eyes, we talked about which girls we liked and how we might get them to go out with us.

I started recording all the dreams I remembered and tried to analyze them using Freud's approach. I learned how important it was to record your dreams, and to analyze them not just once, but to go back to them after 10, 20, or more years. You can learn things from your old dreams that you just cannot learn when they are new. Repression is too powerful a force. As Emily Dickinson wrote: "The Mind is so near itself/it cannot see, distinctly/and I have none to ask" (Dommermuth-Costa, 1998, p. 70). As time passes, though, the mind can start to see its old self more clearly.

I remember a dream from when I was seven years old, in which I helped out the most popular boy in my class. My help looked innocent enough, but it involved a lot of body contact. I recognize today that I had a crush on him, although if you had told me that back then, I am sure I would have denied it.

When I was 19, a man I disliked appeared in my dream in a frilly dress. I used Freud's technique of writing down your associations to every element of the dream, and that led me quickly to the interpretation of the dream as a way to ridicule him. I did not yet know Jung's alternative approach to dreams—that everyone in the dream is an aspect of the dreamer—which would have meant that the man in the dress was also an aspect of myself that I was ridiculing. Nor did I consciously connect it to the line from *West Side Story*: "My sister wears a moustache/My brother wears a dress," but our dream images bring together things that we have dissociated, things that we don't know that we know (Blechner, 2001, 2005d).

When I was in college at the University of Chicago, there were no undergraduate courses given about psychoanalysis. In fact, many of the psychologists-researchers who dominated the psychology department made fun of psychoanalysts. Robert McCleary, a pioneering neurobiologist and an expert on subcortical mechanisms of behavior, gave me the chance to work in his laboratory on a study of the hippocampus and memory in cats, which was a great opportunity, but he was hostile to psychoanalysis. His idea of a good joke was to say to one of his colleagues, with a mock, highly empathic tone, "How do you FEEL about that?" and then they all would burst out laughing.

There was a psychoanalyst in the psychology department, Erika Fromm, but she taught only graduate courses. Each trimester, I looked at the course catalogue and imagined registering for one of her courses, which seemed delectable but out of reach. It took quite a while, but I finally worked up the nerve to call her and ask to take her graduate course on "Ego Psychology" as an undergraduate. She said she had never admitted an undergraduate into her courses, but she invited me to come speak to her about this in her office.

I was thrilled. The day came; my heart was pounding as I climbed the stairs to her third-floor office. Erika Fromm sat imposingly behind her desk; she had a large head, what I think could be called a "handsome" face—powerful features, erect posture, a strong German accent, thick blond hair in perfect order, a severe and commanding presence. All of this could also describe my maternal grandmother, so in some way I felt immediately at home.

She asked me about my interest in psychoanalysis and what I had already read. I had already read not just Sigmund Freud, but also Anna Freud, Charles Brenner, and other contemporary psychoanalysts. I told her I wanted to be a psychoanalyst, and I was not learning what I needed in my courses. She finally told me she would let me register for her course, reminding me several times that she had never let an undergraduate do so before, and that I would be carefully watched. That was fine with me. It felt like a miracle just to have been admitted into her course.

This was the heyday of ego psychology, when positivism ruled and Freud's concepts and models of the mind were taken literally. We drew diagrams of the id, ego, and superego that looked like plumbing plans. Erika spoke of the ego as if it were a real thing, and we read and wrote papers about how the ego was related to the id and superego, and, Erika's favorite, how the ego was related to "reality." Reality was not put in quotation marks as I just did. Reality existed in those days in a way that would shock today's post-modernists, and the ego had to accommodate that reality. Of course this was very relevant to me: The reality of the world at that time made homosexuality a sin, a crime, and a sickness, but that was where my id was taking me, so what was my ego to do?

I then also found another psychologist-psychoanalyst at the university. Philip Holzman was ensconced in the psychiatry department, where he taught a course on schizophrenia. He was already interested in whether there were neurological differences in how schizophrenics perceived the world, differences that might be inherited through genetics—an idea that eventually led to his discovering (Holzman, Proctor, & Hughes, 1973) or rediscovering (Diefendorff & Dodge, 1908) the pathology of eye movements in schizophrenics and their relatives. I decided to try to take Holzman's course in the psychiatry department, too. It seemed like a stretch, but by now I already had the credential of taking one of Erika Fromm's graduate courses, which gave me more courage.

So I called Holzman. Again, I was invited to come to his office to talk about my wish to take his course. He mentioned during that telephone conversation a book he had recently published, *Psychoanalysis and Psychopathology* (1970), so I decided to read it before meeting with him. It was not an easy book to get. I checked with bookstores all over Chicago, until I finally found one on the North Side that had a copy. I read it cover to cover in the few days I had before the interview.

Holzman was a balding man with a kindly face. His speech was calm and thoughtful. You got the sense that he was always thinking very seriously about something; there was no small talk. The analysts in those days were the smartest people, or so it seemed to me. I mentioned to him that I had read his book. He said, "How did you find my book?" I replied, "Oh, it was very difficult. I called all over town and finally had to go all the way to the North Side to get a copy." It was only after the interview that I realized that he meant, "How did you find my book?" in the sense of "What did you think of my book?" What a humiliating mix-up! I thought, "He'll never take me into his course; he probably thinks I'm psychotic myself."*

Holzman let me into his course; my error apparently did not ruin my chances. His course was thrilling. He did not want us just to read about schizophrenia; he wanted us to see and experience it firsthand in all its forms. For that, he sent us on weekly visits to the back wards of the Illinois State Psychiatric Institute with patients who had been hospitalized for years or decades. There, you could still see the old pre-medication syndromes like "word salad," where patients utter mixed-up jumbles of words that seem to have no meaning. I learned something very important from those visits: No matter how seemingly degenerated the thinking of a longtime schizophrenic, there were glimmers of rational thought if you were willing to hear them. Some patients who seemed mostly involved in their own fantasy worlds occasionally showed remarkable concern for me and my interest in what they were saying (Blechner, 1995e).

For example, one elderly man told me he was a member of a delegation from outer space. I found his story to be fascinating and asked him many

---

* It was like the famous joke that Freud (1905b) discusses in his book, *Jokes and their Relation to the Unconscious*: Two Jews met in the neighborhood of the bath-house. "Have you taken a bath?" asked one of them. "What?" asked the other in return, "Is there one missing?"

detailed questions about his mission. He answered my questions, more or less, sounding crazier and crazier, but in the midst of this stream of words I heard "Don't believe a thing I tell you" uttered without pause or demarcation, just part of the string of what he was saying, and then he went on to tell me that he was here as a Moslem specializing in circumcision. But I had heard his message.

In much of the twentieth century, psychiatry was influenced by Freud's idea that paranoia and paranoid schizophrenia were caused by unacceptable homosexual impulses. The idea was that a person defensively transformed his love for another man. "I love him," became "I hate him," which then became "he hates me." Yet in an entire course on schizophrenia, I don't think Holzman gave much attention to this hypothesis. He was a man who was more interested in data than theories.

I did well in the courses, and my reward was being allowed to take Erika Fromm's other courses, one on "Dream Interpretation" and another on "Clinical Hypnosis," of which Erika was one of the world experts. Working with her and Phil Holzman made it clear to me that my path in psychology would be through psychoanalysis. At that time, my professional aims did not seem daunted by the prevalent hostility to gay people in psychoanalysis.

Section I

Psychoanalysis, Sexuality, and Prejudice

1

Homosexuality and the Rorschach Test

Reality is what refuses to go away when you do not believe in it.

Philip K. Dick

In the mid-twentieth century, most clinical psychologists learned how to administer and analyze the Rorschach inkblot test. Originally developed in Switzerland by Hermann Rorschach, the test is used to diagnose personality and psychopathology. It is a *projective test*. The patient looks at a series of 10 ink blots and tells the psychologist what he sees (projects). The psychologist can then analyze the patient's responses to look for many things—including which issues are troubling him, how accurately he perceives the world, and what kinds of themes or emotions throw him off track. In 1972, I took a graduate class at the University of Chicago on the Rorschach from Samuel Beck, one of the acknowledged masters of the test.

Beck was quite old by then; he was a professor emeritus and came to class wearing slippers. It was clear that he was a kind and well-meaning man who had devoted his life to the Rorschach. It was also clear that he considered homosexuality to be pathological, as did most clinicians of his generation. He mentioned in passing some signs on the Rorschach of homosexuality. This piqued my interest; most of those signs were not on my own responses to the Rorschach test, which I had taken before the course. How valid were they? When it came time to do a paper for the course, I decided to research and summarize the available literature on the Rorschach test and homosexuality, thus continuing my library research into what people knew or thought they knew about homosexuality. I also planned to collect my own data on the subject.* The paper was my first step out of the closet professionally, at the age of 22. I considered that some people might wonder why I was so interested in this topic. No one asked me outright.

This was three years after the Stonewall rebellion. Gay liberation had come to the University of Chicago. The first gay and lesbian dance was held in one of the dormitories. In line with the progressive nature of the time, groups of gays and lesbians from the university picketed several gay bars in town that refused admission to Blacks and got the bars to change their policy.†

Openness to gay and lesbian rights had not yet spread into mainstream psychiatry. In the three decades from the 1940s to the 1960s, one of the hottest topics in Rorschach research was the diagnosis of homosexuality. My paper, besides summarizing the research literature, also captured the sensibility of psychiatry and psychology at the time: Homosexuality was viewed as pathological, an illness that needed treatment. I could not find a single study until 1957 that questioned that assumption. While I was collecting the data, I kept wondering how these articles were being used; who was trying to find out who was gay or lesbian, and what did they do with the supposed information once they got it? Many of the studies were done during the McCarthy era and seemed tainted by it; were the studies of homosexual signs on the Rorschach going to be used to root gay people out of the government?‡

I felt it to be important to question the prejudicial assumptions of much of the Rorschach research. And yet, I now realize that I was taking a cautious intermediary position, between challenging and accepting the attitude of the time. I accepted, at least in my words, that homosexuality was something to "diagnose," yet I had already begun to question whether homosexuality was psychopathology or merely an aspect of a person's life.

---

* There was another reason for my interest that I only realized as I was writing this book. My parents were great believers in graphology. When I was nine, a woman was interviewed by my parents to become our housekeeper. I liked her tremendously, and so did everyone else, but my mother sent a sample of the young woman's handwriting to a graphologist. The graphologist's report stated that the handwriting was that of a lesbian, and so she was not hired. I did not really understand then what lesbian meant, but I knew it was considered something bad. My parents feared that she would have seduced the children, at least my sisters. Instead, a heterosexual woman took the job. She, it turned out, had been a prostitute, and late one night she packed her suitcase and was whisked off in a stretch limousine, never to return. When as an adult I read about the "signs" of homosexuality on the Rorschach, it must have connected unconsciously with the "signs" of homosexuality in people's handwriting.

† The joint fight against racism and homophobia was an admirable alliance that is less alive today.

‡ Peter Hegarty (2003) notes, in hindsight, that the two main purposes were the rooting out of gay people from the military and the government.

It is also quite astonishing, in retrospect, how many psychoanalysts who are prominent today were publishing articles about diagnosing homosexuality with the Rorschach, notably Martin Bergmann, an expert on Freud; Otto Kernberg, the most prominent diagnostician of the twentieth century; and Roy Schafer, one of the best-known American-born psychoanalysts. Many of them continued to pathologize homosexuality for years,* although some have admitted more recently, in print or otherwise, that the therapeutic attempt to change the supposed psychopathology of homosexuality has caused a good deal of suffering (Schafer, 1995; McDougall, 2001; Kernberg, 2002).

It is also impressive how frequent was the finding that gender identity confusion was no more common in gay men and lesbians than heterosexuals. In fact, in a study of nonpatients (Hooker, 1958), gender identity confusion was *more* common in heterosexuals. This fact should have made psychoanalysts aware that sexual orientation and sexual identity can be quite independent, but the cultural stereotype, of the gay man as feminine and confused about gender, has been slow to yield its influence on professional thinking. In 2000, when I led a seminar entitled "Talking About Sexual Orientation in Psychoanalytic Supervision," a psychoanalytic supervisor told me that she knew that her feminine-acting male student was gay, no matter what *he* thought (see Chapter 8, "Maleness and Masculinity").

My paper on "Homosexuality and the Rorschach" demonstrated an important basic principle: It is possible, under the guise of science, to get data to support a falsehood. But if you bring in good data from well-controlled studies, science is vindicated, and old, faulty beliefs fall away. This was achieved by Evelyn Hooker, who conducted a brilliant study. Hooker collected Rorschach records of people who were not psychiatric patients. She then sent pairs of records, one from a straight person and one from a gay person, who were matched for age, intelligence, and other factors, to famous Rorschach experts and asked them to judge who was straight and who was gay. The experts couldn't do it; their judgments were no better than chance. Exasperated, one of them said to her, "These are so similar that you are out to skin us alive."

After writing the paper and reviewing all the literature, I was serious and earnest about the possibilities of objective research and planned to conduct a big Rorschach study. However, I had second thoughts the

---

* Martin Bergmann (1987) asked, without irony, "Can homosexuals love?" and answered in the negative.

next year, when the American Psychiatric Association decided no longer to consider homosexuality as a psychopathology. As one gay physician quipped: "The Board's vote made millions of Americans who had been officially ill that morning officially well that afternoon. Never before in history had so many people been cured in so little time."* With such a fundamental shift in psychodiagnosis, many of us realized how we had been caught up, overtly or implicitly, in the presumption that there was something pathological about homosexuality that needed diagnosing. So I set aside any plans to study further the Rorschach and homosexuality, realizing I needed to rethink the fundamental conceptions of psychoanalysis, psychopathology, and homosexuality before I could speak and write about them with any confidence.

I rethought for 20 years.

---

* In 2002, when the Supreme Court ruled that sodomy was legal throughout the United States, one could say that "Millions of people who that morning had been criminals were upstanding citizens that afternoon." Through changes in society, gay men and lesbians went from being sick criminals to healthy criminals to upstanding people.

2
Psychoanalysis In and Out of the Closet

Author's Introduction

I did not write about sexuality during the late 1970s and the 1980s, but I was actively thinking about it, working on it, and living it. And reading about it—in those days, a few landmarks of gay scholarship shook the world like earthquakes, or so it seemed to me. One of the first was *Gay American History*, published by Jonathan Ned Katz in 1978. Just the title was a landmark—no coyness, no secrecy, a title revolutionary for its plainness. I devoured its pages, which to me yielded one revelation after another.

What was life like for gay men and lesbians throughout American history? Jonathan Katz unearthed documents. Now we knew that in pre-revolution America Thomas Jefferson recommended that sodomy be punished by castration instead of death, a progressive proposal at the time. Now we knew that Lincoln was probably attracted to men. Now we knew that President James Buchanan and his longtime partner, William Rufus De Vane King, were called, respectively, Aunt Fancy and Miss Nancy. Now we knew that Native Americans were relatively tolerant of homosexuality and transgender behavior, until Christian European invaders attempted to change those traditions. Now we knew that medicine had tried to cure homosexuality in the twentieth century using shock treatments. I turned those 1063 pages, and devoured all those facts. Most important, the book implicitly stated, "These gays and lesbians of the past were real people. Major things were done by them and happened to them. Attention must be paid."

If you deny a group its history, you deny its identity. Think of what it means to say: "Columbus discovered America." If he did, what were the Native Americans doing all those centuries? The implication is that they *were not people*, but Columbus and his shipmates *were people*. A Mohawk woman once told me that her grandmother

said, "Columbus discovered America? When he landed, my ances-
tors were on the beach to greet him!" That is the essence of most
prejudice—in words and deeds, the very identity of the minority
group is denied its existence as present, living humans. In rural
Poland in 1945, a child asked: "Mommy, was it a human being that
was killed or a Jew?" (Franklin, 2006, p. 37). And during the era
of American slavery, slaves were considered property, not people.
The runaway slave, Margaret Garner, on being recaptured, killed her
daughter so she would not have to live a life of slavery. At her trial,
there was a debate about whether she should be accused of murder
or merely destruction of property.

In graduate school at Yale, I became friends with Bill Sutherland,
a chemistry post-doc who had done his graduate work at the
Massachusetts Institute of Technology (MIT). Bill and I were both
gay, but we had many differences. Bill was of Scottish descent, and
he was very conscious of who was a "Jewish fellow." We broke the
ice by giving each other nicknames. He called me McBlechner, and
I called him Sutherlandstein.

Bill told me that in Boston there was great excitement about John
E. Boswell, an openly gay history scholar who was finishing his dissertation about minorities at Harvard. Shortly afterward, Boswell
came to Yale, and I got to know him during my last two years there.
All his friends called him "Jeb," a nickname formed from his initials.

Jeb was the perfect historian. He knew Arabic, Hebrew, Greek,
Catalan, Turkish, and many other languages. He spoke in long, sin-
ewy sentences, beautifully formed. I often thought that talking with
Jeb was like talking with Socrates. His knowledge seemed endless,
and his reasoning was captivating. He had original ideas about
almost any subject I brought up, and his ideas were always backed
up by facts.

The first time I was at Jeb's apartment, his lover, Jerry Hart, was
lying on the floor. He had hurt his back and lay on the floor the
whole evening. Jerry was from a blue-collar background, as different from Jeb as one could imagine. They were an odd mix, but I
was learning that no one can gainsay what works in another person's marriage.

Each of Jeb's books was an event that shook my universe. He
gained wide notice in 1980 with the publication of *Christianity, Social
Tolerance and Homosexuality: Gay People in Western Europe from
the Beginning of the Christian Era to the Fourteenth Century*. Most
people had presumed that the Catholic Church had always been
bigoted against homosexuality, but Jeb showed us that there were
times when homosexuality was accepted by the church. Although I

was not Catholic, Jeb's book changed my view of the world. Besides the facts about Christian civilization, it implied a larger point. If you study the facts, you may find that people may be quite wrong when they assume things have always been as they are today. Historians are vital in this way to civil rights struggles. In 2003, attorneys for the state of Texas argued in the Supreme Court that laws against sodomy should be maintained, since such sexual relations had always been condemned in Western society. But historian George Chauncy proved that assumption wrong, and his arguments were one of the main reasons the court struck down laws against sodomy.

Jeb went even further with his book, *Same-Sex Unions in Premodern Europe* (1994), which showed that there were early forms of same-sex marriage sanctioned by certain monasteries. If the medieval church allowed sanctified relations between same-sex couples, why couldn't modern society, too? I was aware myself that such rites did not only happen in the Middle Ages. One of my closest friends at Yale, a Protestant graduate student, was romantically involved with the priest of a European Catholic church. They spent the summers living together in the tower of the cathedral. One night, at 2 a.m., they held an improvised marriage/commitment ceremony in the chapel of the church. The priest eventually moved to the United States, and they are still together, 35 years later.

In 1986, I was invited to join a study group entitled "Psychoanalysis and Sexual Difference" at the New York University (NYU) Institute for the Humanities. It was started by four feminist psychoanalysts who were interested in rethinking ideas about gender and sexuality. There were about 30 women in the group and 3 men. One of the other men, to my delight, was Jonathan Katz! Here was the man whose book had taught me so much. We became friends, although we argued constantly. I had never considered myself an essentialist, but next to Jonathan, I was. He was convinced that most categories of knowledge were constructed by human civilization, and I held onto the belief, which Jonathan considered outmoded, that some categories were based on essential characteristics of things. Homosexuality and heterosexuality themselves, Jonathan argued, were arbitrary categories that were created. He wrote a book entitled *The Invention of Heterosexuality*. Next to him, I felt like the last of the British empiricists.

The NYU group was thrilling, but it taught me a new way to experience prejudice. I was a gay man, but I was nevertheless a man in the group. One day, one of the group leaders was speaking about "them." I was having trouble understanding what she meant by "them," until I suddenly realized that "them" meant "men." She was talking about them, about men, as if none of them were in the room. There were three of us there, but for an instant I felt as if I had been erased from the world.

A major strategy against prejudice is not to allow oneself to be erased, by speaking up and making one's presence inerasable. Jonathan Katz did that for the gays of the past, showing that they were there, they were people, and good ones to boot. The same thing needed to be done in the profession of psychiatry, too. At the hearings at the American Psychiatric Association (APA) in the early 1970s about whether homosexuality should be a diagnosable disease, there could be no better source of data than a gay psychiatrist. There certainly were gay psychiatrists, but which gay psychiatrist would dare speak up in public about it? The job of testifying was finally taken up by Dr. John Fryer, a courageous iconoclast. In May of 1972, Fryer stood before the APA, wearing a mask. In a disguised voice, he described his painful experiences as a gay psychiatrist, of being expelled from a residency program and fired from jobs. Fryer said:

> We homosexual psychiatrists must persistently deal with a variety of what we shall call "Nigger Syndromes."…As psychiatrists who are homosexual, we must know our place and what we must do to be successful. If our goal is academic appointment, a level of earning capacity equal to our fellows, or admission to a psychoanalytic institute, we must make certain that no one in a position of power is aware of our sexual orientation or gender identity. Much like the black man with the light skin who chooses to live as a white man, we cannot be seen with our real friends—our real homosexual family—lest our secret be known and our dooms sealed. There are practicing psychoanalysts among us who have completed their training analysis without mentioning their homosexuality to their analysts. Those who are willing to speak up openly will do so only if they have nothing to lose, then they won't be listened to.…Just as the black man must be a super person, so must we, in order to face those among our colleagues who know we are gay.…as homosexual psychiatrists, we seem to present a unique ability to marry ourselves to institutions rather than wives or lovers. Many of us work twenty hours daily to protect institutions that would literally chew us up and spit us out if they knew the truth. (Scasta, 2002, p. 80–81)

Fryer's testimony shook the audience; many of them had never actually spoken to an openly gay psychiatrist.

There was also progress in understanding the presence of homosexuality not just in humans, but throughout the animal kingdom. One of the main arguments about homosexuality involved its naturalness. The word "unnatural" was just a step away from "pathological" if you were a clinician or "sinful" if you were a theologian. So it was very exciting when each discovery of homosexuality in animals was publicized. The news that male and female homosexuality were common in chimpanzees was intriguing, but chimpanzees were relatively close to humans. Imagine the excitement when, in 1977, the journal *Science* published an article that found lesbian seagulls (Hunt and Hunt, 1977). Each year brought more and more findings of homosexuality in the animal world. It was starting to become clear that same-sex pairings had long been observed by biologists, but they had been dismissed or ignored. Even gay animals could be denied their identity! In 1999, Bruce Bagemihl summarized the research in his book *Biological Exuberance: Animal Homosexuality and Natural Diversity*. The conclusion was inescapable: Homosexuality was found in most forms of the animal world, from dolphins to spiders, from elephants to fruit flies.*

I gradually discovered that homosexuality was prevalent not only in most kinds of animals, but also in most kinds of people. I had started in childhood with the idea that all gay men were hairdressers or interior designers. As an adult in the 1970s and 1980s, each year brought a thrilling revelation of a gay person in a different field. There was often a pattern: a rumor, a report that someone trustworthy knew that so-and-so was gay, and then a gradual outing process. At a party I would hear: "There is a gay reporter working at the *New York Times*. His name is David Dunlap." I would hear that five or six more times, and then it would morph into: "They found out at the *Times* that he's gay." Then there would be a confrontation: Would the bosses fire him, or would they change their attitudes? When the organization changed, there was a sigh of relief among many gay people—one more small notch toward normalization, toward sexual orientation just not being a big deal. And then organization: Dunlap formed a group of gay journalists.

It happened in one field after another. David Kopay (1977) wrote his book about being gay in professional football. Of course, if there was one person in professional sports who announced that he was gay, there probably were many more still in hiding. Soon we knew about Martina Navratilova and Billie Jean King, the famous tennis stars who happened to be lesbians.

---

* In 2006–2007, the Natural History Museum at the University of Oslo in Norway organized "Against Nature?—An Exhibition on Animal Homosexuality." It demonstrated the ubiquity of homosexuality in the animal world, concluding that it is simply false to claim that homosexuality is unnatural. The exhibit was exceptional, but the most striking thing about it for me was that many of the people attending it were Norwegian heterosexual couples with young children. The organizers of the exhibit offered to bring it to New York, but the American Museum of Natural History turned them down.

Each one of these professional "outings" made it easier for the next generation. The great British actor Ian McKellen announced that he was gay; his career was not destroyed, and eventually he was knighted. The same happened with the singer Elton John.

For me, the role model of how to be a gay psychoanalyst with dignity was Dr. Bertram Schaffner, whom I met in 1981. I was two years into my psychoanalytic training at the William Alanson White Institute for Psychiatry, Psychoanalysis, and Psychology in New York. As part of my training, I needed a psychotherapy supervisor, and I was sent to Bert, at the time the only openly gay psychoanalyst at the White Institute (and, for that matter, probably the most openly gay psychoanalyst in the world). My being assigned to Bert was, I believe, not a coincidence, although no one acknowledged it.

Bert had been an openly gay candidate at the White Institute from 1949 to 1953. It is amazing to think how courageous Bert was back then, when not only psychoanalysis was homophobic, but Senator McCarthy was scaring the nation about Commies and perverts. It was the clinical custom of the time for an analyst to encourage a gay patient to pursue heterosexual relationships. Bert had planned to fly to Europe to become engaged to a woman he knew there. He feared that otherwise he would not be able to have a psychiatric practice, and he knew that his analyst was pleased about the engagement. However, he had a dream in which he was in an airplane that had no roof and was flying upside down. He realized the dream's message and felt that his plans violated his core sense of being and mental health. He canceled the trip and changed psychiatrists (Schaffner, 1995).

Bert's office was in his apartment on Central Park South. He was a great collector of Indian antiquities. He bought up Indian terra-cotta sculptures at a time when they were considered insignificant and worthless. Eventually he amassed one of the most significant collections, which he donated to the Brooklyn Museum. When you walked into his apartment, you were transported to a world of Indian deities, hundreds of them. The living room was also filled with chairs and couches, more than most interior decorators would allow, but it provided a warm and comfortable locale for meetings, and Bert loved to host meetings in his apartment, which became in my mind "Gay Psychiatry Central."

Bert was a superb supervisor. He was especially attuned to cultural differences, and we mainly discussed my work with a heterosexual woman from South America.

When I first met Bert, he wore a light brown toupee, which jutted out an unnatural distance from his forehead. He looked like an old young man. One day, I came into supervision, and sitting there was a distinguished-looking gentleman with thin gray hair neatly brushed back. It was Bert! I hardly recognized him without the toupee, but that was his look from then on.

A few months later, I went into Bert's office and noticed on his desk an announcement of the first meeting of GPNY, a new organization of gay psychiatrists in New York. I asked Bert about it with studied casualness, and he answered me equally straight-faced, saying that the first meeting would take place soon in his apartment. He added, "You're welcome to attend." Thus, we came out to one another.

When I started working with Bert, he was about 67 years old. He already had had a brilliant career. He had entered college at Harvard when he was 16. After the Second World War, as an army psychiatrist, he had studied the roots of German authoritarianism, which he published in a book entitled *Fatherland* (Schaffner, 1948). He had collaborated with Margaret Mead in cross-cultural studies, and he had spearheaded a program of psychiatric services in the Caribbean. Yet he had never been fully accepted by his White Institute colleagues. He was always grateful that they had accepted him for training as an openly gay man, but he felt hurt that he had been bypassed for promotion and that his institute colleagues rarely referred patients to him, and usually only gay men.

Bert told me that if I became completely open about my homosexuality, I would probably receive only gay referrals. That did not turn out to be true for me, although I took his warning seriously. People who knew and respected my work sent me male and female heterosexual patients, although I am sure some colleagues may have thought twice about it. (A woman who was a college friend once said, "Well, of course, no one is going to send a man and woman to you for marriage counseling!" —which also was not true, but I appreciated her candor in telling me that *she* would not.)

We were all very excited about the prospects of change in the mental health world concerning homosexuality. In 1973, the American Psychiatric Association had removed homosexuality from the *Diagnostic and Statistical Manual* (DSM-III), which was the bible of psychiatric diagnosis. The change had been bitterly opposed by most psychoanalysts, and you could still hear the homophobic murmurings of many analysts, even at the relatively progressive White Institute. The first year of my training, I heard one of my teachers brag about having cured a "cruising homosexual." He told us that, contrary to his usual practice, he attended his patient's wedding. I thought, but did not say, "Was it to make sure he went through with it? And how is he doing now?"

I already was seeing in my practice people who had been through such "cures" and now were agonizing over what to do with their homosexual wishes. They usually were stuck between a wish not to hurt their wives and children, whom they sincerely loved, and the impossibility of suppressing the bulk of their sexuality, which still was driving them toward members of their own sex. They knew they had been strongly influenced but not cured, and they were furious at the practitioners who had pushed them into the painful situation of being gay and married to someone of the opposite sex.*

At professional meetings, you still could hear psychoanalysts railing against homosexuality. Otto Kernberg, the inveterate diagnostician, wrote of different kinds of homosexuals, such as homosexual narcissists and homosexual borderline patients. Always, there was the implication that their homosexuality was part and parcel of their psychopathology.

A particularly significant meeting was held at the New York Academy of Medicine on April 6, 1976, which featured a panel of supposed experts on homosexuality, including Irving Bieber, Lionel Ovesey, and Charles Socarides, who had written books about the causes and treatment of homosexuality.† In the audience (and, it turned out, in some of the stairwells) were gay activists, and they were prepared for the challenge. They asked why there were no openly gay people on the panel. They disrupted the meeting. It was thrilling. You could feel it; the days of psychoanalytic homophobia were numbered.

In the early 1990s, Dr. Barbara Gerson, a colleague at New York University, told me that she was planning to edit a book with the title *The Therapist as a Person: Life Crises, Life Choices, Life Experiences, and Their Effects on Treatment,* in which different psychoanalysts would write about how their personal lives affected the way they worked clinically. She asked if I would write a chapter for her about being gay and how it affected my work as a psychoanalyst. I accepted the invitation and quickly set to work on the chapter. To my surprise, it was the most effortless piece of writing I ever did. It poured out of me, as if it had already been written. It seemed as if I had been writing it unconsciously for years.

It also turned out to be one of my most popular written works. I received calls and letters from dozens of people. Gay people said

---

* Whitney (1990) has published an excellent study of women married to gay men.
† I had already heard from a friend that Socarides' son Richard was gay, but I was, at the time, sworn to secrecy. It became public knowledge years later (Nagourney, 1995). It was significant primarily because Socarides asserted that homosexuality was caused by faulty parenting. It later emerged that *two* of his sons are gay.

it gave them courage. Straight people, especially straight psycho-analysts, said it gave them insight into how the world is prejudiced, how they themselves are prejudiced, and how such prejudice causes damage. Parents told me it helped them understand what their gay children were facing and how they might help them better. Here is the chapter. I have updated the text with several footnotes.

Psychoanalysis In and Out of the Closet*

I would like in this chapter to do a number of things. I wish first to sum-marize my own growing awareness of my homosexual feelings, their role in my development, and the integration of my own homosexuality into my personal and professional life. This indulgence in autobiography is not so common in psychoanalytic writing. I do so here, not because I find my life so fascinating, but because it shows some of the major psychological hurdles faced by a gay or lesbian person growing up in our society. It is my hope that I can sensitize and educate heterosexual readers to the special problems gay people face. In all of my training, I was never once taught about such issues, neither in coursework nor in supervision, and this may be true of many readers. A lack of such knowledge may lead therapists to be unhelpful or even destructive to their gay patients, as Isay (1991) has noted. I would also like to consider how the mores of society have changed over the last four decades and the effect of those changes on psychoan-alytic practice. Finally, I would like then to address how these changes in society and my own personal development can interact with patient dynamics and affect the course and outcome of clinical work.

I would like to start with a fact that may seem so obvious that it can be taken for granted. All of us need role models, which allow us to form goals and ideals that guide our lives. The heterosexual world is so filled with role models that people can pick out models that are most conducive to them. For gay people, it has not been so easy. The tyranny of the closet is that it hides, from young lesbians and gay men, the broad range of lesbian

---

* Originally published as a chapter in Gerson, B. (1996). *The Therapist as a Person: Life Crises, Life Choices, Life Experiences and Their Effects on Treatment*. Hillsdale, NJ: Analytic Press, pp. 223–239.

and gay adults who have led fulfilling lives.* When I was 15, I had my first summer job in Manhattan. It was at a data processing company, and I was becoming gradually more aware of my attraction to men. At the company, there was one obviously gay person. He was loud and nasty, and would refer to men with women's names. He had a clerical job that was going nowhere, and he was bitter. I remember thinking, "Is this what life is like if you are gay?" Unfortunately, at that time, people did not talk frankly to teenagers about homosexuality; there were usually only furtive remarks, usually with a tone of disdain, statements like "All homosexuals are hair-dressers or interior decorators." Since I had no talent in either area, what would become of me?

In the mid-1960s, I had dear friends in high school with whom I shared many interests, and who, I now know, were gay, too, but we never spoke about it. But others saw it. My close friend Roger and I were inseparable. One day, the biology teacher threw a baseball at us during class and said, "Blechner, do you go home and wash Roger's back at night?" The meaning was obvious, but, dissociation being what it is, I only vaguely apprehended that he was suggesting Roger and I were having a physical affair. And since we weren't, surely we weren't gay. After all, we only loved being with each other every moment of the day.

Some of my friends of that time who turned out to be gay managed the difficulties well, but a few suffered seriously from being closeted. One became extremely obese and spent most of his adult life living with his mother. Two of them dropped out of college and "disappeared," although one of those turned out to have moved to another part of the country where he felt he could live life as a gay man without constant exposure to the disdain of his family.

Each of us had to struggle to "come out." Some excellent articles have been written on the coming-out process, and psychoanalysts should become familiar with them (e.g., Martin, 1991; Troiden, 1988). But I think we should also look at the need for "coming out" as a sign of social pathology. Society will be cured of this pathology only when there is *no more need for coming out*. When homosexuality is not something publicly condemned, but merely acknowledged as one of the acceptable variants of human development, then children and teenagers will be free to discover

---

* This has changed somewhat in the United States. The American television series *Queer as Folk*, which began in 2000, has gay men with a broad range of occupations, including an advertising executive, an accountant, a university professor, a football player, and a drugstore clerk. The show *The L Word*, which began in 2004, has a lesbian tennis star and a museum executive. In reality, I know of no profession or career in which there are no gay people.

the vagaries of their own sexuality openly and without fear. It will still be a difficult process. Adolescence and the discovery of the self are always difficult tasks. But at least the need for secrecy and shame will have been removed or reduced, as well as the hiddenness, the excessive emphasis on sexual acts over loving acts, and the lack of preparatory rituals, like open dating, that will allow young gays and lesbians the opportunity to test out their social-romantic yearnings.*

In the current world, because of widespread anti-homosexual prejudice and the resultant secrecy surrounding homosexuality, there is often a conflict between a gay person's self-concept and public opprobrium of gay people. How does one deal with this discordance between what one knows of oneself and the images that one receives from society? Often, without guidance, one can try identification with the aggressor. One can start to feel contemptuous of gay people and give others the impression that "I'm certainly not like that." I did this on a limited scale. In high school, we read the novel *The Devil's Advocate*, which, if I remember correctly, had a sinister homosexual character in it who tries to seduce a young man, and we made jokes about people in the class who were like that young man. Fortunately, we never went beyond that, but I can see how, under different cultural circumstances, a budding gay adolescent may try to deny his homosexuality by beating up openly gay people.

When I got to college at the University of Chicago, I immediately formed an extremely close friendship with Dan Kozloff. We met in the music practice room of our dormitory. We were both pianists, and we started to explore the section of the library where four-hand piano music was stored. In this way, we could study together huge amounts of the symphonic and chamber repertory. I loved the time I spent with him, and we were nearly inseparable. But I was also dating women and did not call myself homosexual.

After nine months of this life, Dan came to my room one day and said, "I have something important I want to discuss with you. Can we talk openly?" I said, "Of course," and he said that what he had to say was difficult, and it would be easier if we had the lights off. I agreed to that, too. We both sat on the bed, and he told me that he loved me and was very attracted to me. I was stunned, but also intrigued. I said, "I need three

---

* Society puts a great deal of pressure on adolescents not to become homosexual, and it is a popular view that such pressure discourages homosexuality. I have seen a number of cases where the opposite is true. People who had the potential for romantic involvement with either sex are sometimes pushed into declaring their identities, prematurely, as gay or straight, and this may foreclose an open understanding of their sexual and affectional makeup.

days to decide." So we spent the next three days in endless discussion. What did it mean to be in love with another man? What would this mean for our futures? Was it normal? Despite all the abstraction, I realized that I loved Dan, too, and so we would see. And we did.

What does a young man in conflict who has strong academic leanings do when faced with a difficult issue? He goes to the library. I went straight to the card index* and looked up homosexuality. I looked up every book and journal article I could find on the subject, and, of course, I took in every detail, no matter how silly, with deadly seriousness. I remember one study of what homosexuals were like. It said that they prefer impressionistic music. I remember thinking, "Dan really likes Ravel and Debussy, while I am not such a great fan of theirs. Does that mean that he is more homosexual than I am?"

There were books on the *Boys of Boise* and *The Tearoom Trade*, which painted a sleazy picture of promiscuous sex in bathrooms. This wasn't part of my life, but the books seemed so authoritative that I worried terribly that that was where my life would end up. And then, of course, there was the dreadful Edmund Bergler, whose titles leaped out at me from the card catalogue: *Homosexuality: Disease or Way of Life*? All the psychiatric texts in those days were discussing how to treat the disease called homosexuality. And yet I was having the most glorious times with Dan. I was in love with him, and we were learning and teaching each other all sorts of new things. We argued about "life" in the way adolescents do, and were constantly inspired and prodded by each other to grand plans and less grand achievements. How did this all fit together with the view that our relationship was diseased?

I began to scrutinize how life was being lived by other gay people. The picture was mixed. There were a number of homosexuals on campus whose suffering was quite public. There was the campus carilloneer, a man who was flamboyant and had wild parties. He killed himself. There was one eternal student, a man who attended the same courses year after year, with no apparent goal in life. What was wrong with him? He was very conflicted about his homosexuality and apparently went from one psychiatric consultation to another, and one treatment to another, but was never "cured." Unfortunately, the psychoanalysts were attempting to cure

---

* Libraries in those days had each book listed on an index card, whereas today all library holdings are listed in a computer. To search the card index was the best way to research a subject, in those pre-Internet days.

his homosexuality, instead of curing his internalized homophobia and his general self-hatred.

But gradually I discovered that there were alternatives. One pair of professors, Roger Weiss and Howard Brown, lived together as a couple on campus and were apparently accepted, since they kept their sexuality relatively discrete. There was a man who was rumored to be the next Nobel Prize winner, who was secretly gay. I got to know him and was impressed at the time by how he managed to make his personal life seem completely irrelevant to his work, which seemed easier perhaps in the hard sciences. But he lived alone and seemed quite lonely.

Gradually, this "research" became integrated with my academic work. I took a course on Rorschach testing with Samuel Beck and discovered the extensive literature on the "signs" on the Rorschach of homosexuality. Why anyone needed such "signs" wasn't exactly clear. Was it mere abstract interest, was it to help clinical assessment, or were they trying to find ways of weeding out homosexuals from situations in which they were prohibited, like the military? Many of the studies were done during the McCarthy era and seemed tainted by it. When it came time to do a term paper, "The Rorschach and Homosexuality" was my topic (see Chapter 1). I found that many of the studies claiming to find different signs contradicted each other. Evelyn Hooker (1957) finally put this area to rest with her landmark study, in which she sent Rorschach protocols to acknowledged experts, and they were unable to distinguish the protocols of gay men from straight men.

That paper was my first step out of the closet professionally. I realized that some might ask, why is he so interested in this topic? No one did so to my face, and I went ahead with the project.

Dan and I read André Gide's *Corydon*, which was one of the more gay-positive tracts around, but still had the tone of an apologia. Today, I think, "What was there to apologize for?"—but in those days, the opprobrium of society was not something I could shrug off. And then there was Gide's *L'Immoraliste*, that moving tale of bisexual torment. Gide's diaries became regular nighttime reading. There was a feeling of constant sleuthing: Where are the homosexuals of our culture hiding?

For example, when I was in high school, I fell in love with the works of Thomas Mann. It started with *Buddenbrooks*, the great novel of a German family (that had astonishing resemblances to my own family). By the time I had finished high school, I had read every work of fiction Mann had written. Besides my interest in his insights into my family and the genius of his writing, there was the prevalent homoerotic element: the crush between

schoolboys in "Tonio Kröger," the thrilling tragic kiss between Mario
and the Magician, and, most of all, *Death in Venice*. It was odd that in
those days, it was considered inappropriate to speak of *Death in Venice* as
a novella about suppressed homosexual desires. I did so in a paper, and the
professor (who I know now was gay) called it grotesque. Mann's work was
supposed to be about aesthetic love, or so we were told, and anyone who
saw it having to do with suppressed homosexuality was a vulgarian.*

Vulgarian that I was, I persisted in trying to discover if Mann himself
had homoerotic interests, and felt vindicated when Mann's letters were
published (Winston, 1971) and I found this in a letter to André Gide on
August 22, 1924: "I received and studied [*Corydon*] with extraordinary
pleasure: the spiritual apology for an area of feeling which I too hold can be
despised and condemned only by barbarians and ignoramuses." And later,
in the 1980s, I heard Mann's son, Golo, give a talk at Columbia University's
Deutches Haus, which included a documentary by a man in California
who told of taking Mann to see Muscle Beach, "and how he stared!"

But in the era before Stonewall, duplicity about homosexuality was
the prevalent ethic—proper manners meant that gays should not identify
themselves as such, and straights were considered ill-mannered if they
spoke overtly about someone's homosexuality.† Certain code words were
devised instead and were even used by psychoanalysts. Clara Thompson
(1964) put it quite bluntly:

> Moreover, we of this Institute [the William Alanson White Institute of
> Psychiatry, Psychoanalysis, and Psychology] maintain that a man's capacity as
> a therapist will be adequately revealed in his work with patients, so that his
> supervisors will be able to judge. The reply to this statement is that there is no
> way of knowing whether a man is a psychopath—by which, I think, is usu-
> ally meant a homosexual—because psychopaths are often good therapists. (pp.
> 58–59)

This tradition allowed prejudice against gays without open acknowledgment—"the prejudice that dare not speak its name"—a phenomenon
still very much alive today.

For someone gay, this crazy tradition is a constant challenge to know
what is really going on; it turned me and many others into devotees of

---

* This tradition was a long one. The anonymous review of *Death in Venice* in the *New York Times*,
  on February 22, 1925, ended with this sentence: "Given the theme of the story, it should in fairness
  be added that it is written with exquisite tact and delicacy and that its implications will only be
  misunderstood by the coarse and literal mind" (p. 9).
† This phenomenon extends to historians and scholars in many fields, which I discuss further in
  Chapter 6, "The Closeting of History."

a kind of counterespionage. Who were the secret, influential homosexuals, and where, how, and why were they hiding? I learned about J. Edgar Hoover's long-standing love affair with Clyde Tolson, which went on while they persecuted gays in America. Roy Cohn was doing the same thing, and so were many others (see von Hoffman, 1988). It is an odd fact that people who are the victims of prejudice often become the purveyors of that prejudice, and persecute their own people.* It is as if they identify with the aggressor and end up doing the dirty work for their persecutors. We have seen this not only with gays, but, often, among Blacks (the Anita Hill investigation, where all the traditional hypersexualized stereotypes about Black men and women were dragged out) and among Jews (the case of Otto Weininger, a Jewish psychoanalyst who converted to Christianity and wrote damning, prejudicial things about Jews [Weininger, 1903]).†

I was very lucky to have begun my gay life with Dan, a relationship that integrated sexual, loving, and intellectual aspects of my self. For many gay men, romantic life can begin quite differently. Their first sexual experiences may be just furtive sexual acts, not coordinated with an ongoing relationship, and this may set up a pattern of a separation between sex and emotional connection that can be problematic in later life. This is made more likely by the necessity for secrecy in a hostile world, and by the lack of social supports to adolescent gays and lesbians to help them in dating. So many of the institutions of the heterosexual world—dances, proms, and other social functions—are not hospitable to gays and lesbians. It is difficult to gauge how important such rituals are to adolescent development, but for gays and lesbians, dances and proms are often a painful experience of either exclusion or false-self development.

Dan went off to California after college, and our relationship ended. I began graduate school at Yale and met John Silberman, whom I quickly decided would be the man with whom I would spend the rest of my life (it turned out to be 14 years). He was in law school in the Boston area, and so we had to commute to see each other every weekend. But during graduate school, most people did not ask many questions about one's sexuality, and life, mostly in the closet, seemed easy and enjoyable. Some people asked why I was going to Boston so often, and one person told everyone she had figured it out: I was having an affair with a married woman, and so I didn't want to tell anyone.

---

* I am indebted to Dr. Kathleen White for this insight.
† Weininger argued that women and Jews were primarily sexual beings who lacked individuality.

John and I moved to New York, where we lived together and settled down to develop our lives. During my psychology internship, I was also not usually asked about my sexuality, but I started to see the phenomenon of the closeted gay or lesbian psychiatrists and psychologists who diagnose homosexuality and its supposed pathology partly to cover suspicion about their own lives. I also came to recognize how pervasive was the belief that homosexuals can and should be encouraged to change to heterosexuality. One particular internship experience stands out: I had a supervisor whom I considered quite sophisticated clinically. I was working with a gay man who was extremely detached and had developed an elaborate group of defenses to avoid connection with any human being. As the therapy relationship developed, he became quite anxious by the closeness of contact with me. One day, he reported a brief encounter with a woman friend, in which she gave him oral sex. I raised in supervision the idea that this was a case of "sexual acting out" in which he was trying to dispel his anxiety about the relationship to me. My supervisor said something I shall never forget: "You are probably right about the psychodynamics. But clinically, it has been my experience that whenever a homosexual patient shows any signs of heterosexuality, he should be encouraged in that direction." This was really my first contact with the way that clinical thinking was skewed by professional and societal homophobia.

I think such thinking is still very prevalent, although it is becoming less ego-syntonic* for some practitioners. Schafer† (1995) writes:

> I believe that, by and large, it is still that way in the analytic treatment of the great majority of patients. Heterosexual tendencies are taken for granted; it is conflict over them that is to be examined, understood, and reduced. In contrast, homosexual tendencies are considered central to psychological problems, and it is the temptation to act on them in fact or fantasy that is to be examined, understood, and reduced. (p. 195)

A survey of members of the American Psychoanalytic Association (MacIntosh, 1994) found that 97.6% did not believe that "homosexual patients can and should change to heterosexuality." Yet, 34.4% believed that "most other analysts think homosexual patients can and should change to heterosexuality." This statistic could be interpreted as a divergence between what psychoanalysts think and do. However, the letter that accompanied the survey was very directive in its implications and defensive of the profession against charges of prejudice, so it is hardly surprising

---

* Something is "ego-syntonic" if you are comfortable with it. If something is "ego-dystonic," it clashes with your beliefs, values, or view of yourself and makes you uncomfortable.

† This is the same Roy Schafer who produced the "Schafer signs" of homosexuality on the Rorschach.

that most respondents disavowed prejudice and a wish to change a patient's sexual orientation on their own part. But given the reality of psychoanalytic practice, it is not surprising, either, that many thought prejudice against homosexuality rampant among their colleagues.

In 1979, I was accepted by the William Alanson White Institute for psychoanalytic training. I wondered whether I ought to be open about my homosexuality during my training or not. During the summer, I met Dr. Ellis Perlswig, a gay psychiatrist from New Haven. About 20 years before, he began training at the New York Psychoanalytic Institute. His training analyst was Dr. Jacob Arlow. During his first session, Perlswig told Arlow that he was gay. Arlow reported it to the training committee of the New York Psychoanalytic Institute, and Perlswig's standing as a candidate of the New York Psychoanalytic Institute was ended.

So Perlswig's advice to me was not to be open about my homosexuality at the White Institute until after I received my psychoanalytic certificate. But then he added, "Of course, the longer you wait, and the more advanced you become, the more you will have to lose by coming out."

I took his advice and went through my psychoanalytic training in the closet, for the most part. I told my analyst I was gay, of course. He was trying to be open-minded about it, but there were many signs of his entrenched heterosexism. When I referred to my lover, he asked what the term "lover" meant. To him, it had the connotations of an illicit paramour, as in "Madame Bovary took a lover." Of course, from an old-fashioned heterosexual standpoint, that was right, but it showed his vantage point. I gave him John Boswell's (1980) book, *Christianity, Social Tolerance, and Homosexuality*, which was at the time a book of revolutionary gay scholarship, with the hope that it would teach him about the history of prejudice and the significance of gay love relationships.

Being in the closet during analytic training turned out to be increasingly difficult. My classmates and I were very close, and we socialized quite a bit. When people came to my house, it had to be arranged for a time when my lover, John, would not be at home. Analysts being the sort of people who are interested in other people's lives, they asked probing questions, which I mostly finessed. Most people began to think of me as lonely and schizoid, with no intimate relationships. It was painful to be misperceived that way, but I stuck with my choice. It was especially difficult when there were weekend events to which everyone brought their spouse or significant other, and I attended alone. It also caused stresses in my relationship with John, although this way of living was mutual; I did not attend the social functions at his law firm either.

Sometimes I slipped. One summer, a fellow candidate from the White Institute and her boyfriend visited me at my summer home. We were preparing lunch, and her boyfriend asked me, "Is there usually someone else here with you?" I asked him why he asked that. He replied, "Because you have set the table with four place settings, and there are only three of us here!"

My reaction to this slip was informative. I did not think, as I might have earlier in my life, "Oh, no! That was a terrible mistake!" Rather, I thought, "I wish I could simply reply, 'Yes, usually my lover John is here with me.'" It signaled to me that I would not put up with such hiding much longer.

I also came to realize how damaging it was to maintain secrecy. One of the problems with being in the closet for a long time is that you get used to it, and you start to lose awareness of how debilitating it is (see Sedgwick, 1990). Heterosexual analysts who work with gay and lesbian patients need to devote special efforts to appreciate this. If you want to understand the agony of being in the closet and of coming out, read first-person accounts of treatment histories, such as Martin Duberman's *Cures* (1991); or Paul Monette's *Becoming a Man* (1992); or the poignant account by Richard Socarides of coming out to his father, the psychoanalyst Charles Socarides (Nagourney, 1995). Also, if you are straight and married, try an experiment on yourself. For one month, do not ever mention your husband or wife or your children in conversation with anyone. When you describe an experience that you shared with your spouse, tell of it as if you did it alone. Always say "I," even when you mean "we." These things are all done by gay men and lesbians who must keep their homosexuality hidden. I know straight people who have gone through this exercise and been astonished at how debilitating it is—to one's sense of self, reality, integrity, honesty, and cohesion. We may ask, how is it that anyone who does this day in and day out, not for just one month, but for years, for a lifetime—how does such a person manage not to have a feeling of loss of self, of false self?

One of the most powerful antidotes to the loneliness of the closet is affiliation with others who are in the same predicament or who have found a solution to it. I certainly benefited from collegial discussions with other gay psychoanalysts including Drs. Bertram Schaffner, Gerald Perlman, Jack Drescher, Richard Isay, and Martin Frommer. Several gay and lesbian colleagues and I founded the Association of Lesbian and Gay Psychoanalysts at the White Institute,* a small group that allowed us to compare our experiences and speak out on them with an official voice.

---

* Bert Schaffner gave our group a nickname: "The Great White Way."

And then there was AIDS. It is impossible to describe in words the impact that the advent of AIDS has had on me personally and in my clinical work. I knew someone in 1980 who started to become strangely sick and was first diagnosed with Hodgkin's disease. It turned out to be AIDS. Now, 15 years of constant death of friends, colleagues, and patients, most in the prime of life, have taken an intolerable toll, all the worse since there is no sign of the epidemic being stopped or the disease cured.* Although I was lucky to be healthy, AIDS gave me a new sense of urgency to live life fully and honestly. Part of the psychology of being in the closet is tenacious procrastination. One thinks that, someday, the secrecy will stop. Someday, I will not worry about what others think of my romantic life. Someday, I will stand up against injustice and inequality. All of these "somedays" can extend into infinite delay. I was really jogged out of such procrastination by working with people with AIDS, whom I saw trying to fulfill long-postponed goals in a shortened life span. It forced me to realize that, someday, there would be no more days left, and no one could say when that time would come (Blechner, 1993b).

With Dr. Bertram Schaffner, I founded and directed the HIV Clinical Service at the White Institute, which provided psychotherapy for people with AIDS and those traumatized in other ways by the epidemic. Our monthly seminars also allowed remarkably free discussions of all aspects of sexuality. They also revealed that many of the younger generation of analysts were relatively free of the homophobia so common in the older generation.

The more I emerge from the closet, the more instances of homophobia within psychoanalytic organizations, which I had once tolerated, seem unacceptable. The great advantage of not being in the closet is that one can speak out publicly against such blatant prejudice. In 1992, I attended a conference on psychoanalysis and musical biography. It was part of a series of conferences organized by the seminar on Psychoanalysis and Music of the American Psychoanalytic Association, which I had been attending for years. At this particular conference, held at the City University of New York, the moderator announced that a paper on the great British composer Benjamin Britten was to have been delivered by a musicologist, Professor Chip Whitesell, who was the head of the Gay and Lesbian Musicologists Association, "an organization that actually exists." (He actually said that.) He also said the musicologist could not attend but had sent his manuscript,

---

* This was written shortly before the anti-retroviral drug combinations were discovered, which changed AIDS in most cases from a nearly certain death sentence to a more treatable, chronic illness.

and that the manuscript could be read to the audience if they wished to hear it. Did anyone want to hear the paper? I replied, loudly and alone, "Yes." The speaker got ready to read it, but there was an interruption from the chairman, and it was not read. When I protested, I was ignored. I left the conference. I since have received a copy of Professor Whitesell's paper, entitled "Britten, Inside and Outside." It is an excellent piece of work and would have provided a much-needed balance to the stultifying patholo- gizing of Britten that occurred at the conference.

Prejudice continues. In the old days, one could be prejudiced against homosexuals with impunity. Now people are a bit more careful, but, still, homosexuals are the one group in America about which openly prejudicial statements can be made with little or no repercussion. People made viru- lently anti-gay speeches at the Republican National Convention in 1992. In 1995, Congressman Dick Armey publicly referred to Congressman Barney Frank as Barney Fag.* States continue to attempt, and at times suc- ceed, in passing laws that allow discrimination against gays to continue. The military continues to bar open homosexuals from serving. To all these aspects of discrimination, most psychoanalysts have been either silent or have actually supported such discrimination through pathologizing theo- ries of homosexuality.†

Certainly there have been exceptions. Harry Stack Sullivan, as a psy- chiatrist for the military forces, attempted to remove homosexuality as a disqualifying factor for admission to military service, although he was eventually overruled by the military establishment (Bérubé, 1990). Judd Marmor (1980) was extremely helpful in combating the homophobia in organized psychiatry.

In their practices, psychoanalysts must become aware of the traumatiz- ing effects such pronouncements have on a gay person's sense of safety. It takes work for a heterosexual analyst to become sensitive and empathic with these issues, which are so much taken for granted in society (see O'Leary, 1997).

One of the most poignant spectacles of internalized homophobia is of a closeted gay analyst saying prejudicial things about gay people. During my

---

* Armey claimed it was a slip of the tongue, but I doubt it. In another context, he said, "Yes, I am Dick Armey. And if there is a 'dick army,' Barney Frank would want to join up."

† In the late 1990s, I heard a forward-looking talk about homosexuality by a psychoanalyst at a meeting of the Columbia University Psychoanalytic Center. During the discussion, a man asked a question, which was amazingly hostile and demeaning. I wish I could remember his words, but I can't. However, I can remember how the speaker responded: "I haven't been spoken to so contemp- tuously since I left my nuclear family!"

psychoanalytic training, I remember one married teacher (whom I presumed to be bisexual, which I have confirmed) discussing a patient who had a severe thought disorder. He asked, "Is his homosexuality treatable?" Besides the essential misguidedness and inherent prejudice of the question, this patient had much more important and fundamental issues to solve besides his homosexuality. I felt hopeful about the future, when one of my fellow students stated this in blunt terms.

In psychoanalysis, things are changing, but the changes are quite a bit behind the progress of organized psychology and psychiatry* (see Tabin, 1995; Blechner, 1995d). People who used to be openly prejudiced against gays now are more likely to say prejudicial things in private. In 1994, a colleague of mine had dinner with a senior analyst of the White Institute and his wife. This analyst had been very supportive of my work when he was my advisor and supervisor during my training, at a time when I was still closeted about my homosexuality. At the dinner, my colleague mentioned my name a few times during the discussion. The analyst's wife said, "Who is this Mark Blechner?" Her husband replied, "Oh, he is the White Institute's resident homosexual." So is one reduced.

Eventually, I began to take decisive steps to being more open about, or at least not hiding, my involvement with my lover from the psychoanalytic professional world. I hardly need to state that I was terrified. I was warned by gay colleagues that if I "came out," many of my referral sources would stop referring to me, and, in any case, I would only receive referrals of gay patients. This has not turned out to be true for me, but I did not know that then. I decided, in any case, that the gain in personal integrity and freedom would be worth it. As I gained courage, I also began to speak and to publish about the anti-homosexual bias that was still so rampant in organized psychoanalysis and that was distorting clinical work (Blechner, 1992a, 1993a, 1994a, 1995b, 1995c, 1995d; Blechner & Casden, 1994, 1995).

Some of my heterosexual patients came to know that I was gay during this time. Mostly this was productive for the progress of their analyses, although there were often difficult times. One woman expressed her thoughts rather freely: Did my being gay mean that I hate women? Did it mean that I thought all women were bitches? Did it mean that I cared less for her than for my male patients? While all of these concerns had special personal significances for her, I found myself rather grateful for the candor with which she expressed these blatant and false stereotypes, for they gave me a view of the sorts of misconceptions held by many heterosexuals.

---

* See Chapter 5.

She also raised the question of what my relationship was like with the community. I really didn't know what she meant by "the community," and it emerged that she meant the community at large, i.e., from her viewpoint, the heterosexual community. This seemed a good example of what Moss (1992) has called the tyranny of the first-person plural. "We" means "we heterosexuals."

There were some quite surprising outcomes. One woman patient felt freed to tell me that she had pervasive fantasies about anal sex. Previously, she had felt too ashamed to admit this, but knowing that I was gay led her to assume that I would be more accepting of such wishes. Those who had the most trouble were those men whose behavioral lives were predominantly heterosexual, but who had strong currents of homosexual feelings with which they were not at peace.

Some people were able to explore areas of homosexual feelings and attitudes toward homosexuality in new ways. A woman patient had the following dream:

> My boss, Elaine, wanted to marry me. She asked me. I didn't want to. I didn't know how to say it. An hour later, I told her, NO. I was so upset by it. It was not what I wanted for my life, to be tied to her.

The dream had obvious implications about being tied to her mother in an eroticized relationship that does not give her independence, and the way she was re-experiencing that in her workplace and in the analysis. But, as is often the case, the dream was followed by an enactment of the dream (Blechner, 1995a). The next session, she told me that she had not been able to tell me all her thoughts about the dream, at the time. "She didn't know how to say it." But now, "an hour later" (i.e., a session later), she could tell me: She thought that being gay would be a fate worse than death.

How prevalent is her view in our society? We would have to surmise that it is quite prevalent, judging from the intensity with which some analysts cling to notions of homosexuality as pathology (see Tabin, 1995; Blechner, 1995d). It shows the complex connection between societal norms and views of psychopathology, an area that has been explored far too little (see Hartmann, 1960; Wakefield, 1992). Psychoanalysts' view of what constitutes mental health is sharply colored by cultural standards and prejudices.

Not being in the closet has had a very healthful effect on all my clinical work. I don't bring up my sexual orientation and my domestic situation needlessly with patients. If patients ask, I may tell them, after suitable exploration of their own fantasies and motives. But even if the subject never comes up, the fact that I am not afraid if it does is certainly freeing. Some psychoanalysts adopt a position of not deliberately revealing personal information to patients; still, there is a great difference between whether one does that out of clinical conviction or because there are important things about oneself that one would really not like to be revealed. This principle applies to all aspects of an analyst's personality, not just social-sexual-familial factors. For me, to bring my true private self into alignment with my public self has given me much more freedom to work as an analyst on any issue with any patient. Even if it has meant facing some ugly and painful discrimination, it has been worth it.

Postscript

Time moved on. One of my friends who is an attorney recommended that I sue the White Institute for discrimination, but litigation is something I do not like. Instead, I decided to change the institute as an insider. This was made possible by a fortuitous political change. In 1988, there was a "revolution" at the White Institute. A very conservative administration, run somewhat like a monarchy, which had been in power for about 30 years, was toppled. Under the new director, Dr. Marylou Lionells, many of the procedures of the institute were revised to be more open and allow greater democracy. The Council of Fellows, the policy-making body of the White Institute, had for many years been a kind of "Politburo," with its members elected by its members, not leaving much chance for "outsiders" to gain entrance and have their say. But in the early 1990s, membership in the Council of Fellows was opened up to election. I ran and was elected.

It was an exciting experience, but often painful, too. The Fellows included many of the people who had acted prejudicially against me. And still, we had to move on and work together.

One of the issues that was considered by the Fellows was the promotion process. Originally, the promotion process was completely secret and mysterious. You had to be liked and admired by enough influential people to get promoted. There was no official way you could apply for a promotion, as you could in a university. You just had to wait until you were told that you were promoted. No news was bad news, and there was no official way to find out why you had not been promoted.

Under the new administration, the old promotion system was changed to resemble a university procedure. You could apply for promotion and present your work to a committee that would evaluate you. Yet old habits died hard. At first, the committees that interviewed people for promotion were often the same old people used to the same old patterns of prejudice from the old regime. The Fellows reconfigured the promotion process, not just the nuts and bolts of the process, but the basic spirit, for it to become inclusive. "Inclusive," a malleable word, basically meant that the promotion process would try to include as many people who were qualified as possible, instead of trying to exclude as many people as possible. The discussions in the Fellows were grueling and often insulting. I often returned home after these meetings at 10 p.m., with cramps in my stomach.

But it was worth it. Things changed, and in the year 2000, I was made a training analyst. There are now two openly gay training analysts at the White Institute (myself and Jack Drescher), although so far no openly lesbian training analyst.* The situation in the American Psychoanalytic Association is no better. As of 2004, 13 years after the American Psychoanalytic Association had passed a resolution banning discrimination against gays and lesbians, only one openly gay man, Sidney Phillips, had been appointed a training analyst.† There were no openly lesbian training analysts in the American Psychoanalytic Association.

---

* Progressive steps against prejudice of all kinds usually go together. The first African American training analyst was appointed by the White Institute in 2004. There are, so far, no female African American training analysts.
† Ralph Roughton, who is openly gay today, was first made a training analyst in 1979, when he was a closeted gay man married to a woman. In 1996, when he was openly gay, he was reappointed.

3

The Experience of Hating
and Being Hated

Author's Introduction

In 1991 I met James Marks, a civil rights lawyer who, at the time, was pressing the Boston Psychoanalytic Institute to state in writing that they would not tolerate prejudice against gays and lesbians seeking psychoanalytic training. James asked me, did the White Institute have such a clause in their charter? My answer was no. I learned something important: Just when you think you have achieved much progress in the way of equality, someone radical will put things in perspective and force you to work much harder against prejudices that you may have overlooked.* If I was still somewhat in the closet at the time, James pushed me out the door and slammed it shut behind me.

It was the right time to be radicalized. In 1992 I was asked by Dr. Sheila Brown to be the program chairman of the William Alanson White Psychoanalytic Society. This involved inviting speakers to give lectures at the institute. As I described in Chapter 2, our theme for the year was "Toward a Psychoanalytic Understanding of Hatred." This allowed me to organize a panel on "The Experience of Hating and Being Hated" that included five speakers: three gay men (Bertram Schaffner, Jack Drescher, and myself, all of whom were White and Jewish), two Black women (Kathleen White and Sherry Ross), and one man born in Germany whose father had been involved with the Nazi regime (Joerg Bose). We were able to draw connections between prejudices of all kinds: racism,

---

* Larry Kramer is the ultimate goad in this respect. No matter how hard you work for gay equality, Larry will tell you that you have achieved little and the situation is still terrible. His attitude annoys many people, but he is a very valuable annoyance. He prevents complacency which is the enemy of progress.

homophobia, and anti-Semitism. Each prejudice is different, but they are all the same in one way: They define a group of humans as less than fully human.

The conference was a breathtaking event. On November 18, 1992, all the 600 seats in the auditorium were filled. It was the first time that I stated in a public forum that Harry Stack Sullivan, the great American psychiatrist and the founder of the "Interpersonal School" of psychoanalysis, was gay, and that Sullivan's famous ward for schizophrenic patients was a gay ward; the patients and most of the staff were gay. The world did not collapse. I heard that some people were angry at me for saying these things, although no one contradicted me. Truth was on my side. Nevertheless, when I submitted the talks for publication, they were rejected. Only one of the talks of that epochal event was published (White, 2002), and only 10 years later, when the forward-thinking Donnel Stern discovered it in the old files. I am publishing my introduction here for the first time.

The Experience of Hating and Being Hated

I would like to welcome you to our panel on "The Experience of Hating and Being Hated." This is the second program in the series of scientific meetings, sponsored by the William Alanson White Society, entitled "Toward a Psychoanalytic Understanding of Hatred." Tonight, we offer a very special program, one that must be rare in the history of psychoanalysis, if there is indeed any precedent for it. Distinguished psychoanalysts who have special identities by virtue of their race, sex, sexual orientation, or national and religious backgrounds are going to speak openly about their own experiences of hating and being hated.

This is not to say that hatred and prejudice have never been studied before by psychoanalysts in a personal way. On the contrary, Freud himself was a pioneer of the self-study of hatred. His book, *The Interpretation of Dreams* (Freud, 1900), was not only a landmark in the science of unconscious processes; it was also a relentless airing and protest of the hatred and injustice against Jews in his time. In *The Interpretation of Dreams*, most of the dreams that Freud analyzes are his own, and there are frequent references in them to the struggles Freud had in attaining a university position because of anti-Semitism, and the shame and anger that he felt at his father's humiliation on the streets of Vienna by anti-Semites. Anti-Semitism and racial self-hatred are also a prominent theme in Freud's book on wit.

Freud resisted prejudice against homosexuality, too, both in his famous letter to the mother of a gay man* and in his strongly worded opinion to Ernest Jones that no one should be excluded from psychoanalytic training because of homosexuality (Jones, 1957). Sándor Ferenczi was a pioneer among psychoanalysts in the fight against homophobia. He defended a lesbian transvestite against involuntary hospitalization (Ferenczi, 1902) and argued that homosexuality is not a disease but a psychic disposition (Lorin, 1983).

A. A. Brill asserted in 1913 that "Homosexuality may occur in persons just as healthy as normal heterosexual persons." (This was 44 years before Evelyn Hooker's [1957] landmark empirical study that showed, in a blind reading of projective tests, that the mental health of homosexuals was no different than heterosexuals!†) Brill also condemned some of the ignorant treatment of homosexuals by physicians of the time. He wrote: "I can never comprehend why physicians invariably resort to bladder washing and rectal massage when they are consulted by homosexuals." He also said that, for a homosexual, the experience of having heterosexual relations was just as much a perversion as for a heterosexual to have homosexual relations.

Harry Stack Sullivan also fought prejudice in word and deed. He wrote (Sullivan, 1964) eloquently about anti-Semitism and what he called anti-Negroism, with startling insights based on self-analysis. He interviewed Black youths in the Deep South, one of whom commented: "Dr. Sullivan was one of the nicest white men I'd ever met. It is unusual to have a white man really interested in Negroes. You can't learn to trust white people by one nice one. I guess there are others but I'll bet they're far between" (p. 98).

Sullivan's own homosexuality may have contributed to his being shunned by orthodox psychoanalysis despite his obvious genius. His most famous clinical achievement, the ward for gay male schizophrenics at the Sheppard and Enoch Pratt Hospital, was also an extraordinary experiment on how the removal of prejudice, homophobic and otherwise, can have a very positive effect on severe psychopathology (Chatelaine, 1981).

Subsequent psychoanalysts must bear the shameful legacy of having become a mouthpiece of homophobia. A few psychoanalysts, especially

---

* In that letter (Grotjahn, 1951), Freud wrote: "Homosexuality is assuredly no advantage, but it is nothing to be ashamed of, no vice, no degradation, it cannot be classified as an illness; we consider it to be a variation of the sexual function produced by a certain arrest of sexual development. Many highly respectable individuals of ancient and modern times have been homosexuals, several of the greatest men among them (Plato, Michelangelo, Leonardo da Vinci, etc.). It is a great injustice to persecute homosexuality as a crime and cruelty too." However, privately Freud often expressed prejudice against homosexuals (see Wortis, 1954).
† I discuss Hooker's study elsewhere in the book as well.

Bergler (1956) and Socarides (1968), issued disgraceful, hateful statements about homosexuals. But for decades, other analysts did not protest such statements openly, as Kenneth Lewes (1988) has documented in great detail. We should remember the words of Reverend Martin Niemoeller, a Protestant minister who was arrested and persecuted in Nazi Germany:

> In Germany they first came for the Communists and I didn't speak up because I wasn't a Communist. They came for the Jews and I didn't speak up because I wasn't a Jew. Then they came for the trade unionists. Then they came for the Catholics, and I didn't speak up because I was a Protestant. Then they came for me—but by that time no one was left to speak up. (Eatwell, 1997, pp. 151–152)

The understanding of hatred is especially important in today's world. When I was growing up in post-war America, we came to think of the ethnic torture of World War II as "that dark period of history." But looking at the world today, the events of the 1930s and 1940s seem paradoxically less distant. In the former Yugoslavia, there are concentration camps and programs of ethnic cleansing. In Germany, rightists are attacking buildings that house foreigners and beating up their occupants. In Hungary, skinheads killed a gypsy on the street. And in America, the keynote speaker at the Republican National Convention of 1992 declared open hatred for gays and expressed the wish to take back "our culture." Skinheads in Oregon threw Molotov cocktails into the apartment of a gay man and a lesbian, killing them, and Colorado amended their state constitution to rescind the rights of gay men and lesbians,* reminding us of the spirit of the Nuremberg laws that took away the rights of German Jews in 1935.†

Since, as psychoanalysts, we ought to be experts on self-awareness, we must begin our search with an examination of our own experiences of hatred and prejudice. The population of psychoanalysts has tended to skew our interest toward particular prejudices. Since there are many Jewish psychoanalysts, and many of them survived persecution in Europe during the Second World War, it should be no surprise that anti-Semitism has received more attention in the psychoanalytic literature than hatred against other groups. The problem of prejudice that non-Jewish Germans, the Japanese, and other national groups may feel in America has not received much attention. The problems of racism, and the particular issues of prejudice against African Americans, has also received

---

* The amendment was overturned in 1996 by the U.S. Supreme Court (*Romer v. Evans*).
† And in 2004, several states restricted marriage to male–female couples, while the federal government proposed a constitutional amendment to that effect.

much less attention, partly because there have been relatively few African American psychoanalysts. The plight of Native Americans is perhaps the most ignored.* And while there have always been gay and lesbian psychoanalysts, most of them have kept their identities hidden in order to keep their standing in homophobic professional organizations until recent years. So explorations of homophobia have been rare among psychoanalysts until recently (Blechner, 1993a, 1993b; Moss, 1992).†

The absence or silence of certain voices from psychoanalytic discourse is itself a symptom; now that that silence is being lifted somewhat, and more Blacks and open gays and lesbians are part of the psychoanalytic community, there is hope that hatred against those groups may have a chance to be understood and ameliorated, much in the way that voices of feminists have significantly altered the psychoanalytic theory and treatment of women. The more diverse the community of psychoanalysts becomes, the more we can be sure that our theories and practices apply fairly to all humanity.

---

* The first Native American psychoanalytic candidate at the White Institute, to my knowledge, began her training in 2004. One hopes that she will bring the psychological issues of Native Americans into greater awareness.
† Now the list is much longer, e.g., Isay, 1996; Drescher, 1996; Maroda, 1997; Gartner, 1999.

4

Homophobia in Psychoanalytic Writing and Practice
A Comment on Trop and Stolorow (1992) and Hanna (1992)

Heresy is only another word for freedom of thought.

Graham Greene

Author's Introduction

In 1992, the journal *Psychoanalytic Dialogues* published an account by Jeffrey Trop and Robert Stolorow of a man uncertain about his sexuality who was treated by a psychoanalyst. The case had the supposedly happy ending of the patient embarking on a life of heterosexuality. The published discussions of the article, by Stephen Mitchell and Arnold Richards, praised the clinical work. I was shocked. The case was such a clear example of the same old psychoanalytic approach of trying to coerce the patient to renounce his homosexuality and embrace heterosexuality. Every time homosexuality appeared in the patient's fantasies or actions, the analyst interpreted the pathology of it, while heterosexual fantasies were encouraged. The approach was blatantly skewed; I quickly wrote an analysis of the implicit homophobia in it and sent it to the journal. I also critiqued the similar heterosexist bias in a case report of the treatment of a lesbian patient by Edward Hanna.

As it happened, two other psychoanalysts, Ronnie Lesser and David Schwartz, had similar reactions to the Trop and Stolorow article and also sent in critiques. Their critiques and mine were published together and represent, as far as I know, the first published criticism by openly gay psychoanalysts (three of them, no less!) of anti-homosexual bias in a clinical case report.

It seemed an extraordinary coincidence that three people were moved to write at the same time. Why did it happen then, when other such articles were being printed in psychoanalytic journals all the time? The difference, I think, was that this article was printed in the progressive journal, *Psychoanalytic Dialogues*, edited by Stephen Mitchell. Mitchell, who died much too young in 2001, was an extraordinary analyst who had published two very forward-looking articles on homosexuality (Mitchell, 1978, 1981), at a time when such viewpoints were rare among psychoanalysts. Since Mitchell's journal seemed to be on the cutting edge of psychoanalytic thought, I think we all felt that this instance of homophobia must not be allowed to stand unchallenged. It was a testament to Mitchell's integrity that he immediately published all three critiques.

I was particularly proud of my test of "bias reversal," in which I changed the gender and sexual orientation of the case description and asked people to judge whether the clinical description still made sense. It turned out to be a very potent way of exposing biased clinical thinking. In the case reported by Edward Hanna, a lesbian's sexual activity was described as a defensive flight from her anxiety about heterosexual closeness. In my bias reversal version, I changed her into a woman whose heterosexual activity signified a defensive flight from her anxiety about homosexual closeness. Such a formulation had never been printed before in a psychoanalytic journal.

Homophobia in Psychoanalytic Writing and Practice: A Comment on Trop and Stolorow (1992) and Hanna (1992)*

Mitchell (1981) described and criticized the directive-suggestive approach to homosexuality, in which the psychoanalyst departs from the "traditional analytic position of non-directive neutrality by actively discouraging homosexual behavior and encouraging heterosexual behavior." The analysts who promulgated such an approach recommended exploiting the idealizing positive transference to push the patient into heterosexual behavior. They also recommended being open with their patients that this was their goal. Ovesey (1969), for example, recommended establishing with the patient at the outset that homosexuality is pathologic and is a treatable illness. Hatterer (1970) recommended what he called the "dehomosexualization process," which included exploitation of the patient's sense

---

* Originally published in *Psychoanalytic Dialogues*, 1993, 3, 627–637.

of shame to prod him or her into heterosexuality. Bieber and Socarides offered similar approaches.

Today, the world has changed. The gay liberation movement has helped many lesbians and gay men to feel content with their sexual orientation, and greater visibility of homosexuals has made it abundantly clear that a deeply satisfying life is the experience of many men and women who choose someone of their own sex for a romantic relationship. As a result, far fewer gay men and lesbians seek psychoanalytic treatment in order to change their sexual orientation. Nevertheless, such a treatment agenda has not completely disappeared, and the ethical and clinical issues raised in earlier dehomosexualization treatments still emerge in contemporary clinical reports about patients with homosexual or bisexual feelings.

Thanks to the work of Schaffner (1992), Isay (1989), Mitchell (1978, 1981), Gonsiorek (1977, 1991), Kwawer (1980), and others, analysts have been alerted to the problems of the directive-suggestive approach. It is rarer today to see articles in which analysts report telling a patient that homosexuality is evil and pathological, and that psychoanalytic treatment will be a failure unless their sexuality is changed. Nevertheless, it is not rare today to find articles in which the line of analytic interpretation is severely biased toward discouraging homosexuality and toward encouraging heterosexuality. Sometimes the authors claim to themselves, their readers, or their patients that they are neutral as to the issue, yet their actual interpretations make it clear that they are not. In a way, this seems like no improvement over earlier reports, and perhaps it is even a more pernicious development. The gay and lesbian patients of the past had to face humiliation and undue influence by their analysts. Gay and lesbian patients today may, in addition, have to face the double-binding experience of those experiences being masked by statements of neutrality. In many cases, the analysts seem to be unaware of their biases, and other analysts reading their reports, who may be sharing the same biases against homosexuality, do not perceive the gross departures from neutrality.

That this is so shows how deeply rooted are the biases against homosexuality in our society. They are most blatantly evident in the gay-bashings that are increasing every year, and the open expression of hatred of homosexuals that made its way into the Republican National Convention of 1992. Psychoanalysts are not saints, and they cannot be expected to operate independently of their culture. They do have a responsibility, however, to try to be as conscious as possible of their attitudes. Examples of covert homophobia can be found in many works of the psychoanalytic literature of the last decade, but I will focus in this communication on only two that have appeared most recently in this journal.

Trop and Stolorow (1992) report the case of Alan, a 34-year-old attorney who has been in analysis for 10 years. In their words: "He sought treatment because he felt deeply depressed about himself and did not know whether he was homosexual or heterosexual. His sexual experiences with women were few, and his primary sexual activities were infrequent, isolated homosexual experiences with different partners." The case ends with Alan engaged to a woman. Again, in the author's words, "Having found an idealizable, guiding, and protecting father in the transference, Alan is now developing an increasingly clear vision of his own future as a husband and father."

The case report is discussed by Mitchell (1992) and Richards (1992). Both see the case as a success. In Mitchell's words, "Because the clinical work is obviously of high quality and also because the tale is told so well, the morals dramatically drawn, the ending so happy, it is difficult to raise questions about it without appearing peevish and disagreeable" (p. 445). Richards writes: "The patient in this case was able, as a result of this kind of therapeutic encounter, to give up his homosexual behavior and fantasy, which were presumably ego dystonic, and to embark upon a more satisfying life of heterosexuality" (p. 462). Stolorow and Trop (1992), in a reply to these discussions, mention that both discussants find that "it is difficult to argue with success." I should like to offer a dissenting opinion. The case is by no means a clear success. It is one of the latest reported examples of the way that conscious or unconscious homophobia can lead an analyst to direct a patient, in conflict over his sexual orientation, to choose a path of heterosexuality that may not be the best choice for him or her. It is a blatant example of the way interpretation can veer far from the neutral, despite an analyst's claims of neutrality. The case also shows the vulnerability of patients with severe self-pathology to the influence of their analyst. In an attempt to retain the analyst's so-called "self-delineating functions," which include affirmation and approval, the patient may compromise his or her own self-delineation.

The case report and its discussions are a clear example of why psychoanalysis is distrusted by gay men and lesbians (Lewes, 1988; Isay, 1989; Drescher, 1992). The organized profession of psychoanalysis in America has a long history of prejudice against homosexuality. Openly gay men and lesbians have long been excluded from training at most psychoanalytic institutes. The writings of psychoanalysts have offered pseudo-scientific rationales for the discrimination of society at large against homosexuals.

Many psychoanalysts, believing that homosexuality per se is pathological, have engaged in treatments that supposedly cured their homosexual patients. Long-term follow-ups of such patients have often revealed that such conversions were ephemeral and superficially behavioral, and that the patients felt that their lives were seriously damaged (Isay, 1989; Duberman, 1991; Brown, 1976). Psychoanalysts were at the forefront in the resistance against the American Psychiatric Association's removal of homosexuality as a diagnosis of pathology (Bayer, 1981). As documented by Lewes (1988), well-known psychoanalysts like Bergler and Socarides have expressed blatant contempt for homosexuals, and their remarks went unchallenged by their peers. The problem has in part been the conscious hatred and bias against homosexuality; but even more problematic is that many well-meaning psychoanalysts often do not recognize their biases and the way their conceptions of mental health conform to the prejudices of society at large (Blechner, 1992a).

Examining the clinical material in Trop and Stolorow's paper, I think it is quite easy to see the slant in the analyst's interpretations. For example, the analyst interprets his patient's homosexual experiences as reactions to either a failure of empathy by the analyst or to a traumatic interchange with his mother. He also interprets the patient's resistance to and fear of getting further involved with a woman friend as reactions to fears of engulfment or being controlled. These are not neutral interpretations. If the analyst were truly neutral regarding his patient's sexual orientation, he would interpret Alan's resistances to involvement with both men and women. His pattern of relationships with both men and women is the same—he puts himself in the position of the one being seduced and the one who is resisting mutuality in the relationship. If the analyst interprets these resistances to involvement with both sexes, then the patient has a better chance to see clearly his resistances to relatedness with both sexes, and once having worked those through, can make a more independent choice about which sex to choose for a deeper involvement. Otherwise, the analyst, despite all claims of neutrality, can be engaging in a subtle form of influencing without being aware of it.

The slant in interpretation appears over and over in the clinical report. The analyst interprets also "that the patient's homosexual activities seemed to substitute for the alignment with him [the analyst] that his father had been unable to provide" (p. 435). This is a plausible interpretation, but it is no more plausible than that the patient's heterosexual activities are a substitute for the quality of acceptance that he lacked in his relationship with his mother. The analyst also interprets that the patient's "homosexual activity, in which he felt intensely desired and admired, represented an effort to avert the feelings of worthlessness and nonbeing that had resulted from the interactions with his mother and to restore his vanishing sense of aliveness and intactness." This is also a plausible interpretation, but it is no more plausible than that the patient's heterosexual activity, in which he also feels intensely desired and admired, also represents "an effort to avert feelings of worthlessness and nonbeing." That the analyst makes only the former sorts of interpretations is further evidence of bias; he interprets the patient's attraction to homosexual involvements as a reaction to anxiety. He interprets the patient's resistance to heterosexual involvements as a reaction to anxiety. This asymmetry cannot help making a strong impression on the patient, even if not consciously formulated. And a patient who is yearning for mirroring and twinship with the analyst will likely comply, at least as long as he is in analysis, with this bias in the analyst.

I think that Alan is aware of this bias, perhaps only fleetingly. He becomes involved with a woman, but "after several months he decided that he wanted to end the relationship because he felt she was intrusive and critical. At one point the analyst commented that perhaps he wanted to escape from her because he had interpreted her wish to discuss their relationship as criticism, which felt very threatening. In response to this defense interpretation, the patient immediately felt crestfallen and depressed and shaken." That night he meets a man and takes his telephone number.

Why is the patient crestfallen and depressed and shaken? Is it the anxiety raised by the analyst's "correct" interpretation? Or is it despair at registering the analyst's homophobia and biased interpretation that feels coercive? At the next session, the patient "said he was still feeling upset and confused. He said that the analyst's comments in the previous session had made him feel as if his whole world had been turned upside down, and he felt completely alone. The analyst commented that Alan had felt abandoned by him because he had failed to help him continue to articulate his own feelings and trust their validity. Instead, the analyst had unwittingly allied himself with the woman's perceptions and had thereby severed the bond between himself and the patient. In consequence, the patient felt suicidal despair and the return of homosexual desires, in an attempt to replace the lost tie with the analyst."

But what if the patient felt suicidal because he realized the bias in the analyst's interpretations, toward interpreting homosexual reactions as defensive and resistance to heterosexual reactions as defensive? That would fit the patient's words to his analyst, that he "felt as if his whole world had been turned upside down, and he felt completely alone." Is he being forced to make the choice that many gay men felt they had to make with analysts who are consciously or unconsciously homophobic—comply with the bias in interpretation or risk losing the positive, otherwise self-affirming bond with the analyst? Is one's essential sexuality too great a price to pay for maintaining the analyst's self-affirming functions? During treatment, many patients have made the decision, consciously or unconsciously, that trading off one's most deeply felt sexual feelings is worth it to keep the analyst's approval. After termination, unfortunately, they may realize that the decision was a mistake.

I have seen many such patients in consultation, as have Isay and others, patients who have been "treated" by analysts for their homosexuality, supposedly successfully. As long as the treatment went on, they avoided the homosexual behavior. But after the treatment was over, sometimes after a fair amount of time, they realized that the behavioral change accomplished in the analysis did not make them happy. Their attraction to members of the same sex had not disappeared; it had only been suppressed. They realized that during the analysis, they yearned so much for the analyst's approval in the transference that they were willing to go to great lengths to achieve it. If the analyst wants to "change" the patient's homosexuality, he may get the impression that he can do it. But he may not recognize that this seeming change itself may represent a transference–countertransference enactment, in which the patient may re-experience the rejection of his or her essential sexuality by one or both parents.

But sexual orientation does not change so easily as sexual behavior. And these patients now found themselves angry at what now seemed like a manipulation by their former analysts. Most often, the former analyst does not hear about this. The patients are usually angry and see no purpose in paying any more fees to register their complaints. And so the former analysts continue to maintain their pathogenic belief that homosexuality can and should be changed. Meanwhile, the patient is left with the difficult task of rediscovering his sexual desire. If a spouse or children are involved, the process is that much more difficult, painful, and complicated.

When such a change-oriented analysis is in progress, the patient may at times feel consciously that the attempt to change his sexual orientation is misguided, and he may protest against the process, either openly and overtly, or if that fails, in his dreams. At several points, Alan seems on the verge of expressing his perception of the analyst's homophobia. After one homosexual experience, the patient states that he

was very apprehensive about disclosing this event and said that he "knew" the
analyst would never find such activity exciting and that the analyst must feel
"sickened" by even imagining it. The analyst then interpreted Alan's belief
that he was required to feel only what the analyst would feel and that the
analyst would not tolerate any sexual feelings that were different from his
own. (p. 433)

Note here that the analyst implicitly acknowledges the validity of the
patient's perception that he is sickened by homosexual activity. The fact
that he interprets the patient's belief that he was required to feel only what
the analyst would feel reassures the patient. But, despite these words, the
bias in the analyst's interpretations, which I have outlined above, belies his
intention to be neutral and to allow the patient to develop in his own way.
The analyst may consciously believe that he is, but he seems to me not to
have acknowledged and dealt with his own biases.

I would also suggest that the patient's last reported dream certainly
gives one reason to doubt his contentment with the outcome of the analysis (p. 439): "A man dies, and then another man dies. Another man is
taken across the country and is progressively cannibalized in each city."
As Richards (1992) legitimately observes:

That the patient would dream, while on a trip about which he was ambivalent,
that "a man is taken across the country and progressively cannibalized" gives
one pause; as his going on the trip was no doubt regarded, by both patient and
analyst, as "making progress," an element of unconscious irony is at least to be
suspected....Nor should we forget the fact that analysts are capable of missing
a patient's conscious or unconscious irony, especially when it is aimed at them.
(p. 463)

That the patient, on waking, tried to reassure himself that he was not
about to be eviscerated makes one wonder if it feels to him that the guts of
his sexuality are being removed. Certainly, the dream has the themes of
being forced and devoured.

The night before his return, the patient dreams: "I was about to go
through a labyrinth in Iran, and it was booby-trapped, and I knew it was
inevitable that I would die. Then someone came and gave me a detailed
map of the labyrinth, and I arrived safely at Tehran airport." Alan says
"gratefully, that the analyst was giving him the map he needed to feel safe
with a woman." But is that what the patient wants, or has he chosen evis-
ceration for safety? Richards (1992) notes, about this dream: "...also telling
is the fact that the dream is set in Iran, a Mideast country to which the
patient's trip to the Far East presumably did not take him (travel there by

Americans has been banned for years)" and that "safety is relative: Tehran airport is not exactly a haven." Does the patient or analyst know that in Iran homosexuality is officially punishable by death? Has the patient accepted a place of relative safety at the cost of being somewhere he really wants to be?

Some readers may find themselves bristling at this case analysis. We are all so steeped in the bias that heterosexuality is better than homosexuality that it is hard for us to see out of these widely held cultural preconceptions. But if one is to work effectively with lesbian and gay patients, one has the responsibility to become aware of such biases. If you want to test yourself, consider the following case description:

> Dr. D's heterosexuality, not deeply entrenched, served mainly to ensure that her partner's emerging sexuality would not lead to a homosexual interest. Dr. D's idealization of her partner was partially a defense against an awareness of feelings of deprivation and the hatred of her father for failing to respond adequately to her developmental needs. Her heterosexuality also served as a defense against incestuous wishes toward her mother. During early adulthood, however, partly motivated by differing professional interests that involved some increased separateness from her husband and partly motivated by Dr. D's wish to experiment with homosexuality, she again made a tentative effort to resume her individuation, and she took a trip with a casual female acquaintance. Shortly thereafter, her husband abandoned her for another heterosexual relationship.

How do you feel about the formulation of this case? About its clinical "success?" I ask the reader to think through these questions before reading further.

This clinical vignette comes from Hanna (1992). I have transformed it somewhat, to illustrate what I call the test of "bias reversal." I have transposed the words homosexual and heterosexual, and changed the sexes of the people with whom the patient was involved. In the original reported case, the patient shifts from a deep lesbian involvement. The original text went as follows:

> Dr. D's homosexuality, not deeply entrenched, served mainly to ensure her that her partner's emerging sexuality would not lead to a heterosexual interest. Dr. D's idealization of her partner was partially a defense against an awareness of feelings of deprivation and the hatred of her mother for failing to respond adequately to her developmental needs....Her homosexuality also served as a defense against incestuous wishes toward her father....During early adulthood, however, partly motivated by differing professional interests that involved at least some increased separateness from her partner and partly motivated by Dr. D's wish to experiment with heterosexuality, she again made a tentative effort to resume her individuation, and she took a trip with a casual male acquaintance.

Shortly thereafter, her partner abandoned her for another lesbian relationship. (pp. 375–376)

Most heterosexual analysts find the transposed version to be bizarre but have little trouble with Hanna's original version, and this indicates their bias. If you cannot consider heterosexual and homosexual activity and ideation to have equivalent potentials to be defensive or expressive of desire, then you cannot consider yourself neutral.*

The question of the analyst's prejudice is particularly important in relationship to the issue that Dr. Hanna discusses: false-self sensitivity to countertransference. For it is exactly false-self issues, such as a tendency to barter compliance for acceptance, that are likely to lead a patient who is essentially homosexual to try to achieve a "heterosexual adjustment," especially if she perceives that that is what her psychoanalyst wants, consciously or unconsciously. Mitchell (1981) calls some other analysts to task for making a change from homosexuality the analytic issue, and strives instead to have the patient's compliance be in the forefront when that is a focal psychodynamic issue.

Mitchell (1978, 1981) has noted, in general, the importance of the analyst's not having an agenda to change a gay patient's sexuality, but rather that he or she gives primacy to an exploration of dynamic issues. While I agree with Mitchell's argument, I think Trop and Stolorow's article shows how difficult it is to bring it into practice, as long as the analyst harbors conscious or unconscious biases about homosexuality. Given the cultural heritage of Western society today, it is unlikely that anyone can claim to be totally free of such bias. Lesbians and gay men themselves often have to struggle with what is known as internalized homophobia, and the resolution of bigotry against the self is not much easier than eliminating bigotry against others. Nevertheless, the first step in eliminating homophobia, as with all kinds of bigotry, is to make it conscious and explicit.

---

* I would like to make two additional comments about homophobia embedded in psychoanalytic language as shown by this translation process: 1) "Heterosexual partner" is not a fair translation of "lesbian partner." A heterosexual partner sounds much less attached than a husband, which may be the truer equivalent of a committed lesbian partner. 2) In writing about a husband, we would not phrase the last sentence: "her husband abandoned her for another heterosexual relationship." We would say he abandoned her for another woman. Notice how subtly degrading "lesbian relationship" is.

5

The Interaction of Societal Prejudice with Psychodiagnosis and Treatment Aims

Author's Introduction

During the 1990s I was often invited to speak about homosexuality, homophobia, and gender issues. The New York University Postdoctoral Program in Psychotherapy and Psychoanalysis was at the cutting edge on these issues. On December 4, 1993, they held a conference, "Perspectives on Homosexuality: An Open Dialogue." It was the first conference (in history, I think) in which an equal number of openly gay psychoanalysts were featured along with heterosexual analysts, some homophobic, some not. It was an amazing event. Roy Schafer* admitted plainly that most heterosexual analysts still considered homosexuality a pathology that needed to be corrected.

The NYU conference started what I think became a regular format—to have the openly gay analyst engage in direct discussion with the homophobic analyst. There was value in this. Homophobia, like homosexuality, had to come out of the closet. The clinical presumptions of the past needed reexamination in public. Much that had passed for "clinical reasoning" was a mask for personal prejudice.

By that time, I had seen enough people in treatment who had worked with analysts who had tried to change their sexual orientation to realize what a futile project that was. The attempts generally failed and much money was wasted, but the worst was that the patients were often wounded by their psychoanalysts' anti-homosexual statements and simple prejudices masked as expert opinion— statements like: "If you continue to be homosexual, you will never have love in your life; homosexuals are just not capable of sustained,

---

* Roy Schafer is an influential psychoanalyst in New York. In 1954, Schafer was the creator of the "Schafer signs" of homosexuality in the Rorschach (see Chapter 1). Four decades later, he changed his views and published them.

loving relationships." If that were so, why did I know so many gay and lesbian couples that had been together for decades? Apparently, these analysts did not know such gay couples or had excluded them from their world view.

I was now out of the closet completely, not only as a gay man, but also as a gay man who was ready to fight entrenched homophobia. Coincidentally, in 1994, an article about the HIV Service at the White Institute appeared in the *Psychiatric Times*, and it mentioned that I, the director, was gay, thus informing virtually all American psychiatrists of that fact. On the next "National Coming Out Day," when you are supposed to reveal to someone that you are gay, I realized I had no one left to tell.

Meanwhile, I was asked by a group of psychoanalysts in Connecticut to speak about how to work with gay patients. They asked me to speak about principles of gay-affirmative work, and they also asked me to discuss a case presented by Dr. Susan Casden of her work with a gay patient. Dr. Casden was truly interested in correcting any heterosexist bias in her work, and in those discussions I began to hear how much misinformation was harbored by some heterosexual analysts. It wasn't always a question of homophobia. There was a lot of knowledge that the well-meaning heterosexual psychoanalysts just didn't have, knowledge that most gay people take for granted.

In dialogues with heterosexual psychoanalysts, I learned that things that seemed obvious to me could come across as revelations to someone straight. For example, there is the fact that gay people, unlike African Americans or Jews, do not usually have the support of their families to help them endure or fight prejudice. Instead, their families are often the source of prejudice. And in the nuts and bolts of sex practices and gender identity, the level of misinformation among heterosexual analysts was staggering.

For instance, at the Postgraduate Center for Mental Health, I was asked to address the entire training faculty about homophobia in supervision. One faculty member spoke proudly of her work with a male supervisee who was, in her words, very effeminate. She confronted him with being gay, which he said he wasn't, but she felt sure he was. This is a widespread misconception; feminine behavior in men is presumed to indicate homosexuality. I told her a story about that. The actor Tony Randall used to live in the same building in which my office was located. I had had some joking conversations with him during the annual meetings of the building co-op board, but I hardly knew him intimately. He was most well known for his portrayal on television of a rather prissy man in *The Odd Couple*.

One evening in 2000, my mother called me. She had read the news that Tony Randall had just married a much younger woman, and she asked, "Isn't he gay? It's so obvious." And I said, "Mom, I don't know. But I don't think that because a man has mannerisms that you consider feminine, you can presume he is gay."

Some analysts stubbornly clung to their bigoted views, such as Johanna Tabin. Tabin is a member of the National Association for the Research and Therapy of Homosexuality (NARTH), an organization formed by psychiatrists and psychologists who maintained the belief that homosexuality was pathological and could be changed by therapy. She had been asked to give a lecture in memory of Irwin Bieber at a meeting of the American Psychological Association (APA). However, the APA would not allow the lecture to take place at their annual meeting, since the policy of NARTH was in violation of APA policy. In notifying Tabin that their sponsorship of her talk would be canceled, they wrote to her: "The premise of your organization [NARTH] that homosexuality is a treatable disorder is in conflict with the APA's position on sexual orientation."

Tabin decided to publish her views, instead, in *The Round Robin*, the publication of the group known as "Psychologist–Psychoanalyst Practitioners." Ira Moses, the editor of *The Round Robin* and the psychoanalyst who had previously arranged my talks on homosexuality in Connecticut with Dr. Casden, asked me to write a response to Tabin. It was a real dilemma. Some of my colleagues encouraged me to write the response, arguing that the flaws in her viewpoint needed to be exposed. Others said it would be better to ignore her; to respond was merely to give a forum to bigots. I decided to take on the assignment, and here is what I wrote.

The Interaction of Societal Prejudice with Psychodiagnosis and Treatment Aims*

What "causes" homosexuality is an issue of importance only to societies which regard gay people as bizarre or anomalous. Most people do not wonder what "causes" statistically ordinary characteristics, like heterosexual desire or right-handedness; "causes" are sought only for personal attributes which are assumed to be outside the ordinary pattern of life.

John E. Boswell

---

* Originally published in *Round Robin*, September, 1995, 10–14 and January 1996, 7–9.

What is the relationship between societal prejudice, psychodiagnosis, and the aims of psychoanalytic treatment? If a human trait, behavior, or belief system is widely condemned in a society, inevitably some of the victims of that prejudice may wish to change themselves to avoid the prejudice. How should psychiatry, psychology, and psychoanalysis approach this wish? Should it be gratified with purported "treatment" that aims to remove the hated feature? Or should the person's relation to societal prejudice, and the societal prejudice itself, and those who exercise that prejudice, be treated?

This is an old question on which psychiatry does not have an admirable record. In the nineteenth century, for instance, there was an accepted psychiatric diagnosis of drapetomania (Cartwright, 1851/1981; see also Wakefield, 1992), which was the pathological wish of a slave to gain his freedom.

For many years in pre-Nazi Europe, Jews were not allowed to serve in many of the top official positions in society. Many prominent Jews managed to bypass the official anti-Semitism of society by being baptized. In the field of music, for example, Felix Mendelssohn, Gustav Mahler, and Arnold Schönberg were all baptized. Of course, those who were able to "change" fooled no one. When Richard Wagner (1850) wrote his notoriously anti-Semitic essay, "Judaism in Music," he attacked Mendelssohn. And when the Nazis came, those Jews who had been baptized were sent to Auschwitz anyway. Schönberg, among others, realized the folly of trying to change or cover up something so essential; he converted back to Judaism and wrote several works grounded in Jewish themes.

Tabin claims that patients seeking the "treatment" that NARTH's members offer do so voluntarily. The European artists who had themselves baptized were not forced. But they certainly faced tremendous societal pressure to "change." That is the trouble—when there is massive prejudice, the desire to conform may be great, and the psychoanalyst faces a serious ethical dilemma: Should he or she help the patient adapt to society's prejudice, by secrecy or conformity, or should he or she help the patient recognize the debilitating effects of such prejudice and seek a solution that does not compromise the integrity of the self? The psychoanalyst's own participation in the societal prejudice can of course seriously skew his or her clinical judgment.

Tabin writes, "Why is homosexuality seen by some in a special light? Perhaps it is because gender identity and object choice are so basic in ego formation that the subject produces such intense feelings." In the previous draft of her communication, which is the one to which I prepared this response, Tabin answered the question thus: "Why is homosexuality seen by some in a special light? Perhaps it is because whether a particular behavior should be regarded, psychodynamically, as a limiting compromise, in this case runs us into social issues that are separate from the meaning for the person that the behavior may have inwardly." I am glad Tabin saw fit to revise this statement, because her original version shows two basic problems that constantly arise in relation to the stance of NARTH:

1. The focus on behavior among those who talk of "treating homosexuality" is notably unpsychoanalytic. It is interesting how many psychotherapists report the cessation of homosexual behavior as a "cure." This focus on behavior is problematic; I believe it often betrays a strong countertransference in the psychoanalyst, based in anti-homosexual hatred, that is satisfied by the eradication of homosexual behavior of the patient.

2. As psychoanalysts, we ought to be more concerned with feeling, and the feelings in question include desire and self-hatred. The idea that such feelings can be analyzed separately from the person's relationship to society is misguided. Probably no one seeks to change homosexuality separately from his or her experience of anti-homosexual bias in society, and no one seeks to "cure" homosexuality without reference to that same bias. Of course, the way we in our time classify people as heterosexual and homosexual is also a function of social issues (see Katz, 1995). Psychoanalysis has fetishized* sexual orientation to an extraordinary degree. That in itself is worthy of analysis (see Blechner, 1995c), but it cannot be done separately from consideration of historical-social issues.

The perpetuation of the false belief that homosexual *desire* is changeable by psychoanalysts causes great harm in society. It continues to mislead parents of gay children that their child's sexuality can and should be changed. It leads many children and adolescents to be brought into all kinds of psychiatric treatments that are severely damaging to their self-esteem, which is exactly the opposite of what they need clinically. If one is going to address clinical and scientific matters, then the evidence clearly shows that the human suffering of gay and lesbian people is caused by homophobia, not by homosexuality per se. The suicide rate of gay teenagers is three times that of straight teenagers (Gibson, 1989; Ramafedi et al., 1989). Generally such suicides are committed when the teenager faces severe taunting by his or her peers, serious condemnation of homosexuality in his or her upbringing, and alienation and rejection by his or her

---

* See the discussion of "The Gender Fetish" in Chapter 10.

family. Any psychoanalyst who wants to understand the conflict and sorrow of growing up amidst homophobia should read the poignant interview with Richard Socarides, who was an official in the Clinton administration and the openly gay son of psychoanalyst Charles Socarides* (Nagourney, 1995).

Probably all of us who have grown up in this society have some prejudices against homosexuality. For those of us who are straight, they may be ego-syntonic. For those of us who are gay or bisexual, they may result in painful internalized homophobia that is severely ego-dystonic, and which may be the underlying psychological dynamic that leads many people to seek out the sort of behavior change promised by NARTH. An analyst who has not worked out his or her own homophobia cannot help a patient work through his own internalized homophobia. If you are predominantly straight, you must make a special effort to understand how your gay and lesbian patients experience their homosexuality and its role in their lives, and not to project onto them your own reactions to your homosexual feelings. Verghese (1994) has coined the term "homo-ignorance," which effectively characterizes many heterosexuals' lack of simple knowledge about homosexuality. We may all be more alike than different, but our differences may be very important and hard to comprehend.

The kind of treatment espoused by NARTH seriously abrogates the principles of analytic neutrality. I have discussed one recent example of such work (Blechner, 1993a; see also Lesser, 1993; Schwartz, 1993). This is the case presented by Trop and Stolorow (1992), which demonstrates the way a self-object transference can be exploited to achieve behavior change. During treatment, many patients have made the decision, consciously or unconsciously, that trading off one's most deeply felt sexual feelings is worth it to keep the analyst's approval, as well as society's. After termination, unfortunately, they may realize that the decision was a mistake.

At the extraordinary conference—"Perspectives on Homosexuality: An Open Dialogue"—at New York University on December 4, 1993, Dr. Rita Frankiel spoke from the audience, saying, "We analysts have to admit that we have committed atrocities on our homosexual patients." This was an admirable statement, but it is rare. Some psychoanalysts seem unable to recognize the havoc that they have wreaked on the lives of gays and lesbians. The writings of psychoanalysts have offered pseudo-scientific rationales for the discrimination of society at large against homosexuals (see

---

* Charles Socarides is also an active member of NARTH and has published a great deal on homosexuality, stressing that it is due to faulty parenting (e.g., Socarides, 1968).

Lewes, 1988). Open gay men and lesbians have long been excluded from training at most psychoanalytic institutes, although recently the American Psychoanalytic Association has passed resolutions against discrimination in the admission of openly gay and lesbian candidates to training and in promotion as training and supervising analysts.

The American Psychological Association has demonstrated a remarkable ethical probity in refusing to sponsor Tabin's lectureship. Tabin speaks of political correctness, but that is not the issue. Rather, it is *clinical and scientific correctness* that underlies the APA's refusal to sponsor work that perpetuates the persecution of a minority that does no harm to themselves, to other individuals, or to society as a whole. The attempt by NARTH to promulgate such "change-therapy" is clinically destructive and scientifically unfounded. No one should stop NARTH's members from their right of free speech, but it would be unconscionable for the APA to sponsor a lectureship from an organization whose therapeutic agenda is unethical and destructive according to the APA's principles. Those who stood by silently in the days when Bergler and Socarides published their worst anti-homosexual diatribes ought to recognize the importance of the APA's integrity and clarity.

I agree with Tabin that the issue of gender identity and its relation to sexuality in development is an interesting and important one. It has received important discussions by several modern psychoanalysts and other thinkers, including Butler (1990, 1991), Goldner (1991), and Garber (1995). Yet such discussion becomes either constrained or impossible when one is speaking to someone who starts with a pathologizing view of homosexual orientation. Such a political stance, which is NARTH's, polarizes and stifles the discussion with the presumption that homosexuality is an illness to be treated and heterosexuality is its cure.

I certainly agree with Tabin that the current data we have on genetic causation of homosexuality are inconclusive and scientifically controversial, and that it is currently premature to draw conclusions. However, I disagree with her when she writes, "If genes do not create these patterns, we must seek psychological explanations for their occurrence." There are many other factors that can influence something as complex as sexual orientation, such as hormones, the prenatal environment, and perinatal conditions. These issues are more fully discussed by Money (1988); they are far from clear-cut.

Moreover, if we are to seek psychological explanations, we must subject ourselves to the same scientific rigor that we demand of biologists and geneticists. If one is going to criticize LeVay, Hamer, and others for scientific objectivity, one can hardly exempt clinical observation in the psychoanalytic consulting room from the same scrutiny. For example, some psychoanalysts for decades asserted that a parental pattern of distant father and intrusive mother "caused" homosexuality, without considering the alternative hypothesis, that a child's homosexuality "caused" this pattern of relationships with his parents (see Isay, 1989; Goldsmith, 1995, 2001; Blechner, 1995c).

I am most concerned about the well-being of children and adolescents who are "treated" for homosexuality or gender identity disorder. As I have written (Blechner, 1995c):

> As society changes, as open gays and lesbians provide positive role models, adult gay men and lesbians increasingly are aware enough not to seek treatment from analysts who are either homophobic or insensitive to their experiences, and are better able to realize when that is the case and get out of a potentially destructive treatment. For most adolescents, however, that is not the case. Think about it: When you are consulted by parents upset about their teenager's homosexuality, what do you do? Do you agree to see the teenager for treatment of his or her homosexuality? How seriously do you question why the parent has condemnatory attitudes? Is the problem the child's homosexuality or the parent's homophobia? (pp. 271–272)

It is precisely children and adolescents that I am most concerned about, because they are the most defenseless against collective societal homophobia and the concordant therapeutic agenda supported by NARTH. The diagnosis of Gender Identity Disorder (GID) is especially problematic. GID is used and misused in modern psychiatry, with disastrous effects for some children whose parents are distressed by atypical gender behavior (Corbett, 1996).

Tabin raises issues concerning the biological causation of homosexuality. Her citation of the literature is selective and misleading. The interested reader should consult Byne, Hamer, Isay, and Stein (1995) and Money (1988) for a more comprehensive and balanced summary of the data. However, I think it is essential to note that the high significance placed on the biological causation of sexual orientation is a fluke of our particular epoch, and is not fundamental to the question of the aims of clinical psychoanalysis. As I have noted elsewhere (Blechner, 1995c), at the turn of the century, the predominant theory of the causation of sexual orientation was biological. Homosexuals were viewed as having a degenerate constitution and were discriminated against because of their supposed congenital defect. When Freud (1905b) shifted the focus of the cause of homosexuality from the physiological to the psychological, it was experienced as very liberating. It is also true that when Hamer et al. (1993), LeVay (1993), and Zhang and Odenwald (1995), in our day, shift the focus of the cause of homosexuality from the psychological to the physiological, that is also experienced as liberating. So we see two opposite movements that are liberating. Is that not odd? I think this tells us less about the roots of homosexuality than about the nature of anti-gay hatred. Those who hate homosexuals will use any account, biological or psychological, in the service of their hatred. Any shift in viewpoint seems liberating, because it liberates one from the old view that was pathologizing and persecutory; but in no time, the new view, no matter what it is, will be used in the service of hatred. The problem is that almost any attempt to question why someone becomes homosexual turns into an exercise in covert hatred, when the unconscious motivation behind the asking is unaccepting and pathologizing.

In Europe in the 1930s, it was common for non-Jews to talk about the so-called "Jewish Problem." What a hateful term! We all know the tragic fact that the "Jewish Problem" led to the "Final Solution of the Jewish Problem." It makes a big difference whether you address the Jewish problem, or the problem of anti-Semitism. Similarly, we might ask: Why have psychoanalysts devoted so much energy to the question, "Why does someone become homosexual?" and so little energy to the question that is more pressing and also more answerable by psychoanalysts: "Why do people hate and fear homosexuals, treat them badly, and deny them normal human rights when they do not harm anyone?" Maybe when that is the question being asked, the problem of homosexuality will have been solved; it will have been resolved into the larger and more pressing question for all mankind, which is why people hate minorities that are different but in no way dangerous. When psychoanalysts stop acting out the problem of homophobia and, instead, address it and analyze it, our field may regain its standing as the solver of irrational problems instead of the reinforcer of problematic irrationality.

6

The Closeting of History

Author's Introduction

One of the reasons people have treated homosexuals so badly over the years is that they have not been aware of how many good and important people have been gay or lesbian. The profession of psychoanalysis had by and large dismissed gays and lesbians as sick, but the profession of history has engaged in a more subtle form of dismissal. Historians have tried to hide, deny, or cast doubt on the homosexuality of important historical figures. This, in turn, leads people not to realize how many good and significant things have been accomplished by gays and lesbians, and how many people from the past whom they admire have been gay or lesbian. I wrote the following chapter to clarify this process.

The Closeting of History

I would like to describe a common phenomenon, which I call "The Closeting of History." The homosexuality of an important historical figure is covered over or completely hidden by subsequent generations. People who admire the work of the historical figure would rather not admit his (or her) sexuality for several reasons, including fear that homosexuality will reflect badly on the person who is otherwise valorized for his work; personal anxiety about having a role model or leader who has an attribute that his disciples find anxiety-provoking or even repugnant; and institutional and political reasons, such as that the homosexuality of a mentor will weaken the prestige of an institution led by him.

The posthumous closeting of historical figures is much more common than most people realize. When we read Robert Browning's poetry in school, we inevitably hear about his wife, Elizabeth Barrett Browning, and her poetry. Most teachers do not refer to the "heterosexual Brownings," but the information suggesting their heterosexuality is taught all the same. But when we read the poetry of Hart Crane, we usually are not taught that he was homosexual.

W. H. Auden, Tennessee Williams, and Allen Ginsberg made it harder to ignore their sexuality, but it can be done. When I was in high school, I could not name the life-partners of Auden, Williams, and Ginsberg since I had not been taught about them. (I learned about Tennessee Williams' partner of 16 years, Frank Merlo, from an interview in *Playboy* magazine, of all places!*) I have asked some teenagers today about this, and none had a teacher who mentioned Auden's or Williams' lovers. In school, I learned about painter Andrea del Sarto's travails with an unfaithful wife; but I never heard anything about the male lovers of da Vinci or Michaelangelo. In classical music classes, I learned about Gesualdo's murderous jealousy of his wife, but I never heard that Aaron Copland was gay, let alone Händel, Schubert, and Mussorgsky. Some people object that these composers' sexuality has nothing to do with their music.† But then why did we hear so much about Robert Schumann's wife Clara, Richard Wagner's wife Cosima, and Beethoven's "Immortal Beloved"? Why did we hear that Bach married twice and sired 20 children, that Mozart married an opera singer but had many affairs, and that Brahms never married but loved Clara Schumann throughout his life? That Chopin had a tumultuous affair with George Sand, the female novelist? That Stravinsky married twice? That Mahler's wife Alma had many affairs and broke his heart?

Usually the great love of one's life has an effect on one's work. It is not the only influence, but it is a big one. When it comes to love lives, there is a great disparity in how much we are told about people who were heterosexual and homosexual. Look through the articles in any printed encyclopedia,‡ and you will see how different it is with heterosexuals and homosexuals. The spouses of heterosexuals are usually mentioned. The personal lives of homosexuals are usually not spelled out; at best, there may be mention that "he remained single throughout his life."

---

* Williams told *Playboy* (April, 1973, 69–84): "Once, when I was working on a screenplay in Hollywood, Jack Warner said to Frank [Merlo], "And what do *you* do?" Without a moment's hesitation, he said, in his quiet way, "I *sleep* with Mr. Williams" (p. 76).

† Susan McClary argues that differences in sexual orientation can influence the composer's harmony and other purely musical aspects of composition.

‡ In the twenty-first century, written encyclopedias are becoming extinct, as online resources take precedence. On resources like *Wikipedia*, the homosexuality of major figures is mentioned more frequently than in the past.

In some instances teachers go out of their way to disguise or hide homosexuality. My Bible teachers skipped over many references to homosexuality in the Old Testament: Noah's sons, Sodom and Gomorrah, David
and Jonathan, Ruth and Naomi. In elementary school, we learned about
all the heterosexual shenanigans of Jacob trying to marry Rachel and the
risqué story of a woman being brought to David as an old man to warm
him up—but not the homosexual implications of the relationship between
David and Jonathan.

Even the ancient Greeks are not immune from posthumous closeting.
One of the most widely read translations of Plato, by Benjamin Jowett,
hides open references to sexual relations between men. For example,
Plato's *Symposium* contains the following passage:

> As Pausanias says, It is honorable for a man to grant sexual favors to the good
> among men and shameful for him to grant them to the unbridled.

The Jowett translation rendered this passage:

> As Pausanias says, The good are to be accepted, and the bad are not to be
> accepted. (Tripp, 1975, p. 231)

The worst was what was done with Franz Schubert, the Austrian composer who most people agree was the greatest writer of songs in history and
is considered by many people to be the most inspired composer who ever
lived. Schubert died at the age of 31 of syphilis. The musicologist Maynard
Solomon (1981, 1988) collected substantial evidence that Schubert was
homosexual. Since Solomon's articles appeared in professional journals,
they did not cause much of a stir. However, the situation changed when his
views became publicized by journalists.

At the 1992 conference "Schubert the Man: Myth versus Reality" that
was held in New York's 92nd Street "Y" in honor of the Schubert bicen-
tennial, the musicologist Susan McClary presented further evidence of
Schubert's homosexuality and how it may have affected his music. Many
people in the audience were enraged. They were loath to hear that their
beloved composer was probably gay and vented intemperate comments,
which were duly reported by the *New York Times* (Rothstein, 1992), well
before McClary's paper was published in 1994 (see also McClary, 1993,
1994; Clark, 2002).

As I discussed in Chapter 2, as a high school student, I was attacked for
discussing the homosexual themes in Thomas Mann's novels and short stories. My English teacher called me a "vulgarian." I did not realize then that

this was part of a much larger trend in academic scholarship. When professional historians mention the homosexuality of a famous man, they are often attacked. It is still not acceptable in most of American society to say that an important public figure was an overt and active homosexual. And so, it is often left unsaid, and that leads the general public not to know how many of the people whose work they value have been gay or lesbian. Eve Sedgwick, the literary theorist, captured the problem succinctly. She asked, in her *Epistemology of the Closet* (1990): "Has there ever been a gay Socrates? Has there ever been a gay Shakespeare? Has there ever been a gay Proust?" She answered: "Not only has there been a gay Socrates, Shakespeare, and Proust but … their names are Socrates, Shakespeare, and Proust" (p. 52).

It is especially difficult to discuss the homosexuality of politicians and their families. In 1971, James Kempner wrote and privately printed an article giving some of the evidence that Abraham Lincoln may have been gay or bisexual. Previously, Kempner had put together evidence suggesting that Eleanor Roosevelt had had a sexual relationship with Lorena Hickok. The Roosevelt family threatened to sue him, until Doris Faber published her study in 1980, *The Life of Lorena Hickok: E.R.'s Friend*, which supported Kempner's conclusion. More confirmation was to come later, with the publication by Rodger Streitmatter (1998) of *Empty without You: The Intimate Letters of Eleanor Roosevelt and Lorena Hickok* and the biography of Eleanor Roosevelt by Blanche Wiesen Cook (1992). You cannot sue a scholar for speaking the truth, but you can attack him.

In the United States there are at least two presidents who are thought by some to have been gay or bisexual. One of them is James Buchanan (Klein, 1962), a life-long bachelor who was called "Aunt Fancy" and who had a close relationship with William R. King. The other is Abraham Lincoln (Tripp, 2005). I do not wish to explore fully the debate about whether Lincoln was gay or bisexual. The data are convincing enough to me that at the very least Lincoln was quite open to thinking and writing about homosexual relationships and even about a homosexual marriage. Rather than ask "Was Lincoln homosexual?" it makes more sense to ask "How homosexual was Lincoln?" "First Chronicles of Ruben," an early poem that Lincoln wrote, contains the following lines (Wilson & Davis, 1998):

> for rubin and Charles has married two girls
> but biley has married a boy
> the girlies he had tried on every Side
> but none could he get to agree
> all was in vain he went home again
> and sens then he is married to natty. (p. 152)

This poem was in the original edition (1889) of Herndon's *Life of Lincoln*, but was expurgated from every subsequent edition until 1942, when the editor Paul Angle reinserted it. Thus do historians try to hide evidence of homosexuality.

With the revelation of evidence suggesting that a major public figure is homosexual, there are usually certain kinds of reactions. The first is to deny it. When denial fails, dismissal usually follows close behind. It is typical to hear, "He (or she) may have been homosexual, but what does it matter?" Such a reaction came from Lincoln expert Michael Burlingame: "I don't see how the whole question of Lincoln's gayness would explain anything other than making gay people feel better ... and I don't think the function of history is to make people feel good."

I think Burlingame is wrong. If Lincoln was gay or bisexual, it most probably had an effect on his character and, since he was president, on the history of the United States. I cannot prove it, but I think the experience of growing up gay in a homophobic world can have a decisive effect on one's character. One possibility is that one develops a respect for the suffering of all minorities. This was the case with both Abraham Lincoln and Harry Stack Sullivan. Both grew up in small towns and achieved intellectual prowess way beyond what might have been expected, given their constrained educational opportunities. And both did extraordinary work in the public sector to understand and undo the realities of prejudice against minorities of which they were not a part. Sullivan (1938), a white Catholic, wrote about anti-Semitism and racism, as well as on the general causes of ethnic and national hatred. And Lincoln, as everyone knows, led the United States through its Civil War and the abolition of slavery.

Experience with one kind of prejudice can make one sensitive to the suffering of all people who experience prejudice. This was the case of Judd Marmor, who, perhaps more than any other heterosexual psychoanalyst, exerted enormous efforts at eliminating psychoanalytic homophobia. Marmor claimed that his distaste for homophobia derived from his experience of religious prejudice himself growing up.* As Marmor recollected late in life: "It seemed to me that what I was hearing was the stereotyping and stigmatizing of an entire group of individuals, a pattern I had already learned to distrust as a reflection of social prejudice in other areas, for example, toward Catholics, Jews, blacks, and other minority groups" (in Rosario, 2003, p. 25).

---

* Marmor's first name was originally Judah, much more obviously Jewish than Judd (Marmor, 1942).

Similarly, Elie Wiesel, a survivor of Hitler's death camps, came to acknowledge that Nazism needed to be condemned not only for persecuting Jews but also gay people. On November 16, 1987, Wiesel was the guest speaker at the eighth annual dinner of the Human Rights Campaign Fund, a national gay rights organization. No one who was there can forget what he said: "Those who hate you hate me."

This is not to say there are no gay or Jewish racists, Black or Jewish homophobes, and gay or Black anti-Semites. Of course there are. Experience of prejudice is no guarantee against prejudice. But experience of prejudice can increase one's sensitivity to other victims of prejudice, in individuals who are open to self-examination.

I cannot prove that Lincoln's homosexual feeling helped make him aware of racial prejudice, any more than I can prove that Eleanor Roosevelt's experience with lesbianism motivated her to fight racism in her time.* I would argue that homosexual experience is at least one plausible factor that contributed to their compassion for other groups suffering from discrimination. Of one thing I am certain: For anyone who wishes to be considered a serious historian, it is irresponsible and intellectually dishonest to hide biographical evidence of homosexuality.

---

* In 1939, the Daughters of the American Revolution (DAR) would not allow the great Negro singer Marian Anderson to sing in Constitution Hall. Eleanor Roosevelt resigned her membership in the DAR and organized a concert for Anderson at the Lincoln Memorial, which was attended by 75,000 people.

7

Selective Inattention and Bigotry
A Discussion of the Film *Trembling before G-d*

People in general know not what wickedness there is in this pretended word of God. Brought up in habits of superstition, they take it for granted, that the Bible is true, and that it is good. They permit themselves not to doubt of it; and they carry the ideas they form of the benevolence of the Almighty to the book which they have been taught to believe was written by his authority. Good heavens, it is quite another thing! It is a book of lies, wickedness, and blasphemy; for what can be greater blasphemy than to ascribe the wickedness of man to the orders of the Almighty!

Thomas Paine

Intolerance is the natural concomitant of strong faith; tolerance grows only when faith loses certainty; certainty is murderous.

Will Durant

Author's Introduction

Trembling before G-d was the first documentary film about gay and lesbian Orthodox Jews. In 2004, the Psychoanalytic Psychotherapy Study Center in New York arranged a conference about the film. It brought together Simcha ("Sandi") Dubowski, the director of the film; Dr. Stephen Greenberg, an openly gay rabbi; Dr. Mary Gail Frawley-O'Dea, a heterosexual psychoanalyst who had worked with pedophile priests; and myself, an openly gay psychoanalyst who was raised in an Orthodox Jewish family. I had until then tried to draw attention to the common issues in all prejudice, whether it was against Jews, Blacks, women, or gays and lesbians, but now I was being asked to address a kind of prejudice that was personally very painful: prejudice by Orthodox Jews against gay people. It was a prejudice that I knew first-hand.

The attitude of Orthodox Judaism to gay people is very prejudiced, yet the attitudes of fundamentalist Christianity and Islam to
gay people are even more persecutory, as I know from my clinical
practice and from friends. One trouble with all orthodox religions is
that they are remarkably slow to change; since the beliefs of religious
faith are not testable by data, they need never change (Harris, 2004).
Usually, when religious beliefs change, it is only because enough
adherents of the religion wish the change to occur. Since gay people are always in a minority in fundamentalist religions, that kind of
change virtually never happens.*

Selective Inattention and Bigotry: A Discussion of the Film *Trembling before G-d*†

If you want to understand the suffering that religious orthodoxy brings
to people whose sexual desires are not in the mainstream, see the film
Trembling before G-d. It portrays the agony of gay and lesbian Orthodox
Jews who face discrimination by their families and society, yet wish to
remain part of their religious communities. It has been shown around the
world to Orthodox Jewish communities, as well as traditional Christians
and Moslems, and it has the effect of making religious bigots of all stripes
question their prejudice. For many such religious people, homosexuality
had been just a word; they felt disgust at the thought of homosexual sex,
and felt justified in condemning homosexuality as sinful, or its psychiatric
equivalent, sick. After they see this film, they realize that homosexuals are
just as much serious people, with real feelings of love and pain, as heterosexuals, and they start to recognize how religious bigotry causes tremendous human suffering.

I was raised as an Orthodox Jew myself. My family ate only kosher food,
and we kept the Sabbath and all the holidays. I went to a Yeshiva, a Jewish
elementary school, and I wore a yarmulke, a skullcap, all day. It was not
just a matter of keeping the laws; I was truly religious. I believed in God,
and I prayed sincerely. I talked to God and felt him as an active, benevolent
presence in my life.

When I was 13, I was bar mitzvah, the ceremony in which a Jewish boy
takes on the religious responsibilities of an adult. I received many gifts,

---

* The same problem of beliefs not being falsifiable by data has plagued psychoanalysis, too
(Grünbaum, 1984, 1993).
† Originally published in *Journal of Gay and Lesbian Mental Health*, 2008, *12*, 195–204.

including a four-volume set of the Shulchan Aruch, *The Code of Jewish Law* (Ganzfried, 1961). I thought I knew most of the Jewish laws, but I found things in those books that the rabbis had not mentioned. Maybe they did this out of modesty, or maybe they were afraid they would give us ideas.* Anyway, I started reading and came to this passage [151:1]:

> It is forbidden to discharge semen in vain. This a graver sin than any other mentioned in the Torah. Those who practice masturbation and the issue of semen in vain, not only do they commit a grave sin, but they are under a ban, concerning whom it is said (Isaiah, 1:15) "Your hands are full of blood;" and it is equivalent to killing a person....Occasionally, as a punishment for this sin, children die when young, God forbid, or grow up to be delinquent, while the sinner himself is reduced to poverty. (p. 17)

I had already started masturbating. Like most teenage boys, I was doing it frequently and with great joy and wonder that anything could feel so good. Now, here was this book telling me that what I had been doing was the gravest sin of any mentioned in the Torah; it was equivalent to murder! Oy, vey! I did not discuss this with anyone, but I took it seriously.

The Code of Jewish Law advised that when you feel like masturbating, you should avert your attention "to a subject of the Torah, which is 'A lovely hind and a graceful doe'" (p. 17). I tried that. I found myself getting images of Bambi, which is not what the rabbis had in mind. Also, that phrase "A lovely hind" was awfully similar to "A lovely behind," so I was not getting very far with that one.

To avoid temptation, *The Code of Jewish Law* warned: "It is forbidden to hold the membrum while urinating" (p. 17). That did not work for me. Messy! Besides, when you are a teenager, with those hormones surging through your body, you do not have to touch your membrum to bring on an erection.†

Like the people in the film *Trembling before G-d*, I tried to accommodate my religion and my sexuality. But when I got to college, I became increasingly aware that my sexual attraction was mainly to men. I dated

---

* In elementary school, we read the entire Bible in Hebrew—or so I thought. As an adult, I realized that the rabbis had skipped over certain passages that they thought children should not read. So we did not read, for example, about Noah sleeping with his sons. We did not read the injunction in Leviticus about homosexuality, although we did learn which insects it was permitted to eat. I still remember that day. The word in Hebrew for crawling creatures is *Shegetz* and the female is *Shigsa*. The word *Shiksa* to mean a non-Jewish woman has become a commonplace in our language, yet few people who use it realize its derogatory meaning.

† Some Jewish scholars today consider Ganzfried's *Code of Jewish Law* to represent ultrastringent views without basis in halakhic tradition.

girls, and I certainly liked them, but those love feelings that I had read about and seen portrayed in the movies just were not happening for me. In college, toward the end of my freshman year, my closest friend told me he was attracted to me. I was shocked, but I realized that part of the shock was that I was attracted to him, too, only I had not let myself be very conscious of that. After much agonizing and soul-searching, I said, "OK, let's give it a try." What a revelation! Suddenly all those clichés about love—love makes the world go round, love is a many-splendored thing—they finally all made sense.

Just one problem—the Old Testament said it was wrong. So here was the next great glitch in trying to reconcile my religious feelings with my sexuality. I imagined talking to God about this. The God of my imagination was kind and eminently reasonable. How could God create me in such a way that I could feel such deep love, and then forbid me from realizing that love? That would be a cruel, practical joke, and I could not imagine God being that petty. I also had to admit that the Bible was wrong about many things. It sanctioned slavery. It said that an engaged girl who slept with a man other than her fiancé should be stoned. Surely, I thought, we do not follow the Bible on those issues. The Bible must be wrong about homosexuality, too.

I have seen the film *Trembling before G-d* four times. Each time, I am appalled by the lack of empathy in the parents and the orthodox rabbis in this film. To smile so broadly while you tell someone to give up their sex life seems to me downright sinful. You violate the most important of God's commandments: "Love thy neighbor as thyself." Anyone who would tell another person to give up his sexuality should imagine being told that himself and living through its consequences.

The psychotherapists interviewed in the film are conflicted about how best to help their patients. It is very difficult, certainly, to work in psychotherapy and psychoanalysis with religious gays and lesbians, whether Orthodox Jews, devout Christians, or Muslims. The work with these groups is different, although they all face prejudice. Gay Orthodox Jews face rejection by their family, friends, and community. Gay Christians face this too, but in addition, they are told they will burn in hell. Gay Catholics have it especially bad, since there is a living pope who continues to issue edicts condemning homosexuality and trying to coerce secular governments to maintain anti-homosexual policies. Gay Moslems have the added pressure of knowing that in many countries, like Nigeria, Egypt, and Saudi Arabia, their gay brothers still are arrested, imprisoned, tried by religious courts, and stoned to death. The Islamic gay rights group, Al-Fatiha, estimates that in Iran alone, 4000 homosexuals were executed between 1979 and 2003.*

As a psychoanalyst, I have worked with many gay men and lesbians from strict religious backgrounds, and at times their suffering is difficult for me to bear. My personal bias is for people not to give up their sexuality. For me, it is too great a sacrifice, but that may not be true for some people. It is important for a psychotherapist to remember that each person must find his or her own solution to conflicts, about homosexuality as well as anything else. It is the job of the therapist to keep all the issues in awareness, but the solution must ultimately be the patient's solution.

I have seen people come to very different personal solutions and compromises. Some orthodox men make peace with the religion by limiting their sexual activities. For example, the famous eleventh-century Biblical scholar, Rashi, said that Leviticus 18:22 is really only forbidding anal intercourse. Rashi said that it is "putting it in like a paintbrush into a tube." So one orthodox man I know decided that as long as he avoided anal penetration, he could make love to his partner and not violate Jewish law.

Similarly, an orthodox lesbian researched the Talmud and determined that the rabbis decided that the sin for lesbians was to imitate heterosexual intercourse, specifically by one woman lying on top of the other as in the so-called missionary position, or by the use of a dildo for penetration. She decided that she could forego those two sexual limitations, which really were not things that she desired much anyway, and could otherwise make love freely to her partner.

I worked with one Catholic man whose life represented a constant back-and-forth struggle between his homosexual feelings and his family's fundamentalist form of Catholicism. They were not just against homosexuality; they were vehemently against any liberalization of the church, including having the mass in English instead of Latin. This man had had one long-term relationship with another man before I knew him, but he claimed to regret it. He tried to stay celibate (not having sexual relations with another person) and chaste (not masturbating). He was more successful at celibacy than chastity, and stayed celibate for longer than anyone else I knew, but his sexuality continued to influence his decision making in unconscious ways that surprised him and that he had to learn to

---

* In 2007, President Ahmedinejad of Iran visited the United States and spoke at the United Nations and at Columbia University. When asked about persecution of homosexuals in Iran, he replied that there are no homosexuals in Iran.

accommodate. He also came to realize how terribly debilitating it was to his sense of identity and self-cohesion to be in the closet.

Islam is generally very harsh on gays and lesbians, even more so than Judaism and Christianity. Yet I have been told that the Koran itself has no passages that specifically outlaw homosexuality. In fact, as one lesbian pointed out, there is a passage in the Koran (36:36) that reads: "Glory be to Him who created all the sexual pairs, of that which the Earth groweth and of themselves, and of that which they know not." She felt that this passage is affirming of all sexual pairings and justified her life with her lesbian partner.

There is an identifiable progression of psychoanalytic and psychiatric thinking about the "psychopathology" of groups that suffer prejudice (Blechner, 1995c; White, 2002). It starts with an acceptance of society's standards, and an identification of the distress and dysfunction of the individual as a problem inherent in the individual. Gradually (often too gradually), there is recognition that the individual may be suffering not from an inherent, intrapsychic neurosis, but from persistent perversion of living caused by unbearable requirements of surviving societal oppression. There is then a second, intermediate stage in which some theorists identify this maltreatment, and a growing recognition that the individual's problems can be cured not by intrapsychic change, but rather by changing the individual's relation to society. Finally, there is the third stage, in which there is recognition that for the ultimate removal of psychopathology, society itself must change.

As a clinician, I am bound to respect the wishes of my patients and avoid imposing my values on them. For myself, though, I still have my own values, and they are quite defined. The psychoanalytic conference organized in 2003 to discuss the issues raised by *Trembling before G-d* described the film as "A portrayal of the conflict *within* gay men and women." That phrase precisely captures the problem. My personal belief is: Get the conflict out of yourself and put it where it belongs—between the bigots and yourself. Between the orthodox rabbi and yourself; the priest and yourself; the mullah and yourself. They claim to know what God wants and forbid you from being actively gay. Do not let them get away with it. Form your own synagogues and churches and mosques, and create an environment where you can be religious and also enjoy a life with passionate love.

Get the conflict out of yourself and put it between yourself and your parents. In the film, many of the gays and lesbians suffer terribly from rejection by their parents, but they do not challenge their parents forcefully. None of them. It's a shame. I know a gay man whose parents were

Holocaust survivors. Hitler wanted them in the death camps right along-side gay prisoners, and yet the Jewish parents were terribly prejudiced against their gay son. He was shocked and wondered: "How could people who had experienced the worst bigotry in history be bigoted themselves?" And he made that argument to his parents, repeatedly and forcefully, and eventually they felt the shame of their hypocrisy and started to treat their son and his life-partner with respect.

That brings me to another factor not stressed adequately by the film *Trembling before G-d*. For anyone who experiences prejudice, it is impor-tant to have a group of like-minded people to bring change in yourself and in society. Harry Stack Sullivan told us that the self is constructed of reflected appraisals. For any minority that experiences bigotry, the self is constantly exposed to reflected appraisals that are degrading and humili-ating. It happened to the Jews in Germany, and it happened to Blacks in white-ruled South Africa. For the Jews, one of the solutions was to found the state of Israel, a nation where their Jewish identity is valued proudly. Similarly, in post-apartheid South Africa, Black people are now in charge, deciding their own fate, and valuing their identity.

Gay and lesbian Orthodox Jews need to foster their own group organi-zations to affirm their identities. Lesbians in the United States now have the group Orthodykes, and there is a smaller group of gay male Orthodox Jews that meets regularly. But they need more. They need an organization of orthodox gay and lesbian rabbinic scholars who can publicly challenge the orthodox interpretation of the Bible, study the Torah and Talmud, and argue with the religion on its own terms.* They also need orthodox gay and lesbian synagogues, where Jewish family life can be adapted to gay and lesbian couples and their children, where gay and lesbian Orthodox Jews can develop their own communities with their own affirmative atti-tudes and rituals, so that gay and lesbian couples can stand under the Chupah and celebrate their marriages, blessed by a gay orthodox rabbi. When such things are in place, many of the mental health conflicts experi-enced by orthodox gay and lesbians will be remedied. Then, the therapists and psychoanalysts who work with them can focus on psychopathology, not problems caused by a prejudiced society.

Harry Stack Sullivan developed the important concept of "selective inattention." Sullivan (1953) defined selective inattention as the situation "in which one simply doesn't happen to notice almost an infinite series of more-or-less meaningful details of one's living" (p. 319). He continues:

---

* A good beginning for this dialogue has been published by Rabbi Stephen Greenberg (2004).

> By selective inattention we fail to recognize the actual import of a good many
> things we see, hear, think, do, and say, not because there is anything the matter
> with our zones of interaction with others but because the process of inferential
> analysis is opposed by the self-system. Clear recognition of the implications of
> matters to which we are selectively inattentive would call for basic change in
> an established pattern of dealing with the sort of interpersonal situation con-
> cerned; would make us either more, or in some cases less, competent, but in any
> case different from the way we now conceive ourself to be. (p. 374)

Anyone who claims to adhere strictly to the Bible's commandments today must exert a lot of selective inattention. The Bible tells us that if an engaged woman sleeps with a man other than her fiancé, she must be stoned. Who would be willing to enforce that today? No one I know in a Western country, although in Nigeria there was a case of a Muslim woman who faced stoning for committing adultery. The woman underwent a grueling and humiliating trial; there was intense international pressure, and she was finally freed. But there are also cases of gay men on trial in Nigeria, with the potential for receiving a sentence of stoning, and international pressure is not being exerted for them, so far.

A religious cleric of any denomination needs to think seriously about whether it is right to persecute gays and lesbians. By current estimates, the rate of homosexuality is between 4 and 10% (Laumann, Gagnon, Michael, and Michaels, 1994). There are approximately 50 million to 200 million gays and lesbians in the world. Why would you persecute so many people who do you no harm? In Canada, the Netherlands, Belgium, Spain, Norway, and South Africa, it has become quite obvious that when you allow gay and lesbian couples to marry, it has no detrimental effect on the institution of marriage. Gay and lesbian couples raise children who are about as well-adjusted or maladjusted as children raised by heterosexual couples, and certainly better adjusted than children raised in foster care.

There is no rational argument for persecuting gays and lesbians or trying to outlaw their expressing their love in ways that heterosexuals take for granted as their right. Many bigots realize that, and so in desperation they argue that the Bible is the word of God and must be obeyed. But if you are going to insist that the Bible's word is irrevocable, then you must cease your selective inattention. Then you will agree that it is moral for a father to sell his daughter into slavery (Exodus 21:7) and that we can buy slaves from other nations around us (Lev. 25:44). You will agree that anyone who works on the Sabbath should be put to death (Exodus 35:2). And if you argue that such laws ought to be modified or eliminated, for humanitarian reasons, then you should argue that strictures against loving relations between persons of the same sex should also be eliminated. "*Kal vachomer*" as the rabbis would say: "If something applies in a weaker case, it certainly applies in a stronger case."

Some of the most breathtaking selective inattention came from Pope John Paul II. In 2003, he issued a strong statement urging people to work against gay marriage and against the rights of gays and lesbians to adopt and raise children. In that statement he said that allowing children to be brought up in gay and lesbian households "would actually mean doing violence to these children." The church is in an awkward position to lecture anyone on doing violence to children—for decades it has been covering up sexual abuse of children by priests. Bringing up children in a loving household created by two people of the same sex is not violence; it is love. In psychological terms, the pope was engaging in selective inattention. In religious terms, it is hypocrisy.

And on October 12, 2003, Cardinal Alfonso Lopez Trujillo, president of the Vatican's Pontifical Council for the Family, announced on BBC-TV that HIV, the virus that causes AIDS, can easily pass through condoms; this is patently false, as many scientists were quick to point out. But such disinformation will probably lead many Catholics not to use condoms and thus contract HIV. The pope did not revoke Trujillo's statement and thus was complicit in killing many innocent Catholic believers through the spread of falsehood.

Many Christians believe that someday Jesus will return. He was supposed to make an appearance at the millennium, but he did not show up. If Jesus came back today, I think he would attack the Orthodox Jews, the fundamentalist Catholics, and the fundamentalist Moslems, because they are all guilty of hypocrisy and bigotry. Read over the New Testament, and you will see how courageously Jesus attacked selective inattention, which he called hypocrisy.

If Jesus did return today, he would not even need to change his words; he could address the religious hypocrites of today with the same words he used 2000 years ago, with just a few adjustments to modern culture.* He could quote himself, from the Gospel according to St. Matthew, 23:23: "Woe to you experts in the law, you hypocrites! You give a tenth of mint, dill, and cumin, yet you neglect what is more important in the law: justice, mercy, and faithfulness! Blind guides! You strain out a gnat yet swallow a camel!"

---

* In the quotations from the gospels that follow, I have removed the words "Pharisees." Jesus addressed these comments to the Pharisees 2000 years ago, but today they would apply to religious clerics of many religions.

To the pope who sanctions the cover-up of pedophile priests but says that allowing children to be brought up in gay and lesbian households "would actually mean doing violence to these children," and who spreads dangerous false information about HIV passing easily through condoms; to the Orthodox Jews who torment their gay and lesbian children; and to the Islamic courts that imprison and kill gay men; Jesus could say, as he did in the Gospel according to St. Matthew, 23:27: "Woe to you, experts in the law, you hypocrites! You are like whitewashed tombs that look beautiful on the outside but inside are full of the bones of the dead and of everything unclean. In the same way, on the outside you look righteous to people, but inside you are full of hypocrisy and lawlessness."

To the church that burned Giordano Bruno at the stake for agreeing with Copernicus that the earth revolved around the sun, and that imprisoned the wise prophet Galileo for the same supposed sin, Jesus would say, as he did in Matthew 23:29:

> Woe to you, experts in the law, you hypocrites! You build tombs for the prophets and decorate the graves of the righteous. And you say, "If we had lived in the days of our ancestors, we would not have participated with them in shedding the blood of the prophets." By saying this you testify against yourselves that you are descendants of those who murdered the prophets. You snakes, you offspring of vipers! How will you escape being condemned to hell?

If there is one thing that religion teaches us, it is to strive for high ideals. "Love thy neighbor as thyself." Treat people as you would want to be treated. Support human love above all else, and combat every cruelty and hatred, since you would not like them to be targeted against you.

Prejudice is a terrible problem, and we have to try to eliminate it. We know that all gays and lesbians have coming-out stories—stories of how they discovered they were gay, how they dealt with it, whom they told, whom they hid it from, and how everyone reacted. But, like the Reverend Martin Luther King, Jr., I have a dream. I have a dream that one day *there will be no more coming out*. No one will need to come out as gay or lesbian. Young people will discover their sexuality and identify themselves, without fear. Their families, whatever their religion, will take in the information matter-of-factly and that will be that. No one will be attacked for their sexuality, by their family or their schoolmates or their religious leaders. They will date and kiss and go to dances and proms, and suffer all the anxieties of teenagers, no more or less than if they were straight. And when they find someone they love, young gays and lesbians will go steady, get engaged, and get married if they want, publicly, with joyous celebrations, religious celebrations if they want, in the company of their families and friends. And they will build families and face life's struggles and pains and pleasures just like their straight brothers and sisters. That is my dream. I hope that we can make it come true.

Section II

Sex, Gender, and the Good Life

If they can get you asking the wrong questions, they don't have to worry about the answers.

Thomas Pynchon

8

Maleness and Masculinity

Author's Introduction

Being part of an "out-group" sometimes gives one the objectivity to see things that those entrenched in the mainstream of civilization cannot notice. And so it is with maleness and masculinity. Since those early days in the college library stacks when I began reading so much literature on homosexuality, I have noticed generalizations that simply did not fit me. Perhaps, I thought, I am an outlier, a weird fellow, not a typical homosexual. I doubt now that there is such a thing as a typical homosexual, any more than there is a typical heterosexual. Still, many psychoanalytic writers continue to make generalizations about sex and gender identity that are simply false.

Men are supposed to be the tougher sex, and on average they are, with respect to muscular strength and bodily mass, but I am not sure that men are tougher with respect to confidence and security in their gender identity. Western society puts such heavy burdens on men to fit an ideal of masculinity and to rid themselves of femininity. Based on this cultural stereotype, Freud conceived of women as defective men, without penises or adequate superegos. The burden of assuming an invulnerable toughness makes many men's masculinity a brittle, fragile thing. I think this masculine fragility is a major contributor to homophobia in its literal sense, a phobia about homosexuality. Straight men who are insecure about their masculinity often attack gay people, thus trying to disavow and undo their own fears of not being masculine enough.*

"All generalizations, including this one, are false," as Mark Twain said. I have heterosexual male friends who have shown me that the fear of appearing or being thought gay is not universal. My favorite

---

* As noted in Chapter 1, in a study of the Rorschachs of nonpatients (Hooker, 1958), gender identity confusion was *more* common in heterosexuals.

example is this: My partner was once in need of a medical specialist, and he asked for a referral from our friend Paul, a heterosexual,
married physician. Paul gave us the name of the most prominent
specialist in his hospital, and my partner went to see him. During the
exam, he mentioned he was gay.

A week later, the specialist said to Paul, "You know, that man you
sent me was gay." Paul said, "I know. So?" The specialist mumbled
some prejudicial things, then paused, looked at Paul worriedly and
said, "Are you gay, too?" Paul just said, "Ha!" and walked away, neither denying nor confirming.

Maleness and Masculinity*

The question "What is a real man?" provokes much humor in our society.
What is a real man? Someone who doesn't eat quiche? Over the Passover
holidays, I heard that the real reason the Jews wandered in the desert for
40 years is that the men refused to ask directions. The fact that there is a
whole repertoire of "real men" jokes betrays the great anxiety, in our culture, about what a real man is. The very word "real" captures the problem.
What is not a real man? Is it a fake man? A woman? What qualities are
condensed into the "realness" of a man?

What is a real man? Is it defined by how big your salary is, how big
your intellect is, how big your muscles are, how big your other things are?
Is it defined by your bravery, your ability to walk on hot coals, your ability to fend for yourself in intellectual debates? Is it defined by a rejection
of dependency, not only not asking directions, but not looking at maps,
and not even letting your wife or partner look at a map? Is it defined by a
propensity for rough-and-tumble play? Is it defined by whom you have sex
with and with what enjoyment? Is it defined by what you do sexually with
your sex partner—which act, how often you do it, how hard your penis is,
how long your erections last?† I think that the answers to these questions
would depend on whom you asked and what their cultural background is.
To address these questions, I would like to take a small detour into philosophy, psychology, and psycholinguistics.

---

* Originally published in *Contemporary Psychoanalysis*, 1998, *34*, 597–613.
† Bernie Zilbergeld (1978, p. 23) has described the typical male fantasy: "It's two feet long, hard as
  steel, and can go all night."

Categories and Metaphors

We have in our culture a presumed dichotomy of male and female. But how are those categories divided? Can every human specimen be fit into one of those categories? How do we make that judgment? Many people may claim that their judgments on such issues are intuitive, but it is one of the tasks of psychoanalysis to deconstruct these judgments.

One psychologist who has devoted much of her research to the question of how we categorize the world is Eleanor Rosch. Rosch's research (1977) indicates that people categorize objects in terms of prototypes and family resemblances, not just through a collection of features. For example, consider birds. Most people consider small, flying, singing birds like robins to be prototypical birds. Other kinds of birds, such as chickens, owls, penguins, and ostriches, are nonprototypical birds. They are classifiable as birds, because they share certain essential characteristics with robins. And there are many quite striking unconscious presumptions that people make about the relations between prototypical and nonprototypical members of a class (Mervis & Rosch, 1981).

Another line of research relevant to our subject is the work of George Lakoff (Lakoff & Johnson, 1980; Lakoff, 1987). Lakoff argues that much of our thought and language is structured by metaphors. We think of many concepts in terms of other concepts. One common metaphor is "Love is a journey." If our relationship is in trouble, we may say, "I don't think this relationship is going anywhere," or, "We're just spinning our wheels," or, "This relationship is a dead-end street." If things are going well, we may say, "Look how far we've come." All of these metaphors are easily understandable, although most of the time they are out of our conscious awareness. Although Lakoff does not call himself a psychoanalyst, his work is in many ways essentially psychoanalytic, because it identifies unconscious and preconscious meaning systems in human psychology.

The work of both Lakoff and Rosch is grounded in the thinking of the great philosopher Ludwig Wittgenstein (1953), whose analysis of human "language games" laid the groundwork for understanding how we think by what we say. Wittgenstein, Rosch, and Lakoff study what today is called the "cognitive unconscious." Their work is, in my view, critical to psychoanalytic understanding.

Let us return to Rosch's idea of the prototype. What is the prototype for a male in our society? Let me ask you to close your eyes for just a moment. Now summon up your image of the most manly male. Take a bit of time to examine your image before reading further. Who did you see?

The Marlboro Man? A president of the United States? An athlete? A ballet dancer? A psychoanalyst? I have encountered people whose prototypic manly male was each of these, with the exception of a ballet dancer. It would be valuable to get quantitative data on this question.

The sexologists John Money and Anke Ehrhardt (1972; see also Stoller, 1968) see masculine gender identity as a confluence of factors: genetic (XX versus XY chromosomes), anatomy (penis versus vagina, flat chest versus breasts), secondary sexual characteristics (facial hair, body shape), and a whole range of behavioral tendencies (athleticism versus sedentariness, self-assertion versus compliance, self-adornment versus utilitarian dress, attention to achievement versus to romance). The list of possible attributes could be quite a bit longer. The relative psychological importance of these factors in judgments of masculinity has yet to be determined, and the question of maleness versus masculinity as possibly different categories also is open to study. But significantly, Money and Ehrhardt notice that many characteristics of masculinity vary in different cultures and can change rather rapidly over time. They wrote in 1972, "It is a popular pastime, nowadays, to talk and write about the American male's loss of masculinity, thereby misinterpreting what should more accurately be interpreted simply as an accommodation of certain traditional facets of gender role, male and female, to changing times and circumstances" (p. 13). In other words, what one person might call a loss of masculinity might be viewed by another person as a redefinition of masculinity.

Corbett (1996) has done just this in his excellent discourse on sissiness. In it, he rejects the social stereotype of sissiness as a preponderance of certain mannerisms and behaviors defined as weak, and instead focuses on sissiness as a particular path in which a young man may experience himself, and which can be a strong-willed self-assertion of a kind of individuality. When, in 1969, the transvestites at the Stonewall Bar refused to be arrested by the New York City police, they proved, in one fell swoop, that being defined as a sissy by someone else does not make you a sissy. That is, those transvestites were very masculine, if brave, assertive behavior by a man is defined as masculine. In their courage during the Stonewall rebellion, which launched the gay liberation movement, they proved that they were more "manly" than the gay men in business suits who let themselves be arrested and paid fines to try to avoid publicity, and more manly than the cowardly police who were persecuting an innocent minority.

But consider this: Was Rosa Parks masculine when she refused to sit in the back of the bus? We men, gay and straight, have appropriated certain virtues for ourselves, so that women who take part in them may have to call themselves tomboys to take them back for themselves (A. Harris, 2005). What about the idea of a sissy girl? On face value, this may sound like an oxymoron. But many people can imagine a potential meaning of a sissy girl, such as a girl with the traits that were once considered prototypical of girls, but which today, in some circles, are considered the effects of oppression of women.

This is an example of how changing the metaphor can change the reality. Lakoff and Johnson (1980) argue that this is possible, even inevitable: "New metaphors have the power to create a new reality.... If a new metaphor enters the conceptual system that we base our actions on, it will alter that conceptual system and the perceptions and actions that the system gives rise to. Much of cultural change arises from the introduction of new metaphorical concepts and the loss of old ones" (p. 145).

One basic metaphor operating in our culture is "Masculinity is a good substance." We say, "Are you man enough for it?"—implying that there is a quantity of manhood required for a task. We don't say nearly as often, "Are you woman enough for it?"* The unconscious distinction is that manliness is a quality of goodness and strength, and more is better. Our representation of womanliness is quite different, and subtly demeaned. Orthodox Jewish men, in their daily prayers, still thank God for not having made them women. Women thank God for making them "according to His will." Such distinctions continue in our language. We say "He has been unmanned," yet we do not say "She has been unwomanned."† "Unwomanned" sounds like a neologism, although it is plausible to assign meaning to the word. If being unwomanned entered common usage, it would signify a shift in our culture.‡

In all these linguistic subtleties are encoded our unconscious views of masculinity as a good substance and femininity as lack of that substance. When Freud characterized the vagina as the lack of a penis, I don't think he was identifying an immutable given of the unconscious; he was iden-

---

* But see Glazer (2001) for a lesbian's concerns about being "woman enough" for motherhood.
† This sentence is true today in American culture generally. However, the definitions of a "real man" and a "real woman" have been profoundly questioned by Bornstein (1994). Those who would like to become more aware of their presumptions concerning gender should read *My Gender Workbook* (Bornstein, 1998).
‡ Similarly, Karen Shore (1998) has pointed out how managed care has attempted to change the self-image of psychologists, psychiatrists, and social workers, and what we actually do, by changing the way we think of ourselves. By calling us "providers," rather than clinicians, they attempt to get us to provide a product that they can regulate, instead of having us think of ourselves as clinicians who take care of our patients.

tifying a metaphor that expresses how Western society has structured masculinity and femininity.

Gays, Straights, Queers, Trade, Men Who Have Sex with Men, and Other Categories

Our coding of traits as masculine or feminine may often be a product of preconceived notions and wish fulfillment. Mitchell (1996) gave us an excellent example of this. He remembered how his father trained him over and over, in baseball, to catch grounders, to keep his eye on the ball, and not flinch in his attention or give way to the reflex to turn away. But when he discussed it with his father later in life, his father told him that such training sessions happened only once or twice. Mitchell then realized that he had recoded his memory according to an ideal of how a father should be. In fact, he tells us, his father was an anxious person, and the lesson of approaching life's difficulties by looking at them head-on was probably something that he had learned from his mother, who was a much "steadier, quietly steadfast, extremely resourceful person."

This example highlights the fact that memory is often an active organization of the past into what could have been or should have been (Bartlett, 1934). But it also highlights the categories that most of us hold about which traits can and should belong to men and women. What are those?

One of the most common ways of defining masculinity is through sexual activity. In heterosexual American society, masculinity is defined sexually by heterosexual intercourse. Therefore, any sexual activity by men with other men is seen as a compromise of masculinity. In several subsets of American culture, however, and in many other cultures, including Latino, a different metaphor applies: Masculinity is penetration. People who operate with this metaphor do not consider themselves to be gay or to be compromising their masculinity when they have sexual contact with other men in which they themselves perform the act of penile penetration.* Thus we find that there is a large group of what has been called heterosexually identified "men who have sex with men (MSM)." These are people who regularly perform penetrative anal and oral intercourse with other men, but consider themselves masculine and not gay (although they

---

* It is significant that in English we do not have a single-word antonym for penetration. We say that someone penetrates or is penetrated. The implicit passivity of being penetrated is reflected in our linguistic usage of the passive verb form. Bieber et al. (1962) bypassed this linguistic quirk by using the neologism "insertee" as the opposite of "insertor."

consider their partners to be gay). Such men could say, quite sincerely, "I'm not gay, but the man with whom I have sex is gay."

While this attitude seemed startling to contemporary researchers, it was actually the most common attitude among New York men in general until the 1940s, according to historian George Chauncey. In his book *Gay New York* (1994), Chauncey outlines how in the early twentieth century men did not divide themselves up into the simple categories of heterosexual, homosexual, and bisexual. Instead, there were queers (or fairies) and trade. Trade were men who considered themselves not queer, but who would allow themselves to be sexually serviced by other men, always taking the insertive role. They were, behaviorally, the equivalent of today's heterosexually identified "men who have sex with men." Queers, by contrast, were the men who solicited trade and who played what was considered the feminine role, whether or not their behavior was otherwise feminine. Two factors seem to have been most important in changing this categorization. The first was the McCarthy era hunt for homosexuals, which bypassed the queer–trade distinction and villainized any man who had sex with another man. This was followed by the gay liberation movement, which took under a single umbrella all people who felt love for members of the same sex.* Many people who were yesterday's trade became defined today as bisexual or homosexual, and some of them stopped engaging in sex with other men, having been thus redefined, according to Chauncey. So here we have a fascinating case, in recent history, of a simultaneous change in metaphor and categorization, which changes the moral and psychological reality of our world, with simultaneous changes in behavior, self-concept, moral precepts, and the law.

The precise causation of these changes is open to question. It would be hard to identify whether the change in categorization caused the change in metaphor, or vice versa. The concepts we have available, the ways we think of ourselves, how we behave, how we think and feel about how we behave, how society judges and regulates these behaviors and self-concepts—all these factors interact in very complex ways.

---

* This may be analogous to what happened to European Jews who converted to Christianity in the nineteenth century. Certain positions in society were not open to Jews, and so many people were baptized in order to advance in society. Some of these people may have considered themselves Christians, until the advent of Nazism, which redefined such converts as Jews and subjected them to severe persecution. Nazism erased several former categories, such as the "assimilated Jew" and the "Jew converted to Christianity." All were simply Jews, and in the wake of this "de-categorization," a number of baptized Jews, such as the composer Arnold Schönberg, reasserted their Jewish identity.

Psychoanalysis: The Once and Future Queer Science

Today we are in the midst of yet another shift. The word "queer" has been rehabilitated. In an ironic reversal of stigmatization, "queer" has been revived to embrace many kinds of expressions of sex and gender that were once considered "deviant" or, in Roy Schafer's (1995) term, "non-normative." "Queer" has come to include transgendered individuals, transvestites, gay men, lesbians, and bisexuals. Even heterosexuality is queer when you look closely at all of its varieties. An academic discipline, queer theory, has provided an intellectual umbrella for the study of all these categories while trying to avoid stigmatization, medicalization, or correction. Of course, psychoanalysis was once a very queer theory. It scandalized traditional psychiatry in Vienna, with its proposition that in our unconscious we are all quite queer ("polymorphously perverse" may be a more scientific term for "queer"). Along these lines, I once heard psychoanalysis called "the analysis of the id by the odd." In mid-twentieth-century America, psychoanalysis became much more reactionary, with an attempt to valorize the supposed normality of middle-class stereotypes. (Women who wanted equal rights with men were told they had penis envy. Women who had as many sex partners as men were diagnosed as nymphomaniacs.) But it is possible that psychoanalysis could be rejuvenated by becoming a more queer theory than today's academic queer theory.

We need to study the defensive roots of the ways that gay and straight men theorize each other's sexuality. We also need to study how fantasies about homosexual acts and feelings interact with personal countertransferences and affect the transference–countertransference picture (Blechner, 1993). For example, there seem to be many reports by male analysts of their male patients wanting to suck the analyst's penis or to be penetrated by the analyst anally. There are far fewer reports of patient fantasies where the male analyst sucks the patient's penis or is penetrated anally by the patient. Is that a product of a power differential between patient and analyst, with the ascription of power to the penetrator and lack of power in the one who is penetrated? Is there a bias among patients along these lines, or do patients pick up their analyst's anxieties and comply? Or is it a reporting bias of male analysts, who might be embarrassed to report a patient's fantasy of penetrating the analyst?

Confusions of the Concrete and Metaphoric

Many straight men who have never been penetrated anally by another man have developed a kind of mythology about the experience. They think of it as an act of submission and passivity, as the abrogation of masculinity, and as a potential dreaded humiliation.* They think of it as something they always have to be on guard about, so they make jokes that express their anxiety, like saying to each other, "Don't bend over to pick up the soap in the shower!" which brings guffaws of released anxiety, with the implication that such a posture might lead to being raped.

For many gay men, on the contrary, being the receptive partner in anal intercourse is not only not dreaded, it is ardently desired (Corbett, 1993). But also for a gay man, being penetrated anally is not necessarily passive surrender; for quite a few men, it is experienced as assertive.† To make things more complicated—and these matters are often quite complicated— the essence of submission for many people is not in the act, but in the interpersonal ramifications of the act. For example, I once worked with a man who had desires for being penetrated anally, although he also could be reasonably satisfied by penetrating his partner. His long-time partner only could function in the receptive role, and so my patient experienced his sexual activity, of penetrating his lover, as something like a passive submission. He always did what his lover wanted.‡

Let us consider passive submission further. There are many psycho-analytic case reports in which a patient talks about submitting to a male authority figure, or even learning from a male mentor, and this experience is then codified in sexual terms, as a passive sexual submission to the father figure in reality or in the transference. It is often not clear whether this sexualization is purely a product of the patient's thinking, or whether it is put into those terms by the psychoanalyst's interpretation, or some combination of the two.§

To a gay man reading these case reports, the metaphor of sexual submission might require a bit of a leap. The sexual position presumably feared by the straight man may not really be something feared by the gay man; on the contrary, it is something that might be welcome. Straight men might

---

* There are women who adopt the prevalent male model of domination through penetration by fantasizing revenge for male domination. I know a woman who, on achieving a particular career success in a male-dominated field, imagined that she was symbolically forcing men to fellate her. She said, "Let them suck mine!" As much as she was a feminist, she was capitalizing on the most stereotyped aspects of fellatio-as-submission.

† They are referred to colloquially as "power bottoms."

‡ These observations could be similarly considered in terms of women's experiences of being penetrated in sexual intercourse.

§ One notable example of skewed sexualization is Miller (1985), who describes a bisexual male patient who prefers penetrating other men anally in his real life. Yet no such fantasied behavior with the analyst is reported. Instead, Miller describes the patient's fantasy of sucking the analyst's penis.

easily say that the gay man does have this dread, or that lacking this dread is psychopathological, or that if the gay man were really allowed to develop his masculinity, he would not have these desires. But it just doesn't work that way. Straight male psychoanalysts, if they are to work effectively with gay men, must learn that their presumptions about what they consider sexual passivity and submission may not hold true for their gay patients, just as gay male psychoanalysts have to remember that overt sexuality between men is something that is frightening and taboo for many straight male patients.

There are many ways that sexual metaphor can be used and understood differently by straight and gay men. I am often impressed, in analyses of straight men, to hear how they think of their maleness, how they experience homosexual ideation, and how they incorporate such ideation in their figures of speech. It is noteworthy how often men who have had no overt homosexual experience use sexual metaphors in describing their interactions with other men. For instance, it is a commonplace for a man to describe finalizing a business deal or partnership with another man as "getting into bed with him." Another businessman, who often needed encouragement from his boss before he could start an aggressive business deal, would speak to me of going to his boss for a "meat injection." There is something quite playful about straight men using such sexual imagery. It is predicated, I think, on a firmly held taboo against any kind of overt homosexual activity. Homosexual men, I think, are less likely to use such language metaphorically, because such language is not a metaphor for them. When a gay man talks about getting into bed with another man, he means it—literally. By the way, although more and more business deals take place today between men and women, I have not yet heard a man use the metaphor of getting into bed with a woman business associate, where he did not mean sexually.

The gay psychoanalyst may hear the homosexual imagery used by straight men less metaphorically than the patient intends. On the other hand, the straight psychoanalyst may imagine the homosexual activity of gay men in his own idiosyncratic terms. *It is in this middle region, in the crossover between the literal and the metaphoric, that many of the misunderstandings between gay and straight men have taken place.*

I would like you to imagine a man coming to you for psychoanalytic treatment. You discover that from age 7 to 12, he and many other boys were taken away from their families to a compound that was exclusively inhabited by men. It was a place where he was pushed to work, and, during leisure hours, he sucked the penises of the older males in the compound.

They told him that it was good for him, that ingesting other men's semen would make him manly, so that the more penises he sucked, the manlier he would become. He was also warned to keep away from women, who, he was told, would sap his energy.

Consider what effect, in your view, such an experience would have on this man's development, his adult personality, and the picture of his sexuality. Would you expect that, as an adult, he would have a predilection for sucking penises? Would you expect him to act in a mode of passive surrender?

The scenario I just described is the norm for adolescent boys in a tribe in New Guinea that has been studied by Gilbert Herdt (1981) and which he calls the Sambians. Among the Sambians in New Guinea, it is standard practice for boys to be sequestered from women for a number of years and to suck the penises of older males. The belief in that culture is that the ingestion of semen will make them manly. So, what heterosexual American men might consider sexual submission is seen, in Sambian culture, as the route by which proper masculinity is achieved. The boys go on to become married to women and to father children, with fairly infrequent homosexuality. But among the Sambia, the boys are not seen as sexually submissive; the older males are seen as generously sharing their semen, their strength, and masculinity to make the boys men. What many in our culture might describe as a ritual of sexual submission is seen among the Sambia as an initiation rite in which older males share their precious, masculine essence of semen with the younger generation.

These observations raise some fundamental questions about how men relate to other men in our culture and how that experience is codified. Butler (1995) even has hypothesized that the incest taboo is not really the strongest taboo in our culture. Instead, she claims, it is the taboo on homosexuality. In my view, the relations between heterosexual men in our culture are twisted by this taboo on homosexuality, because it creates anxiety whenever men want to have intimate exchanges with other men.

It is probably significant that many of the most widely held definitions of masculinity in our culture are definitions of the individual. Society has defined masculinity in such a way that the term "masculine relatedness" is almost an oxymoron (Bergman, 1996). Sándor Ferenczi knew this. He noted that many heterosexuals have such a dread of homosexuality that it interferes with the ability of men to develop friendships and close ties with other men. Ferenczi argued that the suppression of homosexual feelings could lead to alcoholism and pugnaciousness, so that bullies are obsessed with denying any trends of homosexuality in themselves by trying to beat up others who do show signs of homosexuality. We could say of such bullies, "Milady doth protest too much." Real men don't need to dread homosexuality.*

Asymmetries of Homophobia

Many straight men feel profoundly threatened even by a noncoercive sexual advance or an expression of romantic affection from another male. It is not infrequent to hear of a man reacting to a sexual advance or a declaration of love from another man with hostility, violence, or even murder (Blechner, 1996). In 1995, a talk show hosted by Jenny Jones invited people with long-standing secret feelings of love to appear on television. One of these people was Scott Amedure, who declared his secret love for another man, Jonathan Schmitz. Schmitz killed Amedure three days later.

What does it mean for a straight man to be approached sexually by another man? For many men, it seems, such an advance is experienced as profoundly threatening. It is felt to undermine the man's masculinity. If there are unconscious or dimly apprehended reciprocations of such feelings, a man may react as if attacked. The fantasy is that even the suggestion of homosexuality takes away or compromises a man's manhood. How fragile a thing is this manhood that fears crumbling at the mere suggestion of homosexuality!

One of the queerest things about homophobia is how asymmetric it is with respect to the sexes. Can straight men bear the sight of two men kissing? I'm not talking here about a peck on the cheek. I mean the sight of a warm, wet, open-mouthed, passionate kiss between two men. In the movie *Jeffrey*, written by Paul Rudnick, when the main characters kiss each other passionately for the first time, the camera shifts to a movie audience presumably watching the movie. Many of the men in the audience look revolted and utter commentary on the scene, like "Yuck!" A few years later, Rudnick scripted another movie, entitled *In and Out*. It also has a sudden, passionate, full-mouth kiss between Kevin Kline and Tom Selleck. This time, the camera did not shift its gaze to the audience. But I did. And I noticed that several men in the audience behaved just as expected, looking away in disgust and yelling "Gross!"

---

* Adams, Wright, and Lohr (1996) showed that homophobia is correlated with penile enlargement to homosexual imagery, providing empirical support to the idea that at least some homophobia is rooted in homosexual feelings that are repressed, suppressed, or dissociated.

What is so threatening about a passionate kiss between men? To me, the revulsion seems awfully queer. There is no comparable public revulsion of gay men to scenes of heterosexual passionate kissing.* And straight men do not usually react with horror to scenes of two women kissing passionately. On the contrary, a perusal of the pornography that sells to heterosexual men will show you that the sight of two women kissing passionately and stimulating each other intimately is very arousing to many heterosexual men. Empirical research (Nyberg & Alston, 1977; Turnbull & Brown, 1977; Kite & Whitley, 1998) has confirmed this fact that has been obvious to pornography dealers. By contrast, North American heterosexual women are nearly equally unaroused by scenes of women kissing women and men kissing men. Why is that? The answer may tell us much about how sexual desire, and sexualized disgust, are different for men and women.†

Cross-cultural research might also tell us important things about how a culture may shape and constrain our sexual reactions. For example, while most North American women claim not to be interested in gay male pornography, that is not true for Japanese women. They love to look at comic books with gay male pornography, which is known as *shounen ai* —boys' love.‡ Why is that? We don't know.

One explanation for the horror that many men feel toward homosexuality, and their general insecurity about any deviation from their ideal of masculinity, has to do with the different developmental lines of men and women. Masculinity, more than femininity, has been viewed as an achievement, not a state of being (Person, 1995, p. 167). In cultures where women are the primary caretakers, males and females usually form their first and most intensive bond with their mothers. As the child grows up,

---

* One of my friends, upon reading this, told me that his gay partner does feel revulsion when seeing a movie with heterosexual kissing, but he keeps quiet about it.

† Chivers et al. (2004, 2007) have found a basic difference in sexual responsiveness of men and women to erotic films. The gender of the people in the picture makes a big difference in men's response; the activity of the people in the film makes the most difference in women's response. A straight man responds sexually more to pictures of women than of men, whether they are pictures of nude exercise, masturbation, or intercourse. A heterosexual woman, by contrast, is quite sexually responsive to pictures of intercourse regardless of gender pairings in the pictures (male–male, female–female, or male–female), while she is relatively unresponsive to pictures of men or women exercising naked. Women have an erotic genital response to films of intercourse between Bonobo chimpanzees, while men do not.

‡ The most popular genre, since the 1970s, is *shoujo manga* or "girls' comics." One of the few that has been translated into English is *Banana Fish* by Akimi Yoshida. It can be found at www.viz.com, translated by Matt Thorn, an American anthropologist whose work (www.ky.xaxon.ne.jp/~matt) focuses on the history and culture of *shoujo manga*. Since writing this, I have heard from some western women that they like to watch gay male pornography.

it must form a stable gender identity. This may be a harder task for a boy than for a girl, for the boy must disidentify with the mother and identify with the father. The girl, already identified with mother from early infancy, does not have to go through this difficult task of disidentification and reidentification (Greenson, 1968; Chodorow, 1978).

In a social situation, I recently met a heterosexual man who told me that he had a good friend who was gay, and that the two of them discussed rather personal things. But, he admitted to me, he found himself very reluctant to hear certain details of his gay friend's life. Really, he continued, it was more an aversion. I asked him which details of his friend's life did he not want to hear? He blushed and said, "This shows you what I mean—I can't even say it." The details of gay sex filled him with aversion and terror. Being a banker, this man was accustomed to framing questions in financial terms. He later described to me what he called the "100 million dollar test" as a measure of the strength of a taboo. "For 100 million dollars," he asked, "would you blow another man in a department store window with your mother watching outside?" He said he would not, indicating how repugnant it would be to him. In this dreaded fantasied scenario, he was mixing oral penetration, public exposure, and humiliation in front of his mother. Under the circumstances, I was not able to ask him what financial valuations he would give to each of these components. But it certainly suggests how strong the taboo on homosexuality and being penetrated can be for heterosexual men.

Very few heterosexual psychoanalysts write about this. One of the few is Irwin Hirsch (1997), who found himself startled by the movie *The Crying Game*, in which, for the first half of the movie, a man falls in love with a woman, but when they finally become sexually intimate, he discovers that she is really a he, genitally speaking. I call this "gender-mischief," in which artists play with the illusion and reality of sex and gender. *The Crying Game* implicitly raises the question: Is there some essential, pheromone-like basis to sexual attraction, or is our attraction to a particular person based on our idea of our partner's gender? It is an important question, and I only have anecdotal data. I know that many presumably heterosexual men who work in Manhattan and live in New Jersey stop on Eleventh Avenue, where street prostitutes will get in their cars and give them oral sex. Many of those prostitutes are actually men dressed as women, but their appearance is usually quite feminine, and they have no trouble satisfying their nominally heterosexual clients. Of course, the nature of the prostitute's own genitalia does not enter into the picture in this situation.

Gender-Mischief in Art and in Life

It may be of value to compare *The Crying Game* with a movie like *Yentl* (based on I. B. Singer's story, "Yentl the Yeshiva Boy"). In *Yentl*, a woman disguises herself as a man in order to be able to study sacred Jewish texts. While dressed as a man, she becomes friends with a young male scholar who finds himself increasingly attracted to him-her. The tension builds, but eventually the friend, panicked about his apparent homosexual attraction, "discovers" that his beloved is really a woman. This movie never shocked people in the way *The Crying Game* did. Partly, this had to do with the fact that the audience was never fooled; while Yentl's friend was shocked by his "homosexual" attraction, we always knew that Yentl was really a woman. But also, whereas *The Crying Game* proposes the subversive notion that our identities as gay or straight could be socially constructed, that we could be fooled, and that a feeling of love could surpass sexual stereotypes, *Yentl* implicitly supports the opposite notion, that our sexual orientations are essential. We can be fooled into believing that someone is of the opposite gender, but in the end our sexual attractions, to one sex or another, cannot be fooled.

The full range of such gender-mischief has not been tested. We may wonder how *The Crying Game* would have been received if the genders had been reversed—that is, if a woman had fallen in love with a man, but in bed discovered that her male lover had a vagina instead of a penis. I think that such a movie would have been much less shocking, partly because nominally straight women in our culture are much less horrified about the possibilities of homosexual attraction or experience than men are.

We could conceive of *The Crying Game* as a kind of experimental paradigm. Any sex or sexual orientation can be substituted into the situation, and we could then study what emotional effect, such as anxiety level, is the result. We could study this in the manner of a thought experiment, or perhaps an experimental psychologist could actually gather data using this paradigm. For example, consider adapting "*The Crying Game* paradigm" to a gay relationship—that is, a self-identified gay man falls in love with another man and then discovers that his beloved has a vagina. Or a lesbian falls in love with a woman and discovers in bed that her beloved has a penis.* All of these mutations of "*The Crying Game* paradigm" might

---

* Some psychotherapists who try to convert homosexuals to heterosexual behavior have advised their patients to fantasize homosexually while behaving heterosexually, that is, for a man to think of a man while actually having intercourse with a woman. This is yet another level of gender-mischief.

yield different levels of anxiety in the viewers, and might thereby reveal the nature and sources of our gender anxieties.

There are many varieties of gender-mischief, and we can learn something important from each one about gender perception.* In 2004, the *New York Times* reported on a young heterosexual woman named Ry, who was raised by her two lesbian mothers. Ry was used to seeing men on the street who were female impersonators, and she developed an intriguing experiment: One summer, just to play around, walking down the street in Provincetown, she started mimicking the drag-queen strut she'd seen her whole life, rolling off her toes, swaggering through her shoulders. She hadn't walked half a block before she successfully passed. "I thought that was a woman!" someone said to a companion as they walked past Ry. So Ry, a woman, was able to impersonate a man impersonating a woman. And she succeeded!

She may not have been the first. Some people consider Mae West to have been a female female impersonator. She satirized cultural stereotypes of women and mimicked the exaggerated versions of femaleness that were typical of female impersonators mixed with their added bold references to sex, such as: "Is that a banana in your pocket, or are you just glad to see me?"†

Nor is Ry the last female female impersonator. In the 2005 film *Transamerica*, the actress Felicity Huffman, a biological woman, played a man passing as a woman and seeking a sex-change operation (while reconnecting with his/her son, conceived years before with a girlfriend).

Psychoanalysis has had trouble adapting to new ideas on sex and gender because Freud's model, and that of several subsequent psychoanalytic theorists, did not adequately differentiate anatomical sex and gender identity (Stoller, 1968; Shapiro, 1996; Dimen, 1997). Today we recognize the relative grounding of sex in the body,‡ but the greater independence, subjectivity, and mutability of the concept of gender. In this respect, psychoanalysis has much to learn from opera. For centuries, some of the most flagrant "gender-mischief" has been achieved by the librettists, composers, and directors of opera. Consider *Der Rosenkavalier* by Richard Strauss.

---

* The following three paragraphs were not in the original article.
† In some accounts of the quotation, it was a "pickle" or a "gun" in his pocket.
‡ The common belief that physical sex is simply divided into just two categories, male and female, is not supported by anatomical data, according to biologist Anne Fausto-Sterling (1985). Fausto-Sterling has proposed that we replace the two-sex model with a five-sex model. Besides males and females, she would add "herms" (named after true hermaphrodites, people born with both a testis and an ovary), "merms" (male pseudohermaphrodites, who are born with testes and some aspect of female genitalia); and "ferms" (female pseudohermaphrodites, who have ovaries combined with some aspect of male genitalia).

The heroine of the opera, the Marschallin, is having an affair with her young lover Octavian, a strapping young fellow who is, however, played by a female singer. So the opera begins with two female singers enacting a heterosexual love scene. Later in the opera, the Marschallin's cousin, Baron Ochs, comes to visit. Octavian disguises himself as a maid with the name of Mariandl, and the Baron lusts after her. So we have a presumably heterosexual man lusting after a boy dressed as a girl, although the boy dressed as a girl is actually played by a girl.

Such gender-mischief is quite common in opera. The unconscious messages are rich and deserve to be analyzed. One message, at least, is that notions of gender, in themselves constructed, can also be reconstructed. Whereas Freud separated sexuality's aim and object, the analysis may be even more complicated. How critical is the actual sex of the object, as opposed to what you imagine is the sex of the object? How far can any fantasy shape actual sexual experience and responsiveness? Perhaps it is as the Italian playwright Luigi Pirandello told us: "It is so, if you think it is."

9

Disgust, Desire, and Fascination
Psychoanalytic, Cultural, Historical, and Neurobiological Perspectives

Author's Introduction

What is the nature of desire? Whom do we desire? What do we desire to do with them? These were questions Freud (1905a) addressed in the *Three Essays on the Theory of Sexuality* when he distinguished between the aim and object of desire. And is disgust the opposite of desire? Or are there circumstances in which disgust may fuel desire? Is this the case only for some people, or is it operative in all people? These general questions were circulating in my mind when I was invited in 2002 to discuss a paper by Muriel Dimen (2005) on what she called "the Eew! factor" in sexuality—sexual circumstances in which one feels like saying "Eew!," presumably in disgust. I found the examples given by Dimen to be rather tame. The disgust elicited by her examples was relatively mild, so I took on the role of describing situations that were likely to elicit sharper disgust reactions (Eew!) along with subtle, or not so subtle, fascination (Wow!). I thought this exploration touched on the essence of sexual excitation, a subject that also has been explored by Jack Morin (1995) and Robert Stoller (1979).

Disgust, Desire, and Fascination: Psychoanalytic, Cultural, Historical, and Neurobiological Perspectives*

All living souls welcome whatever they are ready to cope with; all else they ignore, or pronounce to be monstrous and wrong, or deny to be possible.

George Santayana

* Originally published in *Studies in Gender and Sexuality*, 6, 2005, 33–45.

I would like to discuss the ideas of Muriel Dimen concerning our reactions to the unsavory aspects of sex, which she calls the "Eew! factor." The Eew! reaction in Dimen's examples is caused by humiliation, degradation, and moral disgust. I will balance her discussion by focusing more on the sensory and bodily aspects of the Eew! factor. I think psychoanalysis has, in recent years, shied away from such bodily issues. Psychoanalysts tend to pay lip service to the polymorphous perverse while avoiding the delicious, disgusting details, and sex, like God (or, some say, the Devil), lies in the details.* I also want to place our discussion in a number of contexts: psychoanalytic, to be sure, but also cultural, historical, and neuropsychological.

But first, I want to highlight the ways that gay men have a special experience of the Eew! factor. Most of straight society goes Eew! at the sight or thought of most of the practices of gay men that we consider pleasurable and downright ordinary. This even includes just plain kissing between two men.

I think it is hard for straight people to appreciate what that experience of widespread disgust is like for gay people. If you are straight, try to imagine living in a society in which most of the population believes that what you think is the most straightforward sex act, say, plain penis-in-vagina intercourse in the missionary position, is disgusting, perverted, and/or even a crime. They tell you that you may have your desires, but you must not act on them. Imagine going through your whole life with that. Or imagine walking down Fifth Avenue and *not* being able to hold your husband or wife's hand because of fear of ridicule or being beaten up.

If you can imagine that, you will understand some of what gays and lesbians experience. And so gay people learn the hard way, year after year, what it is like to have something that subjectively feels wonderful and life-enhancing be called sick, disgusting, and perverse by much of society. As therapists, then, gay people may learn to *mentalize* their sexual disgust more readily than most straight people. We can look at disgust reactions, our own and other people's, and recognize how arbitrary, personal, and defensive those reactions can be. We know that all people sometimes feel disgust, we may feel it ourselves, but we gay men and lesbians should learn it in our bones not to project our personal reaction onto another person's sexual experience. It has been done to us too often and too painfully for us not to learn a lesson from it.

---

* According to *The New Dictionary of Cultural Literacy* (2002), the proverb "The Devil is in the details" means that "Even the grandest project depends on the success of the smallest components." The positive version of the proverb, "God is in the details," is often attributed to the architect Le Corbusier.

And also, since there have been such dramatic changes in public attitudes toward homosexuality in the years since the official beginning of gay liberation with the Stonewall riots, we gays and lesbians have great hope that internal reactions of disgust can change, along with political and social attitudes and laws pertaining to sex. You might think that the internal reactions must change first, but the data so far suggest that public, official attitudes sometimes lead the way.

All of which is to say that reactions to sex have many vicissitudes in our society. The same thing can in some cases cause disgust and in other cases cause pleasure. And, as with all aspects of sex, different subcultures in different times may experience these things quite differently.

Holding onto that perspective, I would like to take you back to 1979, when Larry Kramer published his novel *Faggots*. It began with a description of felching. Felching is the act of sucking the semen out of a man's anus after intercourse. I had never heard of felching before that, I had never even thought of doing it, and my initial reaction was shock, followed swiftly by fascination. I wondered, "Do so many people really do that that they have given the act a name?" Shock and disgust are just a short distance from fascination. Eew! is just a short distance from Wow!

Felching has not gone away, but younger people have informed me that sexual experimenters have moved far beyond felching. I will not give you the complete list, but one current gold-medal candidate in the Olympics of sexual adventure is "sounding," in which a ball-point pen, or another cylindrical object, is inserted into the male urethra. It seems to cause extra pleasure if withdrawn near the time of ejaculation.* Eew! Wow! (Or is it Ow?)

To our study of the dialectic between desire and disgust, I think we have to add the relation between disgust and fascination. The closeness between disgust and fascination is visible everywhere, once you are ready to notice it. In our waking sane lives, most of us cannot kill people and eat them, but judging from the box-office receipts of the Hannibal Lecter movies, we surely are fascinated by the prospect of it.

Psychoanalysis has a mixed history when it comes to sex. On one hand, Freud opened up the discussion of the varieties of sexual experience and blurred the distinction between the unusual and the so-called normal. But psychoanalysts, in line with many scientists in the twentieth century,

---

* If you are interested in learning about other sexual experiences, see the film *Beyond Vanilla*. Not only will you learn a lot of facts about less-well-known sex practices, but you will also find it informative to monitor your own emotional reactions. You will find out where your personal boundaries are on the Eew!—Wow!—Ow! axis. By the way, Alfred Kinsey, ahead of his time in so many ways, did research into sounding.

also indulged in much judgmentalism and prejudice, and helped reify terms like perversion and paraphilia, which have caused more harm than enlightenment and certainly close off inquiry and discovery. I would like to expand our view of the varieties of sexual experience and consider them from several perspectives.

First, our perceptions of sexual situations are very much shaped by our own sexual experiences, as well as what we have learned we should think and feel. We all know, or we all should know by now, how intersubjective are judgments about sex. A promiscuous person, it is said, is someone who is having sex with more people than I am.* The same logic could be applied to most of the other old judgmental terms about sex. The pervert is someone who does things that I would never do. The person who is inhibited and constricted about sex is someone who never does what I would readily do. The oversexed person is someone who wants to have sex more than I do. You may remember the scene in the film *Annie Hall*, where Diane Keaton complains to her therapist, "He wants to have sex all the time; maybe three times a week!" and Woody Allen complains to his therapist, "We hardly ever have sex, maybe three times a week!"

In order to do good clinical work with sexual issues, a psychoanalyst must be constantly aware of how relative and intersubjective our sexual judgments are. In the consulting room, some clinicians may presume that their disgust and other subjective reactions have their counterparts in their patients, such as by projective identification, but that is a very risky presumption. Sometimes we have to wonder about the idiosyncrasy of our own reactions and allow for the possibility that our countertransference is not in touch with the patient's experience. The psychoanalytic history of so-called treatments of homosexuality is filled with those horror stories. In the 1990s, when Richard Isay was presenting his paper on the homosexual analyst at the Chicago Psychoanalytic Institute, a man rose during the questioning period and exclaimed, "But you're a pervert!"

At our best—and we are not always at our best—we use our reactions to sexual material not to judge but to stimulate our inquiry. Dimen described her patient, A., who laughed nervously after telling that she took $50 from a man after having sex with him. How did she feel? Many people raised with traditional morality might expect the woman to feel shame about accepting money for sex. But we must be open to all the possible permutations

---

* How many partners are too many? Michael Quadland (1985) reported on two therapy groups of gay men, one "normal" and the other "sexually addicted." Members of the "sexually addicted" had had sex, on average, with 2067 men. The "normal" group had had sex with 481 men. Would those numbers for "normals" be different after so many years of AIDS?

of feeling that she might have, and even incongruous mixtures of feelings: Maybe she felt used and cheapened, but maybe she felt proud to have gotten the man to pay her, or maybe she felt both at the same time, what Hannah Arendt used to call the "two-in-one." Or maybe her shame was that she didn't get more. Could A. have said, "Just $50? I charge $500!"*

We also have to be open to the nuances and paradoxes of cultural mores. People in the white middle class are taught that exchanging money for sex is bad. But the exchange of other material goods for sex is not judged so harshly and often valorized. Was most of America writhing with disgust when Liz Taylor received jewels worth mega-thousands of dollars from Richard Burton? Hardly. So, with Dimen's patient, what if the minor celebrity had given her, instead of cash, a double-stranded pearl necklace? And she had taken it? Would you feel as much Eew! in that case? And what would A. have felt?

An exchange of goods for sex has many ramifications in our society. In some cases, it causes disgust and in other cases, it causes pleasure, admiration, and even envy. And, as with all aspects of sex, different subcultures in different times may experience these things quite differently. Abjection is not a given for any sexual situation. Sex certainly can make us abject, especially when our attraction is not reciprocated, our love thwarted or cheapened or disdained.

There are so many ways one can be hurt in love and in the bedroom, not least of which are sexually transmitted diseases. Sexually transmitted disease is a topic that has not gotten enough attention in psychoanalysis. Actually, Freud wrote about syphilis quite a bit (he often called it "tabes dorsalis"), since it occurred in the families of so many of his patients and was incurable. But he was more attentive to the neuropsychiatric contribution of syphilis to psychopathology than to the psychological ramifications of sex-related disease in general.

Many parents may feel squeamish enough just talking to their children about sex at all. They are usually even more squeamish at the prospect of discussing syphilis, gonorrhea, genital warts, herpes, crabs, scabies, pelvic inflammatory disease, and AIDS. I never wanted to pay much psychoanalytic attention to them either. Then, when the AIDS epidemic hit, I was deluged by such issues, professionally and personally, and the

---

* In 2008, Eliot Spitzer, governor of New York, was reported to have paid more than $4000 for an assignation with a prostitute. While there was public outrage, there was also fascination and perhaps envy that prostitutes could be so well paid. A psychoanalyst colleague said to me, "It used to be that prostitutes and psychoanalysts were paid approximately the same for an hour's work. Now, I can never catch up."

psychological ramifications of sexually transmitted diseases were forced on me (Blechner, 1997). Suddenly, at the HIV Clinical Service of the White Institute, we brought up all these subjects. You could often feel the splitting and dissociation that went on in discussions, as people tried to think of AIDS as something that endangered somebody else. Gay people tried that too, for a while, but we were forced to stare right into the gun barrel of AIDS. Talk about abjection! Here the discomfort of sex moved from disgust to downright dread.

Yet even when the negative stakes seem so high, Eew! can shift into Wow! Thus we see people glorifying HIV by cultivating unsafe sex, and people on the barebacking Web site asking for someone to give them the so-called "gift" of HIV (Blechner, 2002), proving once again that there are no absolutes when it comes to disgust and fascination (I will discuss barebacking further in Chapter 12).

Are there, then, *any* universals in sexual experience, not subject to modification by social, cultural, and historical factors? No one seems to know how much the boundary between disgust and desire is innate or culturally determined.

It probably helps, too, to keep a historical perspective. In the last century, people were talking about fellatio and cunnilingus as perversions. These days, oral sex is an average expectable sex act, almost required foreplay in some cultures. Similarly, in the nineteenth century, masturbation was seen as an enormous problem, and all sorts of procedures were developed to stop it. Sylvester Graham, after whom Graham Crackers were named, preached vegetarianism and avoidance of highly seasoned foods as a means limiting prurient imagination, sexual excess, and masturbation (Graham, 1834).

This link between healthy eating and avoidance of masturbation was picked up by John Harvey Kellogg, who wrote *Plain Facts for Old and Young: Embracing the Natural History and Hygiene of Organic Life* (1888), which vividly described the many ailments caused by masturbation (which he called "secret sin"), including tuberculosis and epilepsy. As a last resort for compulsive masturbators, Kellogg recommended suturing the foreskin so that erection is impossible. Few people today, when eating their Kellogg's Corn Flakes, are aware of their once touted anti-masturbatory properties.

Not only Americans worried about masturbation. The German philosopher, Friedrich Nietzsche, was a big masturbator, and was terribly humiliated when his friend, Richard Wagner, reported the masturbation to Nietzsche's physician. That was the end of that friendship.

There is a gap between what is deemed disgusting and pathological in one generation and acceptable or even desirable in another generation. There is also much hypocrisy to deal with; there is always a divide between what people do and what they say. While society as a whole condemns anal sex, at least among gay men, a study by AIDS researchers found that in one subpopulation, 25% of the heterosexual women practiced anal sex (Laumann and Paik, 2001; Voeller, 1991). It works well for preventing pregnancy, if not AIDS. It is hard to get good data on this; the government usually does not fund it, and you probably will not get tenure for conducting such studies. So, unfortunately, sex shops and prostitutes know more about this subject than scientists. An informal study of sex shops found that the favorite purchase by heterosexual men was a set of butt plugs, which allow self-exploration of anal-erotic sensations. So while most straight men express revulsion at anal penetration, many of them may be privately exploring the experience at home. It may be Eew! in public, but Wow! in private.*

The same sex act can feel very different at different times. D. H. Lawrence (1928/2003) told us all about that. In *Lady Chatterley's Lover*, there is a wonderful scene in which the heroine is not feeling sexual, and her gardener-lover fucks her anyway. Instead of feeling hot, she thinks about how silly sex makes us.

> And this time the sharp ecstasy of her own passion did not overcome her; she lay with her hands inert on his striving body, and do what she might, her spirit seemed to look on from the top of her head, and the butting of his haunches seemed ridiculous to her, and the sort of anxiety of his penis to come to its little evacuating crisis seemed farcical. Yes, this was love, this ridiculous bouncing of the buttocks, and the wilting of the poor insignificant, moist little penis. (p. 182)

But her lover knows she was not with him in feeling and starts to talk compassionately and sweetly to her. She is touched, everything changes, and when he enters her again, she is completely involved, and the silly behavior becomes a cosmic experience, as we read one of the most erotic passages

---

* Jack Morin (1998) confirms this informal finding:

I get letters from all over the world thanking me for writing about anal sex, and one of the biggest subgroups is from straight guys who say, "I'm so glad I'm not the only one who loves this stimulation—I've always wanted to tell my partner about it but I'm too embarrassed so I just enjoy it on my own, but I've worried in the back of my mind that this means I'm gay, even though I'm not attracted to men." It really concerns a lot of guys when they like anal stimulation. I've even had guys who came in and said, "Well, my girlfriend [or my spouse] put her finger up my butt while she was giving me a blow-job and I had the best orgasm of my life—does that mean I'm gay?" By what train of logic I'm not sure: "Gays like the butt stuff" I guess is the thinking there.

in all literature. "And it seemed she was like the sea, nothing but dark waves rising and heaving, heaving with a great swell, so that slowly her whole darkness was in motion, and she was ocean rolling its dark, dumb mass" (p. 184) It goes on quite a bit. You may want to read the original in its entirety.

This brings us to one of the most profound and unexplored aspects of sex, which I think needs to be addressed by psychoanalysts and by cognitive neuroscientists. What makes something sexual is mostly not an intrinsic property of the stimulus, but of our perception of it. The subjective, phenomenological component of sex is greater than in most of our perceptions. We use "sexual" as an adjective to describe a stimulus, but sex is a special case in our perception. Things are sexual because they make us feel sexual. Nothing is intrinsically sexual. When the Supreme Court Justice said, "I don't know how to define pornography, but I know it when I see it!" he was speaking a profound philosophical truth. In most stimuli in our environment, we can connect the properties of our experience to physical properties of the stimulus. When we see the color blue, it is connected with a wavelength of light in the 450-Hz range. But when we describe a stimulus as sexual, the property of its being sexual is primarily located in our subjectivity, in the perceiver. Even genitals can be a turnoff in the wrong context.*

The same changeable boundary of disgust and desire can be seen in the olfactory sense. There was a study published in 1975 of men's reactions to smelling vaginal fluid when it was presented to them in a test tube without their knowing what it was (Doty, Ford, Preti, and Huggins, 1975). In general, they found the odor unpleasant. This set off a vivid exchange of letters. Gordon Globus objected to the study since it did not take into account the state of the sniffers. Had they been sexually aroused, he said, they would have found the aromas attractive. The authors responded, that may be so, but male hamsters find vaginal fluid deposited on inanimate objects appealing. It *makes* them sexually excited. So humans are different from hamsters. Human noses do not lead their feelings; their feelings lead their noses.

---

* Stephen Fry (2004) noted this:

    I would be greatly in the debt of the man who could tell me what would ever be appealing about those damp, dark, foul-smelling and revoltingly tufted areas of the body that constitute the main dishes in the banquet of love…. Once under the influence of the drugs supplied by one's own body, there is no limit to the indignities, indecencies, and bestialities to which the most usually rational and graceful of us will sink.

Interestingly, in another study of male hamsters, vaginal fluid smells were paired with an injection that causes acute gastric distress (Johnston & Zahorik, 1975). Just one experience like that, and the male hamsters stop being so excited by vaginal fluid. So, in hamsters, aversive experience can change Wow! into Eew! quite easily.

We need studies like this in humans. If, for example, men react differently to vaginal aromas in and out of sexual contexts, then we should study that difference by getting brain-imaging data. We might then see what changes in the brain are necessary to make something be perceived as sexually attractive, how the brain can turn Eew! into Wow!

We could do a similar study with the Lady Chatterley phenomenon. What is happening in the brain, if the same stimulus, say, penis thrusting in vagina, can in one moment be just another tactile sensation, as when Lady Chatterley feels removed from the experience, and then in another moment can feel deeply sexual? With fMRI and other brain-scanning techniques, we should be able to determine which parts of Lady Chatterley's brain are active when she is uninvolved in intercourse and when she is most passionate about it.

Through such neuroscience studies, we can get a more detailed and less speculative understanding of the ephemeral and paradoxical sensations that underlie the profundity of sex. The exact same act can seem silly or world-changing. As the depths of our bodies are touched, so too are the depths of our psyche. If all goes well, we feel the union of the bodily and the mental, and the miracle of mutuality. It does not happen every time, but the hope for it is there. The best sex destabilizes our world. Tristan becomes Isolde, Isolde Tristan. Good sex disorients our neatly arranged world of categories. We may think that delight and disgust are diametrically opposed, but they are just around the corner from each other. Things we consider opposite become experiential neighbors, through the magic of subjective alteration of experience. Pleasure can turn quickly to pain and back again. The boring becomes fascinating, the clumsy becomes exquisite, the beautiful ugly, the dearest becomes the most hated, the abject becomes delightful. Eew! becomes Wow!

10

The Gay Harry Stack Sullivan
Interactions between His Life, Clinical Work, and Theory

Author's Introduction

I developed my views about sexuality in general and came to recognize that, while I certainly had my own blind spots, being gay allowed me to see some things that many heterosexuals could not. After 10 years of discussing my views of sexuality in so many places except the White Institute, I realized it was time to come home. And the issue that most needed airing was the homosexuality of the great American psychoanalyst, Harry Stack Sullivan, and how it affected his theory and clinical work. Many people in the world, even psychiatrists, are unfamiliar with Sullivan's work, even though it has had an enormous influence on psychiatry and psychoanalysis throughout the twentieth century and still today in the twenty-first century. His seminal ideas have permeated the thinking of most psychiatrists and psychoanalysts, even if they never heard of Sullivan. He had more success treating schizophrenics than anyone else in his time. He was the founder of what is now known as "milieu therapy," in which the total environment of a psychiatric hospital is coordinated to help the patient recover. And he developed the idea of the therapist as a participant observer; he made us aware that the psychiatrist can never be an anonymous technician working on the mind of his patient, but that all the characteristics of the psychiatrist affect the way the patient is. Sullivan's ideas were great, but for a number of reasons he has not been given the credit that is due to him. *In psychiatry and psychoanalysis, Sullivan is the primary victim of the closeting of history.**

---

* See Chapter 6.

An invitation from Dr. Jay Kwawer, the director of clinical education, to present a paper on any topic at the White Institute was the
impetus to get me writing. I wrote and presented it in 2004. As with
the chapter on psychoanalysis in and out of the closet, a lot of this
one was already written in my head. It picked up themes that I had
broached in Chapter 3: Sullivan was gay, he fought against prejudice during his life, and his homosexuality was integral to his clinical
theory and practice of psychoanalysis.* But it was time to spell out
each of those things in full detail.

As I reread Sullivan's work, I found something that I had long
known but not formulated clearly: that Sullivan had thought a great
deal about sex and sexuality and had written about those subjects
extensively. Freud and his followers believed that sex was one of the
main motivators of all human behavior, and the difficulties with the
sexual drive were behind many forms of psychopathology. Sullivan's
work questioned this basic Freudian assumption, arguing that human
behavior was at least as much the result of a drive for interpersonal
relatedness and achieving a level of security and safety. However,
while Sullivan's theory undercut many of the presumptions of classical psychoanalytic drive theory, especially concerning the centrality
of sexual and aggressive drives in determining human psychology,
this did not mean that he thought sexuality to be unimportant or tan-
gential to human experience.

I spent a lot of time re-analyzing Sullivan's extraordinary chapter
on "Male Adolescence" in his book *Personal Psychopathology*. In
it, Sullivan discusses quite frankly the specifics of sexual practice
in homosexual and heterosexual men. He wrote about these things
in a strange language with unusual words, and most readers, when
confronted by the weird words, simply skipped over them. I decided
to try to really understand them. I used the Internet, many different
dictionaries, and other research tools to figure out what those words
mean. A major breakthrough occurred when I realized that many of
the terms had their roots in the work of European sexologists in the
nineteenth and early twentieth centuries.

I hope my translations of Sullivan's terms are accurate. If not, I
hope others will improve on my work. When I first presented the
paper on March 23, 2004, I expected that some of the older Sullivan
scholars would have more authoritative knowledge about these
terms than I did; but it seemed that no one had worked out this ter-
minology before me.

---

* I had by this time published the fact that Sullivan's famous ward for schizophrenic patients was
a gay male ward (Blechner, 1995e, 1997), but both times the fact had been mentioned in passing,
without working out its important theoretical and clinical implications.

When you understand Sullivan's language, you discover someone who was thinking deeply about sexuality, with great attention to the specifics of bodily experience. Sullivan may have been wrong about some facts, or things may have changed since his time. Nevertheless, many of his observations, different from the mainstream views of his time, were remarkably accurate. Some of these facts were established more empirically by Kinsey 20 years later (facts that many psychoanalysts were loath to believe).

In the 1980s, while in Baltimore, I met with Kenneth Chatelaine, who collected landmark data about Sullivan's famous ward for schizophrenics at the Sheppard and Enoch Pratt Hospital. I also wanted to look at the home that Harry and Jimmie Sullivan shared in the Baltimore suburbs, but alas it had been torn down. In its place was a branch of the appliance store named "Two Guys."

The Gay Harry Stack Sullivan: Interactions between His Life, Clinical Work, and Theory*

Was Harry Stack Sullivan gay? Dr. Arlene McKay asked that simple question when the William Alanson White Institute was celebrating its 50th Anniversary by having a panel on Sullivan. Helen Swick Perry avoided a direct yes or no answer, but as in her biography of Sullivan, she told stories that suggested Sullivan might have had a romantic interest in a number of women. It was an example of the fog of distraction, avoidance, and dissociation that has surrounded Sullivan's homosexuality, an example of the "closeting of history."

I would like to take a different approach to Dr. McKay's question, and answer it directly: Yes, Sullivan was gay. It is quite clear to anyone who has no personal barriers to seeing it. The evidence is overwhelming. I am going to describe some of that evidence from first-hand accounts of people who encountered Sullivan. I am also going to show how Sullivan's homosexuality, far from being an incidental aspect of his life, was a major issue with which he struggled and how, way ahead of his time, he was a pathbreaker in dealing with many of today's issues of gay civil rights. Finally, I am going to look closely at some of Sullivan's writings about lust and sexuality that have been relatively ignored, to show how he was working toward a radical new formulation of sexuality's place in human living. I

* Originally published in *Contemporary Psychoanalysis*, 2005, *41*, 1–19.

will also explore how Sullivan's homosexuality was integral to his clinical and theoretical innovations.

When I was in graduate school, Jerome Singer, who was the head of the psychology department and is a graduate of the White Institute, told me that Sullivan was gay. With the assumption that such a simple fact was a given, I came to the White Institute for psychoanalytic training. Imagine my surprise when, during my first year of training at White, I mentioned that Sullivan was gay to a senior analyst, and he became noticeably defensive and challenged me: "Do you know anyone who slept with him?" Well, no, I didn't. Nor did I personally know any women who had slept with Freud or Erich Fromm, although no one was challenging me to find them. Nevertheless, I decided I would try to find out what I could.

That analyst's question was the first sign I observed of the tremendous dread that many Interpersonal psychoanalysts* have felt about Sullivan's homosexuality. Sullivan was a genius, and he was the theoretical and clinical mentor of the Interpersonalists. But many Interpersonalists, prejudiced against homosexuals, have had great difficulty with Sullivan's sexuality. They routinely hedged the issue by saying that Sullivan's sexuality was questionable. "We don't really know whether or not Sullivan was gay"—a gay man told me his Interpersonal analyst said these very words to him in 1995.

This is the fate of being in the closet. Others may see you as asexual or schizoid or simply mysterious. In the middle of the twentieth century, this was a common spectacle. People were called confirmed bachelors and surrounded themselves with rumors of possible marriages, thus quelling suspicion of homosexuality, which could damage your career. This was frequently done by men and women in all walks of public life, including show business and politics.

In the context of such obfuscation, the late Dr. Ralph Crowley was a breath of fresh air. Crowley said unambiguously that Sullivan was homosexual, and he was able to talk candidly and nondefensively about it. In 1986, Crowley told me this story: He once attended a lecture of Sullivan's

---

* Interpersonal psychoanalysis is a branch of psychoanalysis that was founded by Harry Stack Sullivan. It rejected many of Freud's original presumptions about personality and psychopathology. Interpersonal psychoanalysis held that the need for human connection, not just sexual, motivated human behavior; that all personality factors were affected by other people; and that the psychoanalyst was not an anonymous blank screen, but a person whose characteristics affect the outcome of the clinical interaction. These views, once considered "deviant" and "renegade," are now embraced by most psychoanalysts.

at a conference. At the end of the talk, Crowley went up to Sullivan to ask him some questions. Sullivan invited the young Crowley to continue the conversation in his room at the hotel where the conference was being held. "We went up to his room," Crowley told me, "and there were two single beds in the room. Sullivan lay on one bed, and I on the other, and we talked. I'm sure if I had been a little less square, he would have approached me."

I sought information from other people who had met Sullivan, including Dr. Ellis Perlswig, a child psychiatrist at the Yale Child Study Center in New Haven, who had the distinction, as a candidate at the New York Psychoanalytic Institute, of having been the first training candidate of Jacob Arlow. As I recounted in Chapter 2, Perlswig told Arlow he was gay, Arlow ended the analysis abruptly, and, within a week, Perlswig was asked to resign from the Institute.

But, it turned out, before all that, Perlswig also had been a guest at Sullivan's house in Maryland. He told me there is no question in his mind today that Harry and Jimmie had romantic feelings for one another and were committed life-partners.

Sullivan did something extraordinary for his time. He adopted James Inscoe, known as "Jimmie," as his son. Jimmie was about 20 years younger than Sullivan. People who admired Sullivan's thinking, but were uncomfortable having a gay mentor, were happy to say that Jimmie Sullivan was just Harry Stack Sullivan's adopted son. But others knew there was much more to it, that Harry Stack Sullivan and Jimmie Sullivan were loving partners for more than 20 years. Helen Swick Perry (1982), in her biography of Sullivan, perpetuates the story that Jimmie may have been schizophrenic, that he was standing on a street corner in a semi-catatonic state, and Sullivan took him in and cared for him. But in the 1990s, she told Michael Allen (1995) that Jimmie had told her he was a prostitute standing on the street, and that is how he first got to know Sullivan.

You have to realize just how daring and creative Sullivan's adoption of Jimmie was, in its time. In our time, gay marriage is such a burning issue. It is seen as the means to give gay couples the same rights, privileges, and protection as committed heterosexual couples. So far, there is gay marriage in Canada, South Africa, and several European countries, but the United States is still fighting about it. Sullivan, by adopting his partner, found a way to secure rights for Jimmie concerning inheritance, medical decision making, and other basics of living, that are usually available only to married couples. In addition, adoption, unlike marriage, cannot be easily nullified by divorce. Thus, between two men who are in love, adoption may be a more binding commitment than marriage.*

Sullivan was gay. If that were simply a fact of his autobiography, then this would be just gossip. But there is more to it. Sullivan was gay, and that led to his being a champion of gay rights. Gay rights, you may ask? Did that exist back then? Well, perhaps the words didn't, but the struggle did, and Sullivan certainly engaged the struggle. Even more importantly to Interpersonalists, Sullivan's homosexuality was integral to his clinical and theoretical innovations. Because there has been so much anxiety and mystification about his homosexuality, the importance of his sexuality to his theory has also been obscured. And that may also be one reason why sexuality has had a hazy and sometimes neglected position in interpersonal and relational theory in general. Let that end.

Sullivan's homosexuality affected his clinical and theoretical work in many ways. First, one of Sullivan's most celebrated achievements was his ward for young schizophrenics, which he started during the late 1920s at the Sheppard and Enoch Pratt Hospital near Baltimore. The ward had an astonishing 86% cure rate for schizophrenics, and this was before the advent of neuroleptic medication. Sullivan was famously skillful at making a connection with very cutoff patients; it was said that when he spoke with schizophrenics, they no longer sounded schizophrenic. Sullivan also developed milieu therapy; every aspect of living in the ward was carefully thought out to lessen the patients' anxiety and help them find new pathways to secure living.

This is all well known. But what seems to be less well known is that Sullivan's ward was a gay male ward. In the 1970s, a psychologist named Kenneth Chatelaine interviewed the last surviving people who had worked on Sullivan's ward, and published their revelations in his book, *Harry Stack Sullivan: The Formative Years* (Chatelaine, 1981). The description of the ward and of Sullivan is noteworthy for its frankness. The staff, handpicked by Sullivan, were either openly homosexual or extremely easygoing about it. The staff and the patients were all male. No female nurses were allowed even to come into the ward.

---

* It is unknown how many gay couples have used adoption to get the rights granted by marriage. In 2007, the composer Gian-Carlo Menotti died, and most of his estate went to his adopted son, Francis Phelan, also known as "Chip Menotti." Another well-known example did not work out so well: Olive Watson, granddaughter of the founder of IBM, adopted her lesbian partner of 14 years, Patricia Spado. Spado was one year older than Watson. A year later, the couple broke up. When Watson's mother died in 2004, Spado claimed to be entitled to the large amount of money left to the grandchildren. Her claim was challenged in court and unleashed a series of lawsuits (Belluck & Cowan, 2007).

According to William Elliott, who started working on the ward in 1929, the staff sometimes referred to Sullivan, behind his back, as Miss Sullivan. The staff members were also encouraged to talk casually to each other about homosexual experiences, to let the patients feel that it was not something to be ashamed of or afraid of.

Elliott told Chatelaine that Sullivan started the ward, being closeted himself, but as time went on, he became more open about his homosexuality. Sullivan wanted, in Elliott's words,

> to take care of the homosexual, knowing that they were homosexual, knowing that he was homosexual. Still and all, he was in the ring but he wasn't playing… that's it. It was just like a ringmaster. You jump but I am not going to jump. And I think toward the end he let the hairpins all come down and this is it. (p. 452)

"Letting one's hairpins come down" was an expression in the early twentieth century that meant for one to reveal one's homosexuality to other homosexuals (Chauncey, 1994), similar to what today is called "coming out."*

It would be extraordinary today if someone established a gay psychiatric ward in a major hospital. It is even more extraordinary that Sullivan did it back in 1930. That took courage. It also represented a brilliant insight into the factors that can lead to serious mental illness and the best approach to helping such patients. Even today, when attitudes toward homosexuality are better than they were in the past, every gay and lesbian person knows how difficult it is to cope with anti-gay hostility. Prejudice against gays and lesbians is still considered acceptable in much of society. No public official can say something derogatory about Blacks in America anymore without running into severe consequences. But as Senator Rick Santorum demonstrated on April 7, 2003, a public official can still say hateful things about gays and lesbians and receive the support of his party and his president (CNN, 2003).

What effect does this have on the mental health of young gays and lesbians? As we know, the effect is highly detrimental. The rate of teenage suicide has been estimated to be three times higher for gay youth than for straight (Archuleta, 1998). And in people disposed to mental illness, either because of a genetic predisposition, a traumatic history, or other

---

* One still sees the expression used today, such as the following statement by Armistead Maupin, author of *Tales of the City*: "My parents subscribed to the newspaper in order to follow the column. So, as the hairpins began to drop, they got more and more concerned. And I eventually used the column as my vehicle for coming out" (Glitz, 2001).

factors, the added stress of homophobia can push them over the edge into psychosis. Sullivan showed, with his ward, that when you remove such a person, even temporarily, from exposure to such hatred, the potential for therapeutic gain can be enormous. The ramifications of this finding, I think, have never been fully appreciated, nor have they been adequately tested in other groups that suffer discrimination.*

I have myself not set up a ward for gay and lesbian psychotics. But interestingly, just by being an openly gay psychoanalyst, I have had quite a number of patients come to me who might have been accepted into Sullivan's ward. These patients had been burned in various ways by homophobia in the mental health system.

I cannot relate to you all of these experiences, but I will give you one example that captures the problem. In the early 1990s, I was consulted by a 33-year-old man for treatment. His presenting complaint was that he felt lost, professionally and personally. He impressed me as very private and cautious. When he called for an initial appointment, he got my answering machine. He told me the name of the doctor who referred him, but didn't tell me his own name and number, so I had to telephone the referring physician to get that information. In our first session, when I asked the patient where he worked, he hesitated for a long time and didn't want to tell me.

You may feel that this man was paranoid. But as his story unfolded, I learned that there was good reason for his caution.

When he was 18, he went away to college and found that he was sexually attracted only to men, a fact that he had suspected but tried to ignore during high school. He knew that his religious family would disapprove of his homosexuality, and so he became extremely anxious about it. On a vacation, he returned home. His father noticed his agitation and asked him what was bothering him. He blurted out to his father that he was gay. The family sent him to a psychoanalyst immediately. When the patient tried to bring up his homosexuality, the analyst said, "Well, of course, doing things with girls is fun." As you can imagine, the patient was not encouraged to tell this man more. Instead, he retreated more and more into himself. He then was hospitalized for two weeks with electroshock treatments every other day. This had no effect on his sexual orientation, but it certainly taught him to beware of the homophobia in his parents, in psychiatry, and in society in general. He waited a dozen years to seek

---

* There have been all-Black hospitals, but these were set up by Whites to give substandard care (Randall, 2004). There have not, to my knowledge, been all-Black hospitals set up by Black medical professionals with the explicit intention of giving excellent care devoid of prejudice, analogous to Sullivan's ward for gay men.

psychotherapy, and did so only when he could be sure to find a therapist who was openly gay himself.

We obtained his hospital records, and they were fascinating. They showed a diagnosis of paranoid schizophrenia, based on the fact that "The patient claims people are saying he is a homosexual." Well, he *was* claiming that people were saying he was a homosexual, because they were, and he was. The use of electroshock therapy was unconscionable. And remember, this was not in a rural hospital. It was in a major New York area hospital in the late 1970s.

I want to tell you one more thing about Sullivan. Later in his career, as a psychiatrist for the military, Sullivan attempted to keep homosexuality from being a disqualifying factor for military service, although he was overruled by the military establishment and eventually fired (Bérubé, 1990). The struggle about gays in the military is still ongoing, but most people working for an end to the military's homophobia today don't seem to know about Sullivan's pioneering efforts 60 years ago.

So Sullivan was, in his day, working on some of the most prominent civil rights issues for gays and lesbians in our day, such as the relations of gays and the military and ways for a gay couple to have the rights and safeguards of marriage. He was a pathbreaker in addressing homophobia-induced psychopathology and the ways it can best be helped by an interpersonal approach. And Sullivan showed that you cannot adequately solve the mental health issues of stigmatized people without also taking a stand against discrimination and bigotry in society.*

Sullivan's homosexuality was also integral to his theory of interpersonal psychiatry. You can selectively inattend to this fact, but if you do, and many have, I think you come up with a skewed understanding of Sullivan's interpersonal theory. In fact, one important source of his understanding of the embeddedness of psychopathology in interpersonal relations was his own experience of his homosexuality. Many a gay man has tried to understand his experience of homosexuality intrapsychically, without reference to how it affects his relations with other people, and how his relations with other people affect his experience of his sexuality. You can scour your oedipal complex and pre-oedipal relations all you want. But if you don't take account of the fact that other people, shaped by social convention, are condemning you for an essential aspect of your being,

---

* As already noted earlier, Sullivan was extremely interested in the destructive psychological effects of anti-Semitism and what was then called "anti-Negroism" (see also *The Fusion of Psychiatry and Social Science* [Sullivan, 1964]).

you will never get anywhere. Sullivan recognized this. It was the insight behind his ward for gay schizophrenic men. By regulating the interpersonal experience of shame, by eliminating homophobic persons from the staff as much as possible, Sullivan drastically lowered the patient's anxiety level to make possible all kinds of therapeutic gains.

Sullivan extended this insight into his theory of good-me, bad-me, and not-me. I cannot prove to what degree Sullivan's general theory of personifications emerged from his homosexuality, but there is some good evidence that it played a big part. Just look at the examples of "not-me" dissociation in his books. You will see that most of them are caught up with disavowed homosexuality. Following are some of them.

In the *Conceptions of Modern Psychiatry*, Sullivan (1940) wrote:

> Our lady entertained fantasies of prostitution not because she simply lusted after many men, but because she had in dissociation a lust after women. She was of the homosexual personal syndrome, but whether by virtue of lack of any permissive acculturation, or of early experience which erected a strong barrier to integrations with members of her own sex, she had no awareness of the homosexual motivation. It existed in dissociation. (p. 135)

In *The Interpersonal Theory of Psychiatry*, Sullivan (1953) wrote:

> Those of you who are men may have discovered, as you're walking down the street, that quite a number of other men look at what is called the fly of your pants, and look away hastily. Many of them raise their eyes to yours—apparently, insofar as you can interpret, to see if they have been noticed (p. 321)

In *The Interpersonal Theory of Psychiatry*, Sullivan also wrote, concerning fugue states:

> The fugue might be called a very massive change of personality. Another, somewhat less massive, disturbance of personality is what I call the eruption into awareness of abhorrent cravings.... The classic instance of this eruption of cravings is the eruption of "homosexual" desires—desires to participate in what the patient feels, classically and outstandingly, to be homosexual performances. I think I can illustrate this, perhaps without misleading you too badly, by mentioning one of my patients, an only boy with five sisters, who had led as sheltered a life as that situation would permit. Shortly after getting into uniform in World War II he was prowling around Washington, and was gathered up by a very well-dressed and charming dentist, who took him to his office and performed what is called fellatio on the boy. The boy felt, I presume, a mild adjustment to the uncanny, and went his way, perhaps in some fashion rewarded. But the next day he quite absentmindedly walked back to the immediate proximity of the dentist's office, that being in some ways, you see, an untroubled

fugue—whereupon, finding himself so very near what had happened the day before, he was no longer able to exclude from awareness the fact that he would like to continue to undergo these experiences. This is a classical instance of an abhorrent craving in that it was entirely intolerable to him. The day before it had been a kind of new experience, but when it burst upon him in this way, it was attended by all sorts of revulsions and a feeling that it would be infrahuman, and what not, to have such interest. And he arrived at the hospital shortly afterward in what is called schizophrenic disturbance. (p. 326)

In the *Clinical Studies in Psychiatry* (Sullivan, 1956, pp. 169–176), in the chapter on dissociation, there is an extensive example, what one could call a short story of gay dissociation. To summarize, Mr. A is a married man whose wife complains that they don't have sex often enough. Mr. A comes to all sorts of rationalizations about this. He meets a man, Mr. X, who, by resembling a boy with whom he had sex as a preadolescent, stirs Mr. A in a dissociated way, which he compensates for by feeling conscious revulsion for Mr. X. Later they are at a dinner party together at which they have to stay overnight.

There are only half as many beds as guests, and the deferences to polite society that Mr. A has to make have the exceedingly unhappy result that he has to share a bed with Mr. X. He is so horribly embarrassed at his disliking this stranger, and so awfully anxious not to make things too difficult for the host and hostess, that, well, the simple thing is to swallow all this stupid feeling of his and act like a good guest, and so they finally wind up in bed together. Mr. X is somewhat embarrassed by the strange casualness and avoidance on the part of Mr. A which he has suffered all day—an attitude that he realizes is quite different from his own feeling that he would like Mr. A if Mr. A weren't so distant. In fact, by this time his feelings have been reasonably well wounded, and he is not much pleased with this arrangement. So he takes reasonable precautions to get undressed and in bed before the other man does, or vice versa. But as he is about to fall asleep, his companion sighs deeply and starts to apologize rather queerly, and gets up and fiddles around a little while; and Mr. X realizes that he is listening to some queer cock-and-bull story about how Mr. A has never really slept with anyone before, and is just horribly angry with himself and so on, but he doesn't know whether he can get any sleep unless he gets under the bottom sheet. And so this is what he does.

What is apt to happen in the course of the night—what, in fact, has in many such instances happened—is the following: During the night Mr. A gets out from under his cotton precaution and goes around and tenderly fondles Mr. X, and then goes back to bed under his bottom sheet. There is considerable evidence of his being in a curiously foggy state of mind, which so impressed Mr. X that he does not say anything about the incident the next morning. Mr. A acts as if nothing on earth like that could conceivably have happened, and Mr. X just says to himself, "Well, this bird is a funny one." Mr. A leaves the house with a feeling that, considering that he had had to share a room with this extremely disagreeable person, he has had a remarkably good night's sleep. He feels fine, and has no trace of any information about what has happened. (pp. 175–176)

Now I would like to turn our attention to the effect of Sullivan's homosexuality on his integration of drives and bodily processes within interpersonal theory. To start with, his earliest publications were very much about the body and drives. His paper, "The Oral Complex" (1925), dealt in great detail with the infant's bodily experience, before and after birth. Sullivan took strong positions about the drives to obtain oxygen and food, and their interaction with pleasurable oral stimulation. He argued that oral experiences are pivotal in the formation of the self and the sense of reality and argued against Ernest Jones' greater focus on anal experience in this regard. And in his paper "Erogenous Maturation" (1926), Sullivan looked into the later development of one's sense of one's body and sexuality. Way ahead of his time, he rejected Freud's notion that vaginal erotism involves a regression, and in general rejected the modeling of female sexual development in terms of male development, rather than in its own terms.

Sullivan, in this paper, was very specific about bodily involvement in pleasure. He discussed erogenous zones like the neck and thighs, and even gave his view of what we today call "hickeys." He also noted that for some people, the navel is both an object of curiosity and pleasure. He was very interested in the significance of male erections throughout the lifespan, and he tried to be precise about the significance of acts that can be called masturbation at different stages of male development. In infancy, Sullivan argued, erections are reflexes responsive to internal stimulation, not external, and so he questioned the notion that anything like masturbation can occur then. Only at the age of about 15 months, he thought, can the baby start to deliberately manipulate the genitals for pleasure, which Sullivan called "juvenile masturbation." At the age of three or four, there is the beginning of inhibition of urination during erection, which Sullivan saw as a significant development in one's sense of the genito-urinary system. But in puberty there is a sudden, qualitative shift in the bodily experience of erections as sexually driven.

Sullivan also was very interested in the ways that notions of sexual sin cause psychopathology; he referred to sexual sin as "the mother of psychiatry" and outlined how such notions of sin lead to psychopathology.

Some of Sullivan's comments strike me as questionable or wrong, at least today. For example, he says that bisexual men are much more easygoing about having a penis inserted in the anus than in the mouth, and he relates that to a primal feeling of vulnerability at the mouth, with its connections to breathing. I do not know if this is true today; whether or not it was true in Sullivan's time, it shows how specific was Sullivan's interest in bodily sexual experience and its links with other primary drives and anxieties.

Sullivan may not always have been right about sexuality, but he gave it a great deal of attention. In his writing, this focus on sexuality was at its peak in the book *Personal Psychopathology* (1972). I think Sullivan scholars have given this work short shrift. Sullivan completed it in 1932. It was not published in his lifetime, but keep in mind that Sullivan thought enough of it himself to finish the manuscript. Sullivan also used the manuscript as a primary text for a seminar he co-taught with Edward Sapir at Yale University on the "Impact of Culture on Personality." I do not think you can know the whole Sullivan without paying close attention to this book.

If anyone doubted Sullivan's homosexuality, they should read his chapter in *Personal Psychopathology* on "Male Adolescence." The chapter might have been more aptly titled, "Homosexuality and the Male Adolescent," since that is its main subject matter. The last six pages are extraordinary. In them, Sullivan discusses the various forms of sexual behavior, especially among gay men, and their significance. I think the chapter has been overlooked in the literature, partly because of homophobia, but partly, too, because it is so difficult to understand. To describe sexual behavior, Sullivan uses terms that cannot be located in any dictionary, at least that I can find. Maybe he had access to a vocabulary that was not popularly known; or maybe he made the terms up.

The obscurity of the language is in the tradition of Krafft-Ebing (1886/1965), who, in his landmark work on perversions, *Psychopathia Sexualis*, wrote in Latin in the sections concerning what he thought were more offensive practices. Sullivan doesn't use Latin, but if he had, at least someone could be sure what he meant. Instead, this section on male adolescence is written in a most unusual language, designed to hide as much as to communicate. I think Sullivan's wording was a compromise formation, an expression of conflicting wishes to be hidden and to be understood. If you want to understand him, you have to put in some effort.

So I have. I have spent a good amount of time looking up the words Sullivan uses. It seems that many of them are neologisms, but if you look up their etymology, you can pretty much figure out what he is saying. I wonder if anyone has done this before me. If they have, I do not know about it.

I am going to describe some of the terms plainly and graphically. My intention is not to shock. However, I think that if you are going to appreciate Sullivan's thinking on sexuality, you need to know the full extent of what he was thinking and writing about the subject. I have no problem if you wish to argue with or reject his observations and ideas; but if you selectively inattend to them, you will never understand what Sullivan thought about sex, drives, and their significance in interpersonal relations.

Let us start with *Stomixis*: *Stomixis** is oral-genital sex. *Parastomixis* is oral sexual stimulation applied to nongenital body areas. *Synstomixis* is simultaneous oral-genital stimulation, what is known colloquially as "69." Finally, *autostomixis* is the stimulation of your genitals with your own mouth.

People involved in these procedures can be *phaledotic* or *thorodotic*. *Phaledotic* seems to mean wanting to have one's penis stimulated. The reciprocal is *phaleleptic*, which I think means stimulating another's person's penis.†

And then there is *thorodotic*. *Thoro*, according to my *Oxford English Dictionary*, is a word root indicating a compound salt, and *dotic* comes from the Greek for "to give." Therefore, I think the word *thorodotic* means "to give semen." The word *thorophagic* means "to swallow semen."

Then there are the terms for anal sex, which Sullivan refers to, in general, as "*Pugisma*." Sullivan gives no source for this word; I think it is a variant of the term "pygism" used by Gustav Jäger in *Entdeckung der Seele (Discovery of the Soul)*‡ (see Hirschfeld 1914/2000, p. 68). The word seems to be derived from *pyge* (Greek for buttocks; the Greek verb for anal intercourse is "pygizein" [Boswell, 1990]). The closest word currently in use in English is "callipygian," which means "having beautiful buttocks."§

People who like to be penetrated anally are called *proctodotic* by Sullivan. Oral-anal sex is referred to as *proctolichsis*.

Now that you know what the words mean, you can consider what Sullivan has to say.

Regarding autostomixis, stimulation of your genitals with your own mouth, Sullivan feels we would all do that a lot, if, as he says, "geometric factors permitted," that is, if you could reach. He says that it is common in young honey bears and cites a case of a boy who could do it until puberty

---

* If Sullivan created this word himself, he may have been influenced by Ferenczi's (1924) term *amphimixis*, which is "the synthesis of two or more eroticisms into a higher unity." *Sto* probably comes from stoma, Greek for *mouth*. Thus, stomixis = synthesis of oral and genital eroticism.

† The etymology from Greek is *phale* (phallus) *leptic* (lambanein = to take hold of). Other roots used by Sullivan in coining words: *chresis* (khresis = use) (cf. Sullivan, 1972, p. 242n), *proctochresic*, and *dotic* (didonai = to give).

‡ The word in Jäger's book was used in the chapter on homosexuality, which was actually written by Karl-Maria Kertbeny. The chapter was omitted by the publisher of the book and was only published in 1900 by Magnus Hirschfeld in his *Jahrbuch für sexuelle Zwischenstufen* (*Annual for Sexual Intermediaries*).

§ There is also "steatopygian" which means very fat buttocks.

and became schizophrenic when he was no longer able to suck his own penis. Sullivan's assertion of the frequency of attempts at self-fellation received support from the research findings of Kinsey, Pomeroy, and Martin (1948, p. 510)* and from the clinical observations of Stone (1954).

Sullivan gave special prominence to mutual fellatio. He made up the word, synstomixis, for it. Colloquially, people today call it 69; Sullivan used the French equivalent, "soixante-neuf."† In Sullivan's words (1962):

> The [active homosexual and bisexual], when oral-erotic, establish sentiments making for behavior in the shape of soisante-neuf [sic] and in these and similar arrangements there is libidinal interchange equivalent to complete satisfaction of demands of the socialized personality. (p. 181n)

You can hear that Sullivan valued this sex act highly. Why? One cannot be sure. One possibility is that he and Jimmie liked it, but it is also possible that Sullivan was influenced by the orthodox psychoanalytic valuation of what was called "mature genitality." Freud's developmental model considered oral and anal interests developmentally immature, and implied that full maturity required sexual satisfaction using the genitals. Following that scheme, I infer that Sullivan may have found that mutual fellatio between men met the criteria for simultaneous genital stimulation.

Sullivan's high valuation of 69 gives an added significance to his insignia, the two horses' heads facing up and down, which Sullivan asked Helen Swick Perry to have printed on the cover of every published volume of his works. It appears that this insignia is a combination of at least two images: mutual fellatio and the Asian symbol of ying and yang (Perry, 1982; Harned, 1998). It may also have intended to integrate the dark and light horses in Socrates' discussion of love in Plato's *Symposium*.

Some of Sullivan's observations about sexuality are surprising to many people today, and it is not always easy to tell whether things have changed or whether Sullivan came across some rather unusual people. For example,

---

* Kinsey et al. (1948, p. 510), like Sullivan, cited its commonness in the animal kingdom: "Self fellation is an anatomic impossibility for most human males, but it is a common means of masturbation among rhesus monkeys, the macaque, mandrille, chimpanzee and other primates.... A considerable portion of the population does record attempts at self fellation, at least in early adolescence. Only two or three males in a thousand are able to achieve the objective, but there are three or four histories of males who had depended upon self fellation as a masturbatory technique for some appreciable period of time—in the case of one thirty-year-old male, for most of his life."

† Sullivan spelled it "soisante-neuf" in his book, instead of the correct French "soixante-neuf." It is not a typographical error; it occurs also in the original article in the *American Journal of Psychiatry* (Sullivan, 1927, p. 780n).

Sullivan wrote (1972, p. 241): "In personalities in whom the homosexual role is very repugnant to the self, but stomixic tendencies cannot be dissociated, a combination of phaledotic and cystholeptic fantasies or even overt behavior may be substituted with some preservation of self-esteem." What does that mean? I think a translation into regular English would be: "In a person uncomfortable with his homosexuality, who nevertheless desires to perform oral sex on a man, he may combine fantasies of fellatio and cunnilingus, or even act on such fantasies, to satisfy himself while still protecting his self-esteem."

Some other people who are uncomfortable with their homosexuality, Sullivan tells us, may limit themselves to mutual masturbation. They might also do so when the only male partners available to them are unattractive. As Sullivan says (1972): "The hands are schematized as less closely identified with the self than are the genital, anal, and oral zones, and their utilization is thus less personal" (p. 243).

In Sullivan's article "Archaic Sexual Culture and Schizophrenia," delivered in 1929, Sullivan (1962) asserted that homosexual experience in men was much more common than the usual estimate at the time of 5%. His figures are quite close to those estimated more scientifically by Kinsey et al. (1948) three decades later. Sullivan also argues that actual homosexual experience can prevent someone from becoming psychotic:

> While the writer is advised by certain colleagues that a history of "traumatic experiences," such as actual homosexual seduction, is not of good prognostic significance in the average case of psychoneurotic individuals, he has been impressed with the contrary significance among schizophrenics. It is to him certain that in this form of mental maladjustment any actual material arising from voluntary or unwilling concrete sexual activities has a beneficial effect in bringing conceptualization and fantasy of a sexual nature within the frame of real criteria. (p. 211)

This rather unusual idea has not, to my knowledge, been tested empirically. However, it may have some truth, at least for young men who are primarily homosexual in orientation, especially if they feel inhibited from having real sexual experiences because of societal or religious taboos. It may be better for them to have real sexual experiences rather than just wallow in their fantasies. It goes along with Sullivan's very important general observation that mental health is not so dependent on the specifics of one's sexual desires per se; instead, whatever one's sexual desires, mental health depends on whether one can integrate them successfully with another human being.

Once you understand Sullivan's language, you can come to appreciate better what he is talking about and the issues he was trying to address. Is this writing of Sullivan on homosexuality psychoanalytically useful? I would answer yes. If it had been more widely read and understood, it might have led to more specific interest and understanding of gay male sexuality. I think some of it is factually wrong, at least today, but it raises many important questions about what is common and normal in homosexual experience, and an extensive discussion of such issues is certainly useful psychoanalytically. Today, even if we dispute some of what Sullivan said, we can at least explore it openly with people who know about it through personal experience. Perhaps that will lessen some of the anti-homosexual bias still present in society. If such discussion doesn't change homophobia, it will at least change homo-ignorance.

Also, I don't think that Sullivan gave up these early formulations. Instead, he kept developing them. They reappear much later in his career, in *The Interpersonal Theory of Psychiatry* (1953), in a new system with, as Sullivan admits, another set of neologisms: orthogenital, paragenital, metagenital, and amphigenital (p. 293). *Orthogenital* involves integration of the genitals of the two sexes. *Paragenital* involves having one's own genitals stimulated by some other organ of another person, such as the hand, mouth, or anus. *Metagenital* refers to using your own nongenital organ to stimulate another person's genitals. (So it would seem that every paragenital act of one person involves the other person in metagenital activity.) *Amphigenital* refers to two people engaging in analogous if not identical relationships to the genitals of each and the substitutes of each, such as Sullivan's highly valued soixante-neuf.

What Sullivan was basically trying to do in both the early and later writings was to assert that the distinction between homosexuality and heterosexuality, by itself, was not so useful in understanding sexuality's place in human functioning. He was trying to draw attention to the fact that there are many sexual practices and preferences for both heterosexuals and homosexuals. What is most important for psychoanalysis about these practices is how much they allow for successful intimacy with another human being. In Sullivan's own words, in *The Interpersonal Theory of Psychiatry* (1953),

> Now I do not like to coin freak terms, but what these terms represent is terribly significant. And the terrible significance is this: in this culture the ultimate test of whether you can get on or not is whether you can do something satisfactory

with your genitals or somebody else's genitals without undue anxiety and loss
of self-esteem. (p. 294)

In my own work (Blechner, 1995c), I have protested against what I
called the "gender fetish" in psychoanalysis and society. By gender fetish,
I mean the obsessive and exaggerated attention to the gender of someone's
romantic partner, to the exclusion of so many other factors of equal or
greater importance. For example, in 1993, I proposed that we give prefixes
to the terms "heterosexuality" and "homosexuality." What we usually call
"homosexuality" should be called "gender homosexuality." Many other
important factors can be concordant or different in any couple, including age, social class, intelligence, nationality, ethnicity, religion, profession, sexual behavior preference, and others. Any one of them could be
a prefix, such as "age heterosexuality or age homosexuality." The prefixes
"hetero" and "homo" could be used to convey that you are attracted to
people who either share certain characteristics with you ("homo") or differ from you in that way ("hetero"). For example, if you are a man and
your wife is almost the same age as you, then you are an age-homosexual.
Similarly, if your male gay lover is your own age, you are also an age-
homosexual. But if your partner is much older or younger than you are,
no matter whether that partner is a man or a woman, then you are an
age-heterosexual. I recently heard about a case of age-heterosexuality; a
woman described her attraction only to men at least 20 years older, which
she said felt to her as obligatory as (gender) homosexuality must to most
(gender) homosexuals.

The gender fetish has led to all sorts of poorly-thought-out formulations,
such as the idea that an attraction to someone of the same sex, regardless of other similarities and differences, necessarily reflects a narcissistic
object choice that needs to be worked on and changed in psychoanalytic
treatment. As I have written (1995c), "If a psychoanalyst marries another
psychoanalyst, does that reflect a narcissistic object choice? And if it does,
in your view, and you work with such a psychoanalyst clinically, do you
aim to get the person to marry a non-psychoanalyst?" (p. 283).

Sullivan also felt that the terms commonly used to describe sexuality
omitted too much of importance. He wrote (1972):

I would like you to realize, if you realize nothing else, how fatuous it is to toss
out the adjectives "heterosexual," "homosexual," or "narcissistic" to classify a
person as to his sexual and friendly integration with others. Such classifications
are not anywhere near refined enough for intelligent thought; they are much

too gross to do anything except mislead both the observer and the victim.* For example, to talk about homosexuality's being a problem really means about as much as to talk about humanity's being a problem. (p. 196n)

In going back to Sullivan's early writings, I have become aware that he was working on the same questions I have been (Blechner, 1995c, 1998a, 2002, 2005b, 2006), as to what is important about sexuality and the body and how that interacts with one's interpersonal relations, although his solutions were different from mine. He focused on the specifics of one's preferred sexual practices, and how they affect one's ability to find mutual satisfaction and intimacy with another person. Again I will quote Sullivan, from *The Interpersonal Theory of Psychiatry* (1953), on why he worked out his classification of sexuality in terms of explicit, bodily interactions:

> The reason why I attempt to set up careful classifications in this field is this: It is almost always essential for the psychiatrist, when he ventures into reme-dial efforts for serious developmental handicaps, to pay attention to the place of lust in the difficulties of the person. And let me make it clear that lust, in my sense, is not some great diffuse striving, "libido" or what not. By lust I mean simply the felt aspect of the genital drive. And when I say that the psychiatrist must usually pay attention to this, I do not mean that problems in living are primarily or chiefly concerned with genital activity. But I am saying, of people in this culture who are chronologically adult, that their problems in interper-sonal relations quite certainly will be either very conspicuous in, or exceedingly well illustrated by, the particular circumstances governing their handling of the emotion of lust. (pp. 294–95)

I also think that more widespread appreciation of these writings by Sullivan would shift our view of sexuality and the body in Sullivan's theory. I have always felt that Greenberg and Mitchell (1983) underplayed Sullivan's attention to the body and bodily drives, what he sometimes called "zonal

---

* Califia (1983) has expressed a similar view: "It is odd that sexual orientation is defined solely in terms of the sex of one's partners. I don't think I can assume anything about another person because I have been told they are bisexual, heterosexual or homosexual.... For many people, if a partner or a sexual situation has other desirable qualities it is possible to overlook the partner's sex. Some examples are: a preference for group sex, for a particular socioeconomic background, for paid sex, for S/M, for a specific age group, for a physical type or race, for anal or oral sex" (p. 94). In the field of sexual orientation, many truths get sabotaged by overstatement. While Califia is correct that the terms "homosexual" and "heterosexual" don't cover all significant dimensions of a person's sexual desire, I would disagree with her that one can't assume anything about another person by the characterization as hetero-, homo-, or bisexual. Specifically, if you are a man or a woman, you can predict the *relative* likelihood that such a person may be interested in a sexual interaction with you. No certainty here, but odds matter. I remember hearing a heterosexual woman at a party ask a gay man about another man at the party whom she found attractive: "Is he on your team or mine?"

needs." Their division of relational and drive theory was a very valuable heuristic. It forced orthodox psychoanalysts to see the one-sidedness of some of their thinking. But it went too far. Greenberg and Mitchell argued that mixed-drive relational theories don't work. In my view, a mixed-drive relational theorist is what Sullivan was. He kept interpersonal relations in the foreground and saw interpersonal needs, like safety and prestige, as sources of motivation as important as the sexual drive. But he included the body and sexuality in his thinking, quite specifically, and so should we present-day interpersonal and relational psychoanalysts. You can appreciate Sullivan's enormous contribution to understanding human behavior in an interpersonal context without stripping him of the drive and bodily aspects in his theory. And you end up with a more complete interpersonal theory.

Postscript

There is an interesting thing that can happen in historical studies. People around the world may work completely independently and come to similar conclusions. This happened with Harry Stack Sullivan's homosexuality. While I was working on "The Gay Harry Stack Sullivan" (Blechner, 2005a), a graduate student in history at Indiana University at Bloomington, Naoko Wake, was working on her dissertation entitled "Private Practices: Harry Stack Sullivan, Homosexuality, and the Limits of Psychiatric Liberalism" (2005). She was able to examine the transcripts of Sullivan's clinical interviews at Sheppard-Pratt, and they turned out to be a gold mine of information about how Sullivan really worked. In what were called "special interviews," we see the full radicalism of Sullivan's approach, in making psychotic patients feel free to speak about their homosexual feelings and anxieties (**bold**: Sullivan):

> Well—about this fellow *** over here—I began to love him and it was discontinued because I was removed from that ward.
> **Had your love for him been permitted to develop—what would have been its end?**
> Wouldn't have been an end.
> **Would have gone on forever, increasing?**
> Wouldn't have amounted to anything …
> **What was lovable about him?**
> Just a mere fact of his being alive—that's all.
> **His extreme misery had nothing to do with it?**
> It might have been. (pp. 77–78)

Sullivan and the patient discussed the patient's love feelings for another man without mincing words or pathologizing.

The patient went on to suggest to Sullivan that there might be curative effects to physical affection.

> Sometimes when he was hollowing* (sic) and crying—and whining—I would hold him and he would go right to sleep. Maybe if you Doctors try some of that instead of so many orders and theories.
>
> **It might be misunderstood.**
>
> Yes—I know you are handicapped. And these orders of attendants—they knock people around—if the attendants had more intellectual powers and the doctors more manual powers I think it would be possible.
>
> **In your own case would it have helped? Shortly after you came here if someone tried to be physically affectionate to you, would that have helped?**
>
> Physically affectionate? There is no such thing as physical affection.
>
> **Well, pardon my ignorance. If one of them had held you, caressed you, or something of that kind?**
>
> If one of them had shown that he wanted to … I didn't want any actual holding or caressing—no.
>
> **Why not?**
>
> I just wouldn't—I don't know.
>
> **What is the difference between you and ***? It worked with ***. But you say you wouldn't care for any physical demonstration of that sort.**
>
> It would seem unnatural to me.
>
> **But it seemed … natural when you did it to him?**
>
> Because he had a trust.
>
> **Which you lack?**
>
> Yes. (pp. 78–79)

Sullivan takes the patient's suggestion and seriously discusses with him the benefits and problems of such an approach:

> **If he had been suspicious it would have been bad business for us to hold him and fondle him?**
>
> Yes—but you could have found some way to remove his suspicion.

---

* This is a transcript, so perhaps this word was misunderstood and the patient said "hollering."

**Would you mind telling me what would be the best way? ...
What means would you recommend for me to overcome
the suspiciousness?**

... Your kindly and sympathetic attitude would be something.

Would it work with you?

Yes—it would work with me.

**Here is a case in which you can be kindly to a patient and we
cannot; because [we are] ... restrained from doing that.**

Well—your being here is—it rests on your reputation. Does it
not?

If you are asking personally—it does not. Continue.

It does not? ... I feel certain that it does ...

**If you failed [to get well] you will expect the social organiza-
tion, to wit; your loved ones, to punish us—would you
not?**

No—no—no. If you do what you thought was right—why, that's
all a man can do. I don't think that you can do what you don't
think was right here.

**Explain. You have said [earlier] that you don't think that I
could do what I thought was right here. Now explain that
to me, if you will.**

... If you thought that holding any one was right ... of course,
you could do that, but something more than that I don't
think that you would do it ... In that case about *** ... I think
you would be embarrassed to hold him ...

Would you be embarrassed to permit me to do them?

I might—I don't know.

**And what would bring about my embarrassment and your
possible embarrassment?**

Your fear to do something foolish.

**... May I ask what that means? ... I suppose it connects with
some experience of yours ...**

I have been afraid to wear a beard.

**Foolish, then, would be something that opened one to the
disdain or criticism of others.**

Yes—exactly ...

Suppose, then, that it was done secretly?

That would be alright.

**... The rub is not what other people may think of our doing,
but what you think of it, isn't it?**

Yes—that's what concerns you and me.

**So why need we drag in these people who prohibit our
methods?**

I think—that—that situation exists between you and me.
And that's all there is to it, isn't it—just what you think?
Exactly.
The other fellow hasn't a thing to do with it?
No.
It is just you and me? …
Exactly. (pp. 80–81)

We already knew from Arthur Linton (quoted in Chatelaine, 1981) that the patients on Sullivan's ward "could hug, embrace, and kiss the attendants without feeling rejected, odd, embarrassed or humiliated" (p. 455). Here we see that one possible source of this clinical approach was one of Sullivan's patients. In psychoanalysis, many of the most important clinical innovations have come from patients. It is said that Anna O. herself worked out the "talking cure" that Freud developed into a clinical method; here, no less, we see Sullivan developing a method by which the patient is insulated from the shaming effects of a homophobic society. The patient is pushing the envelope with Sullivan, with the suggestion that permitting or encouraging physical contact might be even more therapeutic.

Interestingly, later the patient backs off from his own radical suggestion and appears to deny it. We see the self-system doing its work, and Sullivan brilliantly continuing the exploration:

What do you suppose you would do if somebody held you?
It all—depends who—and when—and how.
You feel you would enjoy the experience, don't you?
No—I feel—I wouldn't enjoy the experience …
… Explain why life is too short for you to try experiments in secret, in receiving the affectionate attention of some of your fellow-men.
Well—just not interesting—that's all.
And yet it seems to me that that was what you recommended—that we should do that towards patients, including yourself.
No—I don't remember that.
Do you have any recommendations to make in that particular?
Well—yes, I would recommend that you go along some high-road and find a way to make your living and then if there were any men to help—help them. As a side line—not as a business.

> **Then you would perhaps suggest that as a preliminary we destroy the existing social system?**
> Yes. I would recommend that—I would fight for it. That I would live for and die for.
> **Do you think that life might be a little too short to accomplish this?**
> Yes—I do. Therefore—I am going to get what I can out of it.
> **Now so much for you. But we continue to be in relationship of the Staff to the patient. While you feel you can't overthrow the social system and reduce everything to a delightful primitive state, what would you recommend we do in the meanwhile, between the Staff and the patient?**
> ... I wouldn't let any man I couldn't trust sleep with me—would you?
> **I have let men I didn't trust sleep with me—yes.* (p. 83)**

Anyone who thought Sullivan never disclosed personal information during therapeutic interchanges must reconsider.

With another patient, Sullivan spoke quite bluntly about misconceptions of the danger of masturbation and how fear of shaming might interfere with one's sexual enjoyment. He also suggests the possibility of a developmental sequence of masturbation to homosexual experience to heterosexual experience:

> **Have you seen any of the homosexual society's members go mad? ...**
> Can't say that I have ...
> **I think there is a large number of the more cultured who are frankly homosexual ... I have received exceedingly few of them as patients in many years past. I have received a great number of people who are terribly concerned lest they are homosexual ... If one says, "To hell with everything, I am going to perform fellatio," the chances are all his training which is directed against immoral practices ... will come in conflict with his impulses to do it and he will find it ... ungratifying ... And I surmise you are one of a large number of people who start by masturbation, ... and then gradually grow to a heterosexual adjustment possibly with a homosexual stage ...**
> Do you mean that a person who had no mental tension and no concern about it—that he could masturbate as often as he cared without injuring himself?

---

* This is probably a confirmation of Sullivan's homosexual experience.

I think if one had … no notion of the evil of masturbation, he perhaps would do himself a wee bit of good.

What is the hope in my case?

To some extent that is determined by your early training and by the weakness and uncertainties in your self-esteem. To a larger extent it is determined by the actual desire you have to get into life, rather than sitting off in a corner and thinking.

… there has been in my mind some trance—rather some homosexual coloring concerning

I think it would have been very unfortunate for you to marry the first one you came in contact with. I do believe you will gain experience which will probably diminish your interest in homosexual fantasies … I … regard you in need of some sexual experience before you … select a satisfactory wife. I don't advise you to go looking for it, but if it comes your way, take it. (pp. 85–86)

Many people have presumed from Sullivan's published writing that his assumption of the role of expert precluded his exploration of countertransference. This, too, is brought into question by the transcribed interviews:

Let us try an experiment and now let us be very candid—you tell me something about myself. We are trying a practical test.

Well, your manner has seemed to be rather affected … especially your enunciation and manner of treating patients … I have often wondered why it is [that] you have never married … And then I tried to … find some association between your choice of work and the reasons you have never married—your professional manner didn't seem affected but I had an intuition that it was the result of some effort anyway. And you seem to be under some strain— that is about all, I think.

All? My goodness! Now you are trying a test as a literary person.

I should have to look at you. I should have to see all of your face.

Do I have to keep my eyes open?

No—seeing all your face enables me to form opinions and theories.

Do so, please. I wish to hear them.

Well, you are not averse to beating around the bush a little and evading the real truth of things just for the purpose of getting a person's mind easy. In other words, certain things which you advocate you don't really believe in yourself sincerely— but by that I mean sex questions.

Do go on.

I am just trying to formulate facts. You seem to be trying to get away from yourself more than you realize and I have often wondered just why a person takes up this sort of work…. I know attendants at an insane asylum take up that certain sort of work for certain reasons—and I was wondering if psychiatrists in an institution take up that work for the same reasons.

Do tell your reason why attendants do take up.

To a great extent they take it up … because of their homosexual traits … they take it up … because they feel a certain affinity for the patient … a man is interested in a certain thing and there is a reason for it.

You see you are continuing a description of me.

You look on things in a sort of calloused way… you … gave me the impression that marriage was an excellent thing yet I knew you had never married … I know that attendants have traits along that line—homosexual traits and they usually come to this sort of work—a great many of them, not all— because they are afraid of being outside of such a place. It gives them a chance to really be a patient without being one actually. May also give them a feeling of superiority where none exists.

… Will you smoke one of these? … Have you any idea that my thoughts would be any good to anyone but me—those that I don't let people know?

No, I don't suppose so.

Do you feel cheated because I don't say everything I think?

No—I merely noticed that.

Do you think I have been sincere with anything to you?

Yes, I think you have been sincere about everything, but I couldn't help but wonder whether they were not, well somewhat of an insincerity of your remarks about masturbation and sex—I thought possibly you were, might say taking the best road out of the difficulties which I was in or thought I was in.

If to avoid argument you should be interested in your characterization of me—do you remember it well? Because if

you don't, I will be glad to give you a copy of it. It would be much more illuminating than anything else you have said. (pp. 87–88)

The patient is invited to describe his psychiatrist, and he does rather bluntly. He says Sullivan is affected, and confronts the disjuncture between Sullivan's valorization of heterosexuality and the fact that Sullivan himself never married a woman. Sullivan does not deny any of this. In fact, when the patient starts to speak in a more general way, Sullivan swerves the focus back to himself: "You see you are continuing a description of me."

We see Sullivan as the prophet of many modern interpersonal trends, such as "mutual analysis" (Ferenczi, 1932), "working in the countertransference, and analysis of the "maybe-me" (Blechner, 1992b; 1994b), and "co-participant inquiry" (Wolstein, 1981; Fiscalini, 2004). Many contemporary psychoanalysts, knowing Sullivan's admiration of Ferenczi, have wondered why he seemed, in his published writings, to avoid countertransference exploration—but here we discover that Sullivan did not avoid it, he welcomed it. We can appreciate now that Sullivan, like Ferenczi, was interested in the potential benefits, as well as the risks, of mutual analysis and physical contact.* Both of these were explored by Ferenczi in his "Clinical Diary," who, like Sullivan, kept those studies private, so that they were discovered only decades later. We can see the crevasse between clinical exploration and publication. As Mephistopheles said in Goethe's *Faust*:

Das Beste, was du wissen kannst,
Darfst du den Buben doch nicht sagen. (Part I, Line 1840–1841)

"The best of what you can know may not be told to the kids." Freud loved this line, and quoted it in *The Interpretation of Dreams* twice (1900, pp. 142 and 453) and again in 1930, when he was awarded the Goethe Prize (Freud, 1930, p. 212).

Sullivan was quite aware that his clinical experiments would be extremely controversial and that he needed to maintain a distinction between the facts he discovered and what was publishable. When one of his friends, Clifton Read, asked him if he had written about what went on in his ward, he grinned and shook his head, saying that all he could do was suggest it in a footnote (Wake, 2005, p. 114).

Wake's dissertation also shows that there was often a divide between the idealized views that Sullivan published and some of his

---

* Wake has evidence that when Sullivan was in private practice in New York, he experimented with physical contact with patients, with troubling results (Wake, 2005, 202–211).

privately expressed opinion. While he decried racism, he seems to have harbored some privately discriminatory views. While he argued against anti-homosexual attitudes in society, he at times published views that were pathologizing of homosexuals. Sullivan used to say, "We are all more simply human than otherwise." To that we may add: "We humans are all not so simple, but otherwise."

11

AIDS

AIDS. It appeared just as I was beginning my psychoanalytic training in 1979. I knew someone then who was diagnosed with a mysterious ailment. They thought it was Hodgkin's disease, but despite treatment, he kept getting worse. He had been one of the handsomest people I knew, with shiny blond hair and a boyish face, but as the illness progressed, he came to look like an old man. I remember seeing him at the opera, walking with a cane, and telling me that next year people would refer to him as "The late...." When he died, he had zero T-cells. By then, the doctors knew that he had a terrible illness that destroyed the immune system.

First it was known, colloquially, as the "gay cancer." Then it was called GRID: Gay Related Immune Deficiency. Finally, when doctors realized that it was by no means limited to gay people, it got the name it carries today, AIDS: Acquired Immune Deficiency Syndrome.

As John Lennon said, "Life is what happens to you while you're busy making other plans." I never planned to spend my early 30s terrified of dying and seeing dozens of friends disappearing in the prime of life. I did not plan to become a specialist on the psychological factors involved in serious physical illness, but AIDS appeared, and we had to deal with it. Although I hardly knew much about the illness at first (no one did), people began sending me patients with AIDS early in the epidemic. They assumed that since I was gay, I would know more than most people about it.

In the early days of the epidemic, we got information any way we could. The mainstream journals and newspapers were giving scant coverage to the epidemic. President Reagan never mentioned it in public until 1987, by which time 20,000 people had died. And the *New York Times* had only brief articles on it for years, hidden in the middle of the paper, while the much less severe Legionnaire's disease, which took 29 lives in 1976, made instant front-page news for 11 out of the first 30 days of the epidemic.

So we had to get information from "alternative" sources. We turned to the venerable "grapevine," but there were as many false rumors as true facts. The best source of information about AIDS, in those days, were the articles by Dr. Lawrence Mass in *The New York Native*, a gay newspaper. With incredible zeal, Mass always seemed to get access to the latest and most reliable facts. He went on to be one of the co-founders of the Gay Men's Health Crisis, the leading service institution for people with AIDS. (He also, it turned out, loved classical music, especially Wagner operas. When I read his autobiography, *Confessions of a Jewish Wagnerite* [Mass, 1999], I discovered that we also shared a love of music, especially Wagner operas, and we became friends. Mass has written extensively about gay composers and performers.)

I have written about the AIDS epidemic at length (Blechner, 1993b, 1997). I won't repeat all those observations here, but I want to discuss the role of AIDS in my relationship to psychoanalysis, my colleagues, and the international professional community. In all the years I had been alive, gay people had endured great unpleasantness from rampant homophobia, but now it was killing us. The actions of the press, the government, and our president sent a clear message to gay people: "We don't care if you die. Your dying is not important news. It is not something to talk about publicly." Once again, the ugly question arose: Were they gays, or were they people?

That message resonated with what I had always heard about the attitude of the world during the Holocaust. The death of Jews was not important. The world would do little or nothing to stop it. And the current answer to that history was, "Never again."

It became imperative for gay people to fight back: to speak publicly, loudly, and insistently about what was happening; to demand public attention and government action. The AIDS activist group ACT UP captured the situation best in the slogan: "Silence equals death." By devising a logo with the pink triangle, which gay men had been forced to wear in Hitler's concentration camps, the link between the AIDS crisis and the Holocaust was made manifest.

When the *New York Times* first wrote about AIDS, it was often inaccurate, colored by the same prejudices and misinformation rampant in the country. Twice I wrote corrective letters to the editor that were published. By the time the HIV virus had been isolated, it was clear to me that this was not intrinsically a disease of "risk groups"—gay people and intravenous drug users—but one that could affect all people. Public officials in the 1980s frequently made misleading statements to assure people that AIDS would only infect "the other," not "the general population," a claim I knew to be false. In two letters to the *New York Times*, I simply stated the facts of transmission as we then knew them, which predicted the dire situation the world would face two decades later. Today, women who have contracted Human Immunodeficiency Virus (HIV) through heterosexual intercourse are the fastest growing group of people with AIDS.

Here are the two letters:

July 23, 1985

To the Editor:

According to "AIDS Cases and Risk Groups" (July 22), Dr. David Sencer, New York City Health Commissioner, says AIDS continues to spread rampantly among those in the risk groups, but not outside them. Of those contracting AIDS, only 1 percent are not in any of the risk groups, as was the case one year and two years ago. The rate remains stable.

Contrary to Dr. Sencer's reassurances, this statistic is alarming. AIDS cases are increasing geometrically among the "risk groups," approximately doubling every year. Thus, if the cases outside the risk groups remain at a constant percentage, then these cases, too, are increasing geometrically. At that rate, in about six years the number of AIDS cases outside the risk groups will equal the number of cases today within the risk groups, which is over 12,000.

Government officials have the opportunity to educate the public on the best ways to avoid the disease, given current knowledge. This includes avoiding sexual promiscuity or sexual relations with promiscuous people. Failing that, using condoms and avoiding the exchange of body fluids during sexual relations may be helpful.

A statement like Dr. Sencer's may calm public fears, but it is a false calm that could eventually cost many lives. Since there is no cure for AIDS yet, prevention of transmission through vigorous public education is the best means we have of saving lives and must become a top priority immediately.

Mark J. Blechner

July 31, 1986

To the Editor:

I applaud your editorial deploring the lack of effective educational action taken against AIDS (July 14, 1986). However, I disagree with you that the case for heterosexual transmission "is still murky," and your emphasis on the political aspects of the argument clouds the scientific facts.

There is convincing evidence from many sources that heterosexual transmission does occur in the United States frequently. The journal *Science* summarized the recent AIDS conference in Paris as follows: "Whatever their discipline, conference participants came to realize that AIDS can no longer be a disease restricted to certain populations. Data from surveys in the United States, including a military study, and on the massive spread of the disease in Africa, indicate that AIDS is passed as easily from women to men as from men to their sexual partners. In its pattern of transmission, AIDS is typical of other sexually transmitted diseases" (July 18, p. 282.).

The cause of public health is not well served by waffling on the issue of heterosexual transmission.

Mark J. Blechner

By 2005, the number of people in the United States who had acquired AIDS through heterosexual contact was 164,850, more than 17% of the total number of AIDS cases (956,666).

No one at the White Institute said anything directly to me about the letters. I heard secondhand that some people thought it unseemly to have published them, but by then I was getting inured to being thought "a vulgarian" for speaking openly and publicly about anything related to homosexuality. The situation was too urgent to worry about such things. People were dying.

Why was there so much irrationality and denial about the heterosexual spread of AIDS and HIV? This was an issue about which psychoanalysis had much to say. Psychoanalysis is the field that established the irrational and the unconscious as areas worthy of study (Blechner, 2005d). Freud and Sullivan taught us how all aspects of human psychology—memory, perception, thinking, and reasoning—can be altered by intense emotional concerns. To understand HIV and the irrational attitudes connected with it, one ought to invoke two of the great concepts of psychoanalysis— Freud's concept of *wish-fulfillment*, and Sullivan's notion of the *not-me*. Both of these concepts were intended to describe the processes of individual psychology, but both of them can be expanded to describe the group psychological processes of distortion and myth making that we have seen rampant in the AIDS epidemic and which still continue today.

Freud (1900, 1901) postulated that when we are under great emotional stress, our reasoning can become illogical by the same mechanisms that can make our dreams so strange. Our waking thoughts can be distorted by primary processes and ego defenses, like displacement, repression, denial, and reaction formation. I think that the great fear and panic invoked by the AIDS epidemic led to those kinds of distorted thinking. But the distortions were not only on the level of individual psychology; they were also on the level of large groups, and ultimately all of society. Over and over during the AIDS epidemic, we saw the distortions of individuals coalescing into distorted group beliefs, which we also call myths. Because these myths fulfill such a strong psychological need, they were very hard to dispel.

Many different AIDS myths were produced, but a theme common to most of them was that the AIDS epidemic affects someone who is "not-me," to use Sullivan's term. In the beginning of the epidemic, when so few facts were available, everyone wanted to project the danger of the epidemic onto someone else, and the most convenient targets were groups that are hated or looked down upon. For instance, in the beginning of the epidemic, there was a rumor among White gay men that the only people getting AIDS were those who were sleeping with Black men. Meanwhile, as Washington (1995) has documented, Black men thought the opposite, that AIDS was a disease of White gay men, and Black men could be safe as long as they only slept with each other. Of course, both groups were wrong. The same phenomenon reappeared in many parts of the world; in Cambodia, for example, a poll showed that most hospital nurses believed that AIDS is a disease of foreigners, and that it could not be passed between Cambodians. It is not very surprising that AIDS is still thought of by many heterosexuals as a disease of gay men and drug users.

Many other myths continued to develop about AIDS, driven by the wish for immunity from the disease. Until 1991, the Centers for Disease Control's definition of AIDS did not even mention several opportunistic infections that occur only in women, such as various forms of cancer and pelvic inflammatory disease, so that many women were not properly diagnosed. One physician put it this way: "In the United States, women don't get AIDS; they just die of it."

The level of irrationality about AIDS produced the most bizarre belief systems. Think about the following question: What do you believe is the risk that two gay men who are HIV-negative can transmit the HIV virus to one another during anal intercourse? Herek and Capitanio (1993) studied this question. They found that about half of the people believed there was a strong chance of HIV transmission between two uninfected homosexual men. Of course, the correct answer is 0. But their study showed how many people irrationally connect HIV transmission with specific behaviors. If anal intercourse is one of the most efficient ways of spreading HIV, then any act of anal intercourse is thought to cause AIDS.

This is an example of the principle of von Domarus (1944) that has been applied to schizophrenic reasoning, in which things that are merely associated with one another are seen to have a causal or inclusive relationship. For example, a schizophrenic may think, "If my mother's name is Mary, and Mary is the mother of God, then I am God."

The most severe forms of irrationality, fear, and ignorance were slow to disappear. In 1995, a group of gay political leaders was to meet with President Clinton at the White House. Secret service members who frisked them wore rubber gloves as a precaution against contracting AIDS. What was their reasoning? The same von Domarus principle seems to have been at work. Many gay people have AIDS. Therefore, all gay people have AIDS. Doctors use rubber gloves when examining AIDS patients where there are bodily fluids. So rubber gloves will prevent my getting AIDS from frisking gay men. Of course, the fact is that you cannot get AIDS by frisking anyone, with or without gloves; but if such ignorance exists at the top levels of American government, what can we expect of those with less education and less public responsibility?

Irrational beliefs and prejudice also limit research into issues of drug use and sexuality that are crucial to AIDS transmission. June Osborn (1992), as chair of the National Commission on AIDS, said that "even our most basic efforts to better understand and respond to this new plague have been hampered. Efforts have been made to constrain or forbid behavioral research." Even though we know that clean needles dramatically reduce the spread of HIV among intravenous (IV) drug users (Hausman, 1993; Karel, 1993), most states do not allow ready access to such clean needles, because of a fear that it will encourage drug use. Even though anal intercourse is known to be the most efficient means of transmitting HIV sexually, the government refused funding for literature that would explicitly mention anal intercourse, for fear that it will encourage such behavior. The unconscious ideas here are that if you talk about a behavior, you encourage it. Not talking about it or thinking about it causes the behavior to be less present. Both of these ideas are false and dangerous. Needle exchange programs do not cause more people to be drug addicts, and safer sex education does not increase the rate of anal intercourse. But while such programs are discouraged in Congress, AIDS has been spreading relentlessly.

I fought against irrational beliefs about AIDS whenever I could, but they affected me, too. When the blood test for HIV was finally released, I wasted no time getting tested. It was a terrifying experience. In those days, you had to wait two weeks from when the blood was first drawn until you heard the results; today you can have the results almost immediately. Those two weeks were dreadful. I felt my mortality acutely and obsessed over every detail that might predict the result. Fortunately, the result was negative; whether it was thanks to my long relationship with John or just good luck, I do not know.

I felt that my personal good luck made it imperative for me to help people with AIDS in any way I could, whether as a therapist, teacher, or friend. A group of people working with AIDS met regularly for several years in Bertram Schaffner's apartment, to share information and experiences. Everyone at the White Institute was invited to these meetings, but very few attended.

This was the era of the cure being around the corner. Every few months, there was the new great hope, the new magic medicine—there was Suramin, which turned out to be ineffective and extremely toxic. People flew to Paris to get HPA-23, thinking that it was the great cure that was available only to the rich and well connected (most famously, Rock Hudson). They were wrong; it didn't work. AL-721, a derivative of egg yolks from Israel, was another great hope, and it did not have a high level of toxicity. People began to drink homemade egg-yolk concoctions, which did virtually no harm, but ultimately not much good, either. There was also the Chinese cucumber, Ribaviran, thermal treatment of the blood, and many other treatments. With each, there was a flurry of great hope, and then, when the results did not hold up, first denial, then disappointment.

It seemed to me that we needed to make the treatment of AIDS some-thing integral to psychoanalysis and to the White Institute, and so I sub-mitted a proposal to set up a clinical service that would specialize in AIDS and HIV issues. This was still in the days of the old, conservative regime at the White Institute, and so my proposal was met with a response typical of society at large: nothing. Not even an acknowledgment that I had submit-ted it, let alone a critique or a refusal. Just silence.

However, I knew that many psychoanalysts at the institute were con-fronting AIDS or the fear of AIDS in their practices, as well as in their families. People would call me or take me aside when they met me and ask me about the facts of AIDS and how to deal with it, often in hushed tones. It was as if psychoanalysts were sharing the public shame about AIDS, and being ashamed that they had to think about HIV.

I suppose I could have made a ruckus about my proposal for a clinical service being ignored. I knew by then, though, that such public protest was not my way. I simply went along, doing the best work with AIDS that I could and trusting that eventually the goodwill of the majority would prevail.

Nevertheless, something active was necessary to tap into that goodwill. On March 10, 1992, I gave a talk at the White Institute entitled "Psychoanalysis and HIV Disease." It was the first talk on the illness held at the institute itself. The room was full but hushed. The talk did, in fact, bring out the well-meaning majority. During the discussion, Dr. Margit Winckler asked, "Why aren't we as an Institute doing something about this? Why don't we set up a program to help people with AIDS?" At this point, the person to whom I had addressed my proposal four years before said, matter-of-factly, "Well, Blechner has written out a proposal to set up a clinical service." This was the first response to that proposal, but better late than never. Also, this was after the "revolution" against the ruling administration of the White Institute. New and innovative things had become much more feasible, thanks to the open and enthusiastic leadership of the new director, Dr. Marylou Lionells. Within weeks, the HIV Clinical Service was up and running.

We held monthly conferences at the institute, inviting experts in the field and presenting our own cutting-edge psychotherapy experiences, and they were well attended. They broke many barriers of what could be discussed at the institute. Jill Ripps gave a talk about safer sex, wearing condom earrings and using dildos to make sure people understood what she was saying. John O'Leary (1997) spoke about running a support group for gay men who had lost a lover to AIDS, during which he struggled with being in the closet as a heterosexual. Karen Marisak (1997) described her attempts to stay helpful as a psychotherapist even while her patient gradually lost his mental faculties from AIDS-related dementia. Sue Shapiro (1997) told us about her anguish and elation as she worked with a heterosexual young woman with AIDS determined to enjoy love and marriage with someone HIV-negative. Seth Aronson ran a group for teenagers in the Bronx who had lost one or both parents to AIDS, for whom sexual abuse by adults was a common fact of life. There were discussions of sex workers and pimps, sadomasochism, and the details of many unusual sex practices. After five years of concentrated work, we held a public conference in 1996 entitled "HIV and Psychoanalysis: Grappling with New Realities" and published a book the following year (Blechner, 1997).

The reality of AIDS was changing. The "cocktail" of multiple drugs was discovered, which was the first really effective treatment for AIDS. People who were near death began to recover. For the first time since the start of the epidemic, AIDS was not a sure death sentence.*

---

* This was true in the United States and other wealthy countries. In most of the world, people with AIDS cannot afford the very expensive treatments. Someday, I believe we will look back with shame about how many people were allowed to die needlessly. Today there is wonderment and shame about how people could have allowed the Holocaust to happen—how, for example, the United States did not bomb the railroad tracks to Auschwitz or abolish quotas on Jewish immigration. And there is wonderment that the founding fathers of the United States could be slaveowners. Someday, there will be the same kind of wonderment and shame about how we could turn away from the suffering of people with AIDS because of financial concerns or even baser motives.

I continued as director of the HIV Service until 2001. By that time, far fewer patients were asking for psychotherapists with special training in HIV. For most people, the illness had become more manageable. If the medication regimen was followed, most people recovered their health. There is still no cure, but the illness can be controlled in most cases. Also, there was less need for specialized training at the post-graduate level in working with AIDS. By the twenty-first century, many of the candidates for psychoanalytic training at the White Institute already had substantial experience in working with HIV issues.

The mainstream psychoanalytic journals were silent about AIDS throughout the 1980s, and there was little mention of the illness, except as a fantasy, in the 1990s. I continued to be appalled at the way organized psychoanalysis ignored HIV, or, when they did deal with it, made shamefully homophobic statements. I often dreaded opening the *International Journal of Psychoanalysis*, lest I saw something offensive that would call for a letter.

For example, I came across the report of a discussion of AIDS at the 1997 International Psychoanalytic Association (IPA) meeting in Barcelona. Homophobia was clearly alive and well at the end of the twentieth century in the IPA. Consider this statement in the report:

> "[Sidonia] Mehler went on to say that we were taught as analysts that liberation of sexuality would improve the relationship between men and women, and would bring about a closer and more empathic relationship. Instead, what we have today after a hundred years of psychoanalysis is an enormous quantity of homosexuals!"

I could not help writing the following letter, which was published:

May 5, 1998

Dr. David Tuckett, Editor
Letters to the Editor
The International Journal of Psycho-Analysis
63 New Cavendish Street
London W1M 7RD England

Dear Sir:

It was painful to read the account of the panel on "Sexuality in the Age of AIDS" [Otero and Escardó, 1998]. The panel was evidence of multiple scotomata* among the participating psychoanalysts. There was ignorance of the

---

* Scotomata are blind spots.

psychoanalytic literature on AIDS and HIV [e.g., Isay, 1989; Aronson, 1996; Blechner, 1993a, 1997], none of which was mentioned. The panel participants tended to ascribe the illness to the other, the "not-me," and to describe the purported psychopathology of those with the illness. When AIDS first appeared, when there was a lack of knowledge and much inchoate fear, this pattern of disavowal was common, but it is not acceptable among professionals 15 years into the epidemic. As further evidence of disavowal and denial, the panel made no mention of psychoanalysts who have died of AIDS and of the many relatives and friends of psychoanalysts who have been lost to the illness. In addition, the obsessive focus on homosexuals at this panel was misguided. Internationally, more cases of HIV infection are spread through heterosexual than homosexual contact, and in the United States, heterosexual women are the group with the fastest rise in the rate of HIV infection [*HIV Center*, 1991].

While the problem of poor relations between gay men and lesbians with psychoanalysis was mentioned, there seemed to be little self-awareness of the homophobia and anti-homosexual hatred among the participants in the panel. Rather than focus on the purported psychotic aspects of homosexuals, as did some of the panel members, the next conference of the International Psychoanalytic Association ought to have a panel that addresses the problem of bigotry among psychoanalysts—the destructive and often delusional fear and hatred of gay men and lesbians. There is now a substantial amount of psychoanalytic literature on this problem [e.g., Schafer, 1995; Schaffner, 1995; Magee and Miller, 1997; Drescher, 1998; Frommer, 1994; Blechner, 1993b; Moss, 1992; Mitchell, 1981] although none of it was cited by this panel.

Yours sincerely,

Mark J. Blechner, Ph.D.

As AIDS became more treatable, the focal issue shifted from dealing with illness and mortality. Instead, there came to be a new spurt in the growth of AIDS cases, which became a great concern. Some people seemed unafraid of contracting HIV and were engaging in unprotected sex, which became known as "barebacking." There were even people known as "bugchasers" who were seeking to be infected with HIV. On the Internet, they could find HIV-positive men known as "gift-givers" who were willing to infect them. A New York psychologist, J. P. Cheuvront, wrote a paper about this upsurge in unsafe sex, and I was asked to discuss his views. It led me to analyze the factors that led to decisions that looked, to some observers, to be totally irrational and self-destructive. Why would anyone willingly contract HIV? I had to think closely about what I had been through and how it was different for a new generation of young gay people.

12

Intimacy, Pleasure, Risk, and Safety*

I speak from the cusp of Boomer/Gen-X. I wobble on either side. I look at my daughter; and her beauty and vitality are so vivid I could faint. I want to lock her up. No, I mean, I want to empower her. Actually, no! I want to scare her. Oh, let's be honest: I'm scared. My generation has melted the polar ice caps, looted the bank, and my inheritance to her is: what exactly?

Susie Bright

The question of safer sex and the current upsurge in "barebacking" has raised alarm among experts in public health as well as in the psychotherapeutic community. While the situation merits serious analysis of risk-taking, it also requires us to examine the fundamental issues of sexual experience and the ways they have shifted during different periods of recent history. Without this perspective, we run the risk of assuming that there are simple truths involved in determining behavior and of losing an empathic perspective on the experience of young gay people coming out today.

In the late 1970s, when HIV was spreading, no one had heard of AIDS. Gay men had spent the previous decade rejoicing in post-liberation sexuality. All sex was, by today's definition, unsafe sex. Virtually no one used condoms. To be sure, there were health risks. Syphilis and gonorrhea were rampant, but they could usually be quickly treated with antibiotics. Intestinal parasites were often tougher to treat, and herpes was untreatable, but generally these were not lethal.

When AIDS first appeared, nobody knew what caused it or how it could be prevented. It was referred to at first as GRID (Gay Related Immune Deficiency), and most gay men were terrified. Was it caused simply by gay sex? By recreational drug use? By unusual sexual practices? No one knew. For the first few years, there was just no way to tell whether you would get sick, and there was at that time no treatment.

---

* Originally published in *Journal of Gay and Lesbian Psychotherapy*, 2002, 6, 27–33.

When HIV was finally discovered and a test for it was developed, the situation changed. Now one could know whether one was infected. For those who were HIV-positive, the news was devastating, since there was no treatment available and premature death seemed nearly certain. Those who were HIV-negative felt extremely lucky. For them, the prospect of staying healthy by regular condom use seemed a small price to pay. They had lived with terror for years, and they were now glad that something as seemingly innocuous as condom use could protect them from HIV. Of course, not everyone practiced safer sex, but much of the gay community did, and the rate of new infections was impressively reduced.

It is essential to realize that young people today did not experience that terrifying period when AIDS was a mystery. AIDS is a relatively known quantity for them. They have been hearing about safer sex since they have been hearing about sex in general. They also have not lived through a period when AIDS was totally untreatable and the death of one's close friends became a horribly regular experience. They may be lucky not to have been through those awful times, but, consequently, many such people today do not share the great sense of relief that the previous generation felt at being able to stay alive by mere condom use. Some instead feel resentment and deprivation at the constraints of safer sex.

I was made poignantly aware of this years ago when, at a discussion of the AIDS epidemic, a 19-year-old gay artist did a "performance piece" in which he expressed great sadness that he might never experience condomless intercourse and never taste another man's semen. His grief was overwhelming and deeply moving to those of us in the audience who, having come of age before the AIDS epidemic, had had those pleasures. It is easy for older people who have enjoyed condomless sex yet survived the epidemic to be smug about how the trade-off between condom use and safety is obviously worth it. For younger people, who in any case tend to feel invincible, the subjective valuation of condoms, risk, health, and pleasure may be different.

Cheuvront (2002) writes: "My sense is that most risk-taking patients feel significant shame surrounding the sexual risks they have taken" (p. 12). I cannot argue with the statistics of his own practice, but I can argue that there are certainly many barebackers who are not ashamed of the sexual risks they have taken. On the contrary, they are proud and defiant, in what some see as courageous behavior against sexual repression and punitive attitudes, sometimes tinged with homophobia (Blechner, 1998b; see also Sheon and Plant, 1997, for several examples). Should clinicians attend only to those individuals who experience conflict and therefore seek psychotherapy? Or should we also attend to the social phenomena that are endangering future generations? Anyone who consults the Web site on barebacking can find many requests from people who claim to be HIV-negative to receive the "gift" of HIV from someone positive. Some of those people may be engaging only in fantasy, but most seem to be quite serious and may succeed in acquiring the gift they seek.

Each clinician must examine closely his or her relationship to sex and risk. Can we talk about risk-taking without identifying our own risk-taking tendencies? Our judgment of risk-taking may be an index of our lack of risk-taking, but it can also indicate our dissociation from our own risk-taking wishes or behavior. It is quite common to find people involved professionally with AIDS prevention who counsel others about safer sex practices during the day and have unsafe sex at night. It is precisely in the gap between knowing and doing that the process of dissociation in human consciousness can best be seen. The danger is great when the clinician pathologizes others and disavows his own vulnerability and fallibility. When our judgment of what is pathological intersects with the "not-me" territory of our own personalities, we run into trouble.

I also don't think we can fully grasp the situation of risk-taking without discussing its opposite, risk-avoidance. Leaders in public health may be made less anxious by people whose avoidance of HIV verges on the phobic, but they suffer, too, and their clinical issues are relevant to those at the opposite end of the spectrum. At the beginning of the AIDS epidemic, there was a great deal of discussion of the "worried well." This is a topic that has receded in prominence. The greater knowledge about HIV and its transmission has eliminated some of the panic that came from lack of knowledge. But nevertheless, the worried well are still with us and many of them claim that no caution is too great. They can cite indisputable facts: There is no absolute criterion for safe and unsafe sex, and we have seen the prevalent guidelines shift over the years of the epidemic. In the early days, when so little was understood, any sex was thought to be dangerous, and all sorts of myths evolved. In our own day, there is still much debate about oral sex without a condom, which ranges in evaluated danger from quite safe to quite unsafe. And with something as serious as AIDS, what amount of risk is acceptable (Blechner, 1993b, 1997; Mujica, 1997; Petrucelli, 1997; Shapiro, 1997)?

If we problematize extreme risk-taking but not extreme risk-avoidance, we may lose perspective on how decisions of risk are made. Risk of HIV infection is serious, but the risk of loss of pleasure and intimacy is also serious. In life, we are constantly making decisions based on conflict, and the parameters of such decisions can vary a great deal between individuals.

For example, when AIDS first appeared, many people living in the inner cities claimed that worry about HIV was not the primary risk that they faced. When one's chance of being shot on the street is high, avoiding a slow illness may not have the same priority as for someone unlikely to be a victim of crime. Similarly, individuals vary in their requirements for pleasure, and the risks they are willing to take for it. And for some individuals, risk-taking is pleasurable in itself.*

The wishes for pleasure and intimacy are powerful, and we humans will go to great lengths to find them. Let us think about the term "barebacking." It comes from the equestrian world, where riding bareback is wild, dangerous, and fun. In the sexual world, when you think of barebacking, do you think of your mother and father having intercourse without condoms? Probably not. The implication of barebacking, at least in the United States, is that it is unprotected anal intercourse between gay men, in a context in which there is some danger of HIV infection. But unfortunately, in the near-panic atmosphere that has surrounded the AIDS epidemic, it has not always been specified precisely when anal intercourse without a condom is most dangerous and when it is most safe. It is most dangerous when the insertive partner is HIV-positive and the receptive partner is HIV-negative. It is most safe when both partners know they are seronegative and are monogamous with each other.

Condomless Safe Sex

Anyone who deals with teenagers knows that excessive scolding and warning are counterproductive. It will mainly ensure that the teenagers will not listen to you. If you want to have any influence on another's behavior, you need to have sympathy with their point of view, including an acknowledgment of the depth of their desire. Especially important is an outlook that offers hope for relative satisfaction. In my view, the possibility of a monogamous relationship makes condomless safe sex a reality. This is what I think has been missing in most safer-sex messages.

---

* The combination of risk and sex can be exhilarating. Bill Clinton was nearly impeached for having sex with Monica Lewinsky, a White House intern, and then lying about it. In 2008, the governor of New York, Eliot Spitzer, hired a prostitute and was thought to have pressured her to have condomless sex. The event destroyed his political career.

Currently, there are many committed gay male couples who practice condomless safe sex. In some cases, they have made the decision that since both partners are HIV-negative and they trust each other enough to sustain fidelity, it is safe enough for them to have unprotected anal intercourse. They do not refer to this activity as barebacking or unsafe sex. If there is no virus or other pathogen to transmit, the sex per se is not unsafe.

During the early stages of the AIDS epidemic, a blanket dismissal of condomless sex developed in many circles. Even people who were certain of their partner's fidelity found out painfully that such presumptions may be wrong. In New York, there developed an ethic that therefore all couples, regardless of serostatus or the commitment of the relationship, should avoid unprotected sex. Theoretically, this would lead to the greatest protection against HIV transmission.

Unfortunately, theory does not always work in our world. Overly prohibiting sexual pleasure may lead to a backlash, and that is just what we are seeing today. Walt Odets (1995) warned about this. He argued that overly restrictive safe-sex guidelines might backfire, and lead people to greater risk-taking. He emphasized that there was an optimal trade-off and a psychological reality to risk-taking that needed to be taken into account. While people must be cautious, excess self-denial may lead to impulsive risk-taking.

Are those the only alternatives? In my view, the answer is "No." I am moving here from purely psychotherapeutic issues to social issues, but I do not think we psychotherapists can ignore the social, and we may consider inserting our views into the debate about social norms. I believe that some people would be able to tolerate the strictures of safe sex better if they could have in mind a future for themselves in which safe-sex precautions would be unnecessary. Obviously, if there were a vaccine against HIV, that would be one solution. But none of us knows if and when such a vaccine will be developed. In the meantime, I think that the prospect of a monogamous, committed sexual relationship without the constraints of safer sex could be a goal for some gay men to consider for themselves. This does not mean entirely mimicking the heterosexual ideal of marriage. On the contrary, because gay men and lesbians have been denied the right of legal marriage,* they have had to find their own

---

* I wrote this before gay marriage became legal in Massachusetts, before a constitutional amendment banning gay marriage nationally was proposed, and before the 2004 election in the U.S. saw many states banning gay marriage. It is quite possible that allowing gay marriage might save lives (Blechner, 2005c).

ways of defining commitment and fidelity with imaginative solutions that provide meaningful, intimate relationships.

I have worked with a number of young gay men, caught up in the New York "scene," who do not know any long-term committed gay couples. There are of course many such couples, but most of them will not be found in the bars and baths of New York, and unfortunately they are not usually the leaders of public discussions of safer sex. It seems a great loss to the gay community that there is not more of a structure in place in which such couples can share their experiences and examples with younger gay men.*

Sometimes the commitment to fidelity in a relationship proves elusive or ephemeral, but sometimes not. It would be a great help for younger gay men and lesbians to come to know gay people who have carved out such lives, and the satisfactions that are possible, as well as the worries and uncertainties. Negotiating that balance is everyone's task, but in considering one's options, it is helpful to know about many alternative solutions, not only those getting the most public attention and publicity.

---

* Already, the publicity about gay marriage has made the existence of long-term couples much more visible. The first couple to be married in San Francisco in 2004, Del Martin and Phyllis Lyon, had already been together 50 years.

13

Love, Sex, Romance, and Psychoanalytic Goals

Truth does not change according to our ability to stomach it.

Flannery O'Connor

Author's Introduction

In the year 2000, the psychoanalyst Stephen Mitchell died suddenly at the age of 54. The psychoanalytic world was shocked at such a great loss, for Mitchell was the most creative and open-minded psychoanalyst of the twentieth century. I was inspired by him, and dedicated my book, *The Dream Frontier* (2001), to his memory.

When he died, Mitchell had been working on a book, *Can Love Last?*, which was published after his death (Mitchell, 2002). There was a conference about the book on the Internet, and I was asked to be one of the panelists. I used the opportunity to develop a more open-minded approach to sex and romantic goals among psychoanalysts. I hoped to bring into question some of the most fundamental questions underlying psychoanalytic treatment—namely, what is the good life? Are there many ways to live it? How do we determine whether something is pathology or an unusual but healthy way of living?

Love, Sex, Romance, and Psychoanalytic Goals*

Psychoanalysis has a history of asking questions that generate much literature, before someone asks, why are we asking this question? Why are we asking the question, "Can love last?" There are really many questions

* Originally published in *Psychoanalytic Dialogues*, 2006, *16*, 779–791.

embedded here: Should love last? Can love last without sexual passion lasting? Can sexual passion last when love does not? What does it mean when each of these things happen? How much do cultural factors enter into the expectation of love lasting? Why do many cultures not believe that love and marriage go together like a horse and carriage?

I will start with the last question. We know that for most of human history, marriage and desire were not presumed to go together. Marriage was primarily for economic and social purposes, to produce children and social and economic stability. Germaine Greer (1971) pointed out, in *The Female Eunuch*, that in the Middle Ages, romantic love was considered adulterous and rebellious, and that in modern times there are tensions when society expects a single relationship to serve both romance and social stability.

In many cultures, past and present, marital stability and sexual love have not been presumed to occur together. In Morocco, there is the saying: "Women for marriage, boys for love." A similar culture exists in Afghanistan, as became more widely known to Americans after the U.S. invasion of that country; an Afghan proverb says that birds fly with one wing over Kandahar, using the other to protect their backsides from the sodomy-loving men of the city (Luongo, 2008, p. 24). In ancient Greece, Socrates, whose disquisition on romantic love was centered on Alcibiades and other men in his circle, was married to a woman and had children.

Lest you think that is all in the past: At the end of the twentieth century, it came out that Fidel Castro had an adult daughter, Alina Fernandez, conceived in an extramarital affair with Natalia Revuelta (Fernandez, 1998). There was a time in the United States when this "scandal" was thought to threaten Castro's hold over Cuba. An acquaintance of mine from South America laughed and said, "In South America, we expect our leaders to have mistresses. If one of our leaders did not have a mistress, the populace would want to know what was wrong with him.'" And many people remember the picture of the funeral in 1996 of François Mitterand, the prime minister of France, showing his wife, Danielle, standing next to his mistress, Anne Pingeot.

Even within cultures, there are subgroups with different traditions. Gay relationships, which have never been socially sanctioned, may be a good place to analyze the intricacies of relationships outside mainstream social expectations, since gay and lesbian relationships have been mostly socially condemned or at best ignored. Some gay couples last a lifetime, and some maintain romantic and sexual interest for most of that time, but there may be more wiggle room for experimentation and for alternative arrangements.

In the *East Hampton Star*, February 6, 2003, there was an obituary for Chrystian Aubusson, an antiques dealer who was born in France in 1920. In 1946, Aubusson met Earl Luick, a Hollywood costume designer with whom he moved to the United States and stayed with for the rest of his life. By 1967, the relationship with Luick had become completely platonic. Aubusson met Kris Kersen, an actor and painter, and all three men lived together for the rest of their lives. They all died within a year of each other, at the ripe old ages of 98 (Luick), 86 (Kersen), and 82 (Aubusson).

I cite this example to highlight that there are many ways for people to have meaningful relationships and satisfying lives, which may differ from the implicit ideal of the couple that sustains love, intimacy, romance, and sexual passion throughout life.

When reconsidering the aims of psychoanalysis concerning love and relationships, I would like to take a perspective that includes historical and cultural variations. It is interesting how many times, in the 100 years of psychoanalytic history, therapeutic presumptions of health and pathology have been reevaluated and changed. Freud and most of his contemporary analysts considered oral sex (when not followed by intercourse) to be a perversion and masturbation to be a problem. Freud also felt that clitoral orgasms were a sign of immaturity and should be replaced by vaginal orgasms. Ambitious women were often diagnosed as having pathological penis envy. All of these presumptions are no longer held or at least seriously questioned by most psychoanalysts. Sometimes younger psychoanalysts wonder, how could the early psychoanalysts have thought that?

I often ask colleagues and students to try to imagine which of our current presumptions of health and pathology might, in 100 years, be considered incorrect and a source of wonder. In reading Mitchell's book, I wondered whether the healthfulness of sustaining love, sex, and romance within a single relationship through the life span might be just one of those presumptions that will not survive this century. What percentage of the population achieves it? If most do not, or if a significant proportion do not, should we still postulate it as a sign of mental health? And should we, in our clinical practices, try to help patients achieve that goal?

Regardless of universal presumptions about health and pathology, Mitchell makes an important point—that the loss of sexual passion within a relationship and the pursuit of sexual adventure outside the relationship can be security operations, that is, they may give a person a sense of security (sometimes a false sense of security). It can be frightening to rely on the same person for sex and for taking care of you. It is often easier to divert your passion to someone on whom you are not dependent. Working through such characterological and psychodynamic issues can often revitalize a romantic relationship.

I have seen this happen quite often in my own practice. One man was married and had a mistress. At first the relationship with the mistress seemed to be free, but eventually it got bogged down in the same control issues that plagued his marriage. He was unaware of the way he constantly sought to control everyone in his life, but worked this through in his analysis. I had the unusual fantasy working with him that one of the walls of my office was gradually moving closer to my chair and would eventually push me into the opposite wall, which viscerally alerted me to the subtle but inexorable way he controlled things.

In one session, he told me his wife wanted to order in food. She asked him what he wanted. He said she should order anything she liked, and it would be OK. She protested: "If I do that, then when the food arrives, you will complain that it's not what you wanted." So he told her what he wanted, she ordered it, and then later, she complained that he controlled everything.

I asked him what he thought would have happened if instead he had told his wife, "You order whatever you like, and it will be OK with me," and then really refuse to direct her in any way. He replied to me, "She'll say, who is this man and how did he get into my house?" The example made him aware of how they together conspired to keep him in control and helped him see how he could change that. He found many ways to break the cycle of his controlling everything. As he did so, paradoxically he discovered that his wife was much more interesting and much more interested than he had realized before. Along the way, the passion between them re-emerged. He said, "After 27 years of marriage, I'm falling in love with her all over again."

Mitchell's argument about the difficulty of sustaining desire takes a number of things for granted that may not be the norm in many subcultures. First, there is safety. Mitchell argues that the safety of a marital relationship is highly valuable, and may lead some people to channel their dangerous romantic feelings outside the marriage to preserve that sense of safety. This may be true for many couples, but not all long-term relationships provide the safety and consistency that Mitchell sees in dialectic with romance. In certain cultures, marriage is quite a dangerous proposition. In Africa, for example, women have little choice about having sex with their husbands without condoms, which has resulted in an out-of-control AIDS epidemic among African heterosexuals. And in Western countries, there are many people who experience their marriages as fraught with dangers to life, safety, bodily integrity, and peace of mind.

Safety is very important, and for some people who have found it in their long-term relationships, it is so important that they prefer to protect the safety of the relationship by taking the sex out of it, in the way Mitchell describes. However, they may not be conflicted about doing so, since it works to some degree. In some parts of Europe, it may even be seen as the norm, enough so that we have the term "European marriage." *Der Rosenkavalier*, an opera by Richard Strauss, portrays such a marriage, in which the spouses sustain a long-term partnership, with mutual social and economic benefits, while each is free to pursue erotic dalliances outside the relationship.

On theoretical grounds, then, we may ask, not only, "Can love last?"—to which the obvious answer is, "Yes"—but also, when it does not last, how do we approach this clinically? There are at least three identifiable approaches:

1. Love should last, and so a patient whose romantic love and sexuality are not integrated into his or her marriage or long-term relationship, if treated successfully, should solve this problem.
2. The clinical goal should be up to the patient. If the patient wants to "fix" a relationship in which love has not lasted, he or she should be helped to do so.
3. The reason for wanting to "fix" such a relationship should itself be the subject of clinical inquiry before attempting any such fixing.

These are not the only possibilities, but I have outlined these three extreme positions for heuristic purposes.

I am particularly sensitized to the question of the clinician's assessment of pathology because of the history of psychoanalytic approaches to psychosexual "problems" in the past. One of the most egregious and telling is the psychoanalytic history of "treating" homosexuality. For most of the twentieth century, the standard psychoanalytic practice was to view homosexuality as a fixation, inversion, or perversion, and to consider changing the patient's orientation to heterosexuality as necessary for a successful treatment, a trend challenged by Mitchell in 1978, but which nevertheless survived for at least two more decades (Schafer, 1995).

If you believed in approach #2, that you only treat patients for the things that they want changed, you still might have tried to convert your homosexual patients to heterosexuality during the twentieth century. Since society so condemned homosexuality, and psychiatry and psychoanalysis claimed that they could help someone get rid of it, many patients actively sought such treatment. Too few analysts devoted time to inquire of the patient, "Why do you want to change?" If you believed in the pathology of homosexuality, you took it for granted that someone would want to change it.

Those of us who have worked with patients so mistreated are very wary about how we define psychosexual goals of psychoanalytic treatment. I try always to ask, and often to re-ask, patients who request treatment to change something in their psychosexual makeup why they want to change it. With patients who have marriages in which sexual love has not lasted, and who seek treatment for other reasons, I am wary of problematizing their marriage. I have worked with a number of patients whose marriages or long-term primary relationships have not been sexual for years. In some cases they consider it a focal clinical issue that they want to change, but in some cases they do not and have found an alternative style of relationship that works for them.

In addition, contemporary relational psychoanalysts do not always give adequate attention to the specifics of sexual expression. In freeing psychoanalysis from the tyranny of drive theory, which implied that sex and aggression motivated all human behavior, many psychoanalysts have downgraded the importance of details of sexual desire and sexual expression. One could completely eliminate drive theory (not that I am advocating doing so) and still pay a great deal of attention to the sexual patterning that John Money (1986) calls the "lovemap." This usually involves a cluster of relational and sexual patternings for the individual that can be relatively enduring throughout the life span.*

Many couples run into sexual difficulties because of such lovemap incompatibilities. I know of couples that have also been together for decades. Although their relationship began with intense sexuality, there were signs right from the beginning that their primary sexual fantasies were incompatible. Each of them had a lovemap that made the other's fantasies noxious. And so, as each tried to realize his or her lovemap, the partner became alienated. Eventually they stopped having sex altogether, although they felt they still loved one another and stayed together, sometimes for decades, and planned to continue to do so for the rest of their lives. In some cases, they have each decided to pursue their particular sexual lovemap with someone outside the relationship. These extramarital relations have shown remarkable staying power, and have allowed them to

---

* Ethel Person (1980) coined the term "sexprint," which is essentially the same as a lovemap. Her term is meant to be connected with the "fingerprint," which is unique and unchangeable. Jack Morin (1995) calls it the "core erotic theme."

have relatively happy and stable lives. Although one might judge the cost to be high in terms of unrealized or diverted passion, it is important, I think, for psychoanalysts to respect those people who have arrived at such a life solution and do not wish to change it.

Sometimes incompatibility is not the problem. Instead, one member of the couple has particular fantasies or desires that he or she considers shameful or perverse and therefore keeps secret from the partner. These can include wishes for enacting particular scripts like bondage and domination scenarios, practices like oral and anal intercourse, special erotic attention to a less-than-usual body part, wearing of particular kinds of clothes, and many, many more possibilities. A psychoanalyst who considers any of these manifestations to be perversions may try to cure the patient of such a desire, usually with little success. An alternative is for the person to overcome shameful feelings and share the proclivity with a partner or to find a partner with compatible desires. If this is done early enough in the relationship, there is a good chance that the partners may be interested in exploring their individual lovemaps together. However, if shame and secrecy prevail for a long time, the eventual frustration and a pattern of sexual avoidance may be hard or impossible to undo.

There is a marvelous portrayal of this dilemma in the Luis Buñuel film, *Belle de Jour*, in which a beautiful, rich, refined housewife, played by Catherine Deneuve, seems completely uninterested in sex and is presumably frigid. Then she starts working, during the day, as a prostitute. There is a wonderful scene in which a Chinese client is having trouble finding a prostitute who will satisfy him the way he wants. He has a small box, and most of the women turn away in revulsion when they see what is inside it. Belle looks inside the box and nods her head, in assent. We never see what is inside the box, and can only imagine what was in it that so revolted most of the prostitutes, but not Belle. This, and her other experiences in the brothel, crack Belle's frigid shell and revivify her sexuality.* The movie touched a nerve in its bourgeois watchers, as most of Bunuel's movies do. If we were removed from our usual social context, would our sexual tastes burgeon and diverge into realms that seem repellant or taboo in our regular lives?

Could Belle have found a way to incorporate her sexual adventurism back into her marriage? That is the outcome that Mitchell (1997) describes in "Psychoanalysis and the Degradation of Romance ," in the case of Susan,

---

* The theme was repeated decades later in the television show *Six Feet Under*, where a female character, uninterested in sex with her fiancé, starts to dabble in prostitution and rekindles her passion.

who has gotten her husband into a very protective, nurturant role with her, and has pursued a wild sexual affair with a somewhat younger man. By the way, Susan considers this situation banal, as if from a made-for-TV movie, although it is also the stuff of great literature, like *Anna Karenina*. In any case, she eventually brings some of her sexual adventurism back to her husband who, she finds out, is more willing to experiment than she had imagined.

Mitchell's patient, George, is a man who feels dominated and controlled by his wife and then, ironically, pays a prostitute to control him. The difference, he notes, is that the man has ultimate control with the prostitute, not only by paying her, but by having a secret word between them that, when he utters it, will stop her domination. One wonders, could George develop such a secret word with his wife? There are a number of couples who have developed such code words, either to alert the spouse that they are acting in an offensive way or to indicate some other private message. However, in my experience, trying to bring home the insight gleaned from the prostitute does not always work, since the patient himself may have characterological reasons *not* to have it work, in which case it helps for the patient to first work out his or her character issues in the treatment.

Psychoanalysts have a history of opening up discourse on sexuality and love, but also of reinforcing the status quo of societal norms. Any sexual practice can be judged pathological, but such judgment does not help clinically. Romance is important to most people, but psychoanalysts (and our society in general) ought to appreciate its many forms; the quality of feeling should be more important than any monolithic standard of correct or normal behavior. Some psychoanalysts have conceived of relational maturity and romance in rather uniform terms. An alternative guideline is the ability of the person to find love, sexual satisfaction, security, and happiness in a combination and arrangement that feels most satisfying and that allows for interpersonal intimacy without coercing or harming another person. That is what Harry Stack Sullivan (1953) observed more than 50 years ago, and psychoanalysis has yet to appreciate and integrate his view fully. To adopt subjective satisfaction, without recourse to any external standard, as the aim of clinical treatment is to draw heavily on the psychoanalyst and patient's tolerance, creativity, and flexibility. It will lead clinicians to more varied and achievable psychoanalytic goals with each patient.

14

Polymorphous without Perversity
A Queer View of Desire

How frightening is the past that awaits us.

Antonin Slonimska

Author's Introduction

In the early 1990s, a doctor referred a heterosexual voyeur to me in my private practice. I did not know anything about treating voyeurs at the time and was puzzled about why I received the referral. Eventually, I discovered his reasoning. The referring doctor thought, "This patient is a pervert, and Blechner is a pervert, so they'll probably work well together." After years of feeling maligned as a pervert, I was discovering that I was now reaping some benefits as a pervert, even developing a subspecialty as a pervert. It turned out that I worked relatively well with voyeurs and other so-called perverts for several reasons, not least of which was that I did not judge them for their supposed perversion, while previous analysts had.

In 2003, I was asked to be a panelist in an international conference on perversion, held over the Internet. So now I was being asked to speak as a professional pervert! All the panelists were asked to circulate a short biographical sketch. I included the usual academic and professional affiliations, but I prefaced them with the statement, "Mark J. Blechner, Ph.D. is a practicing pervert in New York City." One of the participants, Paul Williams, the editor of the *International Journal of Psychoanalysis*, withdrew in a huff. He was shocked that the word "pervert" could be used, ironically, as a calling card and professional credential.

My next opportunity to appear as a professional pervert came in the fall of 2004, when the White Institute sponsored a conference on "Longing and Desire." It was just a few weeks before the pivotal presidential election of Bush versus Kerry. Although I had originally planned to speak about strictly clinical problems of patients with difficulties feeling or sustaining desire, the political climate led me to change my course. The dark clouds of religious censorship were gathering on the American horizon. George W. Bush had assembled in his government a group of religiously minded ideologues who were reinstating taboos that restricted hard-won American freedom and liberty. It seemed more important than ever for psychiatry and psychoanalysis to speak clearly about the importance of sustaining and expanding values of tolerance and independence in private matters, sexual and otherwise.

I had felt the danger in a very personal way. I had an article in press that included some "dirty" words, that is, colloquial sexual words. The text had already been set in galleys, but the editor asked me if we could "translate" those passages using more scientific terms. He was afraid that, in the current climate, the publication of the colloquial sexual words could lead to legal trouble and maybe even shutting down the journal. I did not want to trigger the journal's demise, so I agreed to the change, but it made me shiver to think that the political climate had led free-thinking editors to fear such reprisals. There had already been precedents of television and radio stations being fined for indecency. How far will we allow such a resurgence of Puritanism to go? I hope the reader will share my sense of urgency that oppression of minorities and censorship of ideas are great dangers. Psychoanalysis was once at the forefront of progressive social attitudes, and I hope psychoanalysis will reclaim that position.

Freud had written about the "polymorphous perversity" of children, meaning that children are inclined to do many things with their bodies and bodily products that would be considered perversions in adulthood. While it was courageous for Freud to discuss these behaviors scientifically (things that mothers and nursemaids already knew), Freud's use of the word perversion brought in a value judgment that I thought was destructive. So I entitled my paper "Polymorphous without Perversity." I am publishing it here for the first time, blended with another talk I gave on "Sexual Facts and Values."

Polymorphous without Perversity: A Queer View of Desire*

There is wisdom in turning as often as possible from the familiar to the unfamiliar: it keeps the mind nimble, it kills prejudice, and it fosters humor.

George Santayana

---

* Portions of this chapter were originally published in "Sexual Facts and Values," *Studies in Gender and Sexuality*, 2007, *8*, 373–380.

The word "queer" was once commonly used as a derogatory reference to a homosexual, but today "queer" has been rehabilitated, with a new and expanded meaning. In an ironic twist, what was once an insult is now a compliment in some circles. "Queer" has been revived to embrace all kinds of expressions of sex and gender, both those considered "normal" and "deviant." In its modern form, "queer" has come to describe transgendered individuals, transvestites, gay men, lesbians, bisexuals, intersexed people, as well as just plain old heterosexuals. Actually, heterosexuality is quite queer when you look closely at all of its varieties (Blechner, 1998a). As Jack Morin (1995) has written: "No one who explores honestly the innermost realities of his or her eroticism finds complete 'normalcy.'... When we deny or reject our sexual idiosyncrasies, we renounce who we are" (p. 320).

If you consider yourself predominantly heterosexual, maybe you are thinking, "What do I care about queerness? I am normal. What does this have to do with me?" But queerness is not about a particular form of sexuality; it is about an attitude—an attitude of acceptance; instead of trying to prescribe normalcy, it takes a different approach to mental health. It proposes that we define mental health in terms of a person's own happiness, whether the person's mental functioning provides satisfaction and integrity. Queerness tries to free psychoanalysts and other mental health practitioners from being unwitting enforcers of dysfunctional cultural norms and prejudices. It is possible that psychoanalysis could acquire a new vitality today by becoming once again a more queer science.*

I am using the word "queer" in a positive way. Queerness means that we do not gloss over or prejudge individual differences; instead, we seek them out, identify them, appreciate them, and try to understand them, without automatic stigma or correction. We recognize that we are all much more simply human than otherwise; but within that simple humanness, there are many variations, and variation does not necessarily mean pathology.

A psychoanalyst is privileged, during years of practice, to learn how variable people's desires can be. What one person may most desire in the world may be something that you cannot imagine wanting yourself. It might even disgust you. It is an easy step for you to judge the other person's desire to be pathological, especially if you have most people in your society agreeing with your judgment. Psychoanalysts and all clinicians must learn to resist such judgments, or at least to question them.

---

* I had made this point earlier, too (see p. 84).

When the AIDS epidemic started, Abraham Verghese (1994), who was a physician working in rural Tennessee, realized how little he knew about homosexuality, and he coined the term "homo-ignorance." It was an important word that helped distinguish between the simple lack of knowledge in well-meaning people and the pernicious bigotry of homophobia. Homo-ignorance was rampant among psychoanalysts, too, who had learned little about gay men and lesbians during their training, and much of what they had learned was false.

Besides homo-ignorance, there is also transgender-ignorance, transvestite-ignorance, voyeur-ignorance, and more. There is a dearth of knowledge among many contemporary psychoanalysts about various expressions of sexuality. This is ironic because Freud's stress on the importance of the sexual drive as a motivator gives many people the impression that psychoanalysts must be very knowledgeable about sex. But today, most are not. Relatively little is taught about the varieties of sexual expression in most psychoanalytic institutes—about heterosexual transvestites, transgendered individuals, men who are attracted to "chicks-with-dicks," voyeurs, exhibitionists, "stone-dykes," and apotemnophilia.* I was taught little or nothing about these in my training, and what I was taught was often haphazard, anecdotal, and not very well informed. At the end of my training, I realized that I needed to educate myself about these things. As a gay man, I had often been displeased with the ignorance of heterosexual analysts about the basics of homosexual experience. I realized that I could be faulted myself for not understanding other sexual minorities.

I have come to espouse a basic principle: When I am referred a person who has a sexual predilection about which I have little or no knowledge, I go out of my way to educate myself about that predilection as thoroughly and as soon as possible. If the case is one I am supervising, I do the same, and I recommend that my supervisee do so, too. In olden days, that required a trip to the library to do a literature search. Today, a search of the Internet will bring you more complete and up-to-date information, and you do not have to leave home.

Besides having basic, factual information, there is a question as well of the psychoanalyst's basic approach when beginning treatment of a person with unusual sexual proclivities. How much does the analyst ask and pay

---

* Apotemnophilia is a term coined by the sexologist, John Money, for people who desire to have a limb amputated (Money, Jobaris & Furth, 1977). It is questionable whether, or to what degree, this wish is connected to sexual wishes. Today, it is more often referred to as Body Integrity Identity Disorder (BIID) (Furth & Smith, 2000).

serious attention to a patient's stated aims and wishes? How straightforward is the analyst about whether he is willing and able to work toward the patient's stated goals? How clearly have psychoanalysts staked out what is possible and desirable clinically in such cases? What are the data about outcome? And how aware is the psychoanalyst of the question of *psychopathology* versus *cultural* pathology, namely, that is, whether the unusual sexuality is intrinsically problematic for the person or problematic because society condemns that sexuality?

Our judgments about sexual experience and behavior can be quite subjective. Consider what you think about male cross-dressers. Despite the popular image of the gay drag queen who dresses up as Barbra Streisand, the fact is that most men who want to dress up as women are predominantly heterosexual. It is much more common than usually thought. That may have changed in 2007, a special time in history when a heterosexual man who had been photographed several times in women's clothing, i.e., Rudy Giuliani, sought nomination as president of the United States.

In 2007, the journal *Studies in Gender and Sexuality* asked me to discuss a paper by a senior psychoanalyst, Dr. Irwin Hirsch, about cross-dressing. I have the highest respect for Hirsch. His clinical accounts are always clear and frank, and, more than with most clinicians, you feel like you know what really happened. Also, like Freud, Hirsch reports his failures, without defensiveness. Hirsch (2007) reported a case in which he treated a man whom he calls Z., who had a girlfriend and an extensive heterosexual history, and who liked to dress in women's clothes. Hirsch tried to influence him away from cross-dressing, even though the patient never expressed a wish to stop the practice. He writes:

> I believed that Z. would have a good life with this girlfriend, and thought that she would help him settle into the hard work of his demanding profession, and as well, help him actualize what I felt would be his considerable potential as a loving father to his yet unborn children....In my misguided zeal to help Z. actualize his career and to solidify his relationship with his girlfriend, my interpretive schema accented the immaturity of his sexual interests, maintaining his archaic girly-boy identification with his mother and avoiding the "stronger" and more masculine emphasis on career and commitment to this, in my mind, wonderfully flexible young woman. Even if I had been largely on target with my insight in linking history to present, the more salient message this sensitive man heard from me was to control his cross-dressing distractions and to settle down to a promising career, and a monogamous relationship with this girlfriend with whom I was so taken. In his charming and seductive way Z. quit therapy for "practical" reasons, never challenging me for my egregiously unwarranted impositions on elements of a life that he desired. (pp. 356–357)

The consensus about therapy with heterosexual cross-dressing seems to be quite similar to therapies that claim to change homosexuals to heterosexuals. They waste a lot of money, put the patient through hell, and they do not work in the long run. For many a heterosexual cross-dresser, what he most wants is *not* to lose his desire to cross-dress; instead, what he most wants is to be able to dress up in the clothes of his wife or girlfriend and then make love to her. This was the case with Hirsch's patient, Z.

Interestingly, the pathologizing of cross-dressing is skewed by certain cultural factors. If you think about it, you will realize that heterosexual cross-dressing is seen in our culture as much more of a problem for men than for women. In our culture, if a woman wears her husband's shirt to bed, it is not considered a perversion; it is usually considered normal, even sexy. But if a man wears his wife's negligee to bed, he is considered abnormal. Marlene Dietrich in a tuxedo was considered very sexy; Jack Lemmon or Rudy Giuliani in a dress was considered comic.

It is evidence of the same "gender ethic" that brings many more boys who are acting girlish into treatment than girls who are acting boyish. Our society still seems to value masculinity above femininity. It is considered much more problematic for a man to act female than for a woman to act male. The so-called "symptoms" of Gender Identity Disorder may be as common in girls as in boys, but parents are more likely to seek treatment of a son who is a sissy than of a daughter who is a tomboy.

And why should male heterosexual cross-dressing be a problem? After all, does it hurt anyone if a man wears a dress? Does it hurt anyone more than if a woman wears pants (which was once considered unwomanly, but no longer)? Maybe it is not that heterosexual cross-dressing patients need to stop putting on dresses; maybe society needs to change, to allow them to do so without censure or punishment.

In fact, cross-dressers are beginning to come out of the closet more. In 2003, the British potter, Grayson Perry, won the prestigious Turner Prize (Jones, 2006). Accompanied by his wife and daughter at the award ceremony, Perry wore a purple silk frilly dress that cost $10,000. He said, "Well, it's about time a transvestite potter won the Turner Prize."

Many psychoanalysts have a vague notion of normalcy, and they have a basic approach to working with people with unusual sexual predilections, which is to seek out the roots of the predilection in the early relationship with the parents, with the aim of "understanding" the sexuality and perhaps changing it. Psychoanalysts are expert at coming up with plausible accounts of anything based on early parental relations, and at that they rarely fail, but unfortunately these accounts often make little difference in the patient's sexual pattern and experience.

The Basic Psychoanalytic Premise

This is what I call the basic psychoanalytic premise: If you can understand the role of a symptom in someone's life as well as its function in the patient's history, you can thereby help the person to get over the symptom. When applied to sexual behavior, the same premise is often applied: Exploration of the developmental history of the patient will clarify the causative psychodynamics of the sexual patterning, and such analysis will lead to the patient's understanding of his or her sexuality and no longer needing the familiar pathological sexuality, or, failing that, at least being able to foster a normal sexual life in addition to the patient's non-normative sexuality. *This sounds plausible, but it is often false*; but because there is so little empirical outcome research in psychoanalysis, practitioners continue to proceed as if this approach will work. The fact is that some non-normative sexual patterns, like cross-dressing, will likely never disappear. It is probably unethical to hold out the hope for such change to someone who may desire it.

Hirsch (2007) applies the basic psychoanalytic premise in his account. He writes, "I attributed his cross-dressing as well as his infidelity largely to his identification with and his desire to overcome his infantilizing mother, and his early life as her soft and overweight momma's boy" (p. 356). It sounds perfectly plausible. But is it true? I don't know. And if it is true, did it make any difference in whether the patient continued to cross-dress? There we have a fact: absolutely not.

A psychoanalyst who is going to work with a heterosexual cross-dresser needs to know many facts about cross-dressing. Some of those facts are:

1. The urge for cross-dressing rarely or never disappears during psychotherapy.
2. Some cross-dressers eventually decide they are transgender and seek sex reassignment surgery. Some never go along that path. They maintain a primarily heterosexual desire throughout their lives, and hope that their wife or girlfriend will allow the cross-dressing to be integrated into their sexual lives. (And this was true of Hirsch's patient. "At no point did Z. indicate to me that he clearly wished to stop cross-dressing. He actually hoped that he might integrate this into his sex life with his accepting current girlfriend" [p. 356])

3. There are social support organizations, such as CHIC (Crossdressers Heterosexual Intersocial Club) specifically for male heterosexual cross-dressers, which allow such men to get moral support and information from others. They may also benefit from reading autobiographical accounts, such as Rowe (1997) and Jones (2006).

4. Some women react with disgust to revelations about their husband's cross-dressing, but some adapt and decide that they want to sustain the relationship. Some require their husbands to keep it private, while others allow their husbands to go out publicly in women's clothing. Women married to cross-dressers can learn from other women in that situation, e.g., Helen Boyd's book (2003), *My Husband Betty: Love, Sex, and Life with a Cross-Dresser.*

5. The later in the relationship that the man reveals the cross-dressing to his female partner, the more likely it is that she will feel betrayed and end their relationship.

These are just some of the practical facts about cross-dressing that the analyst and patient need to know if they are to proceed with treatment.

The more you examine how flawed and changeable psychoanalytic judgments of pathology were in the twentieth century, the more you have to question the entire psychoanalytic approach to psychopathology. The concept of perversion has been especially problematic. Freud (1905b) defined perversions as follows: "Perversions are sexual activities which either (a) extend, in an anatomical sense, beyond the regions of the body that are designed for sexual union, or (b) linger over the intermediate relations to the sexual object which should normally be traversed rapidly on the path towards the final sexual aim" (p. 150). Sexual activity ought to end in penis-in-vagina intercourse. If you got there, congratulations. If you did not, you are a pervert.

Thus, for Freud, cunnilingus and fellatio, which do not lead to intercourse, were considered perversions. Today, in America, they are considered normal parts of sexuality, acceptable and even expected in some subcultures.

And then there is masturbation: The circle of psychoanalysts around Freud spent many evenings debating the pathology or normalcy of masturbation, never coming to any consensus. But if the European psychoanalysts were undecided about whether masturbation was pathological, American psychiatry was not. When I was growing up in the 1950s, masturbation was listed in the DSM-I as a psychopathology. If it was a pathology, then I and most of my friends were pathological, as were most of the people who wrote the DSM. There is the old quip: "95% of men masturbate. The other 5% are liars." How could the authors of the DSM-I dissociate so much from their own experience?

I think that a hidden influence on psychiatric and psychoanalytic thinking about psychopathology has been the Judeo-Christian tradition, which outlaws any genital sexual behavior that cannot lead to impregnation. Much of the behavior considered pathological by psychiatrists was the same behavior that was considered sinful by the strictest Jews and Christians. For Orthodox Jews, masturbation is still considered a sin, as is oral sex and homosexuality, and the Catholic Church holds similar views. I think it is important for psychoanalysts, other mental health practitioners, and society in general to disentangle their views of what is psychopathological from what is sinful among traditional religions.

In fact, the word *perversion* has its roots in religion. If you look it up in the *Oxford English Dictionary*, you will find: Perversion: "turning the wrong way; turning aside from truth or right; diversion to an improper use; corruption, distortion; specifically, change to error in religious belief."

You see the trouble with the whole concept of perversion: In orthodox religion, there is a right way to do things, and if you do things differently, even if it makes you happy and you do not harm anyone, you are still wrong, perverted, and sinful. Many clinicians have bought into such a translation from sin to psychopathology, even if the connection between pathology and sin is not fully conscious. That has caused a lot of clinical mischief and a good deal of suffering for patients.

So, it may be that if you think perversion, you are also implicitly thinking, "I know the right way to behave." Not just the right way for me to behave, but *the* right way to behave.

In this respect, the great American psychoanalyst Harry Stack Sullivan gave us an important alternative. Most people know that Sullivan was the founder of Interpersonal psychoanalysis, and that his theory formed the groundwork for what today has become relational psychoanalysis. Yet few people know well what Sullivan wrote about sexuality, and he wrote about it quite a bit. Sullivan was queer, in the old sense of the word and the new one; he was homosexual and he was a rather unusual person. Because many of Sullivan's students had difficulty with his homosexuality, they tended to selectively inattend to his extensive writings on sexuality. These writings are part of what I call the lost Interpersonal tradition. Many people have thought that Sullivan gave short shrift to sexuality and bodily experience, which is simply not true.

Sullivan was raised as a Roman Catholic and was acutely aware of the influence of religious taboos on psychopathology. Sullivan tried to formulate a view of sexuality that would evade old religious formulas and would instead define sexual health in practical terms. He argued that there are

many sexual practices and preferences for both heterosexuals and homosexuals, and what is most important for psychoanalysis about these practices is how much they allow for pleasurable intimacy with another human
being. In Sullivan's own words, in *The Interpersonal Theory of Psychiatry*
(1953, discussed in Chapter 10), "In this culture the ultimate test of whether
you can get on or not is whether you can do something satisfactory with
your genitals or somebody else's genitals without undue anxiety and loss
of self-esteem" (p. 294).

I call this Sullivan's postulate on sexual functioning. If you really take
this postulate seriously, you may have to reconsider most of your judgments of sexual health and pathology. Sullivan does away with the religious idea that healthy sexuality must culminate in at least the potential
for pregnancy, as well as the psychoanalytic derivative of this so-called
"mature genitality." Sullivan does not judge whether any sexual desire is
in itself healthy or pathological; instead, he focuses on how feasible it is to
integrate any particular sexual desire with interpersonal intimacy, without
excessive anxiety or danger. Queer forms of sexuality, oddnesses of various
kinds, are not a problem if you can find a willing and satisfying partner.

Think how this might have changed psychoanalytic practice for the
better. In the last century, if psychoanalysts had paid more attention to
Sullivan's postulate, cunnilingus, fellatio, and homosexuality just would
not have seemed problematic. In addition, where in her body a woman had
an orgasm, whether in her vagina or clitoris, which was a concern of many
psychoanalysts, would not have mattered, only whether she could enjoy
her orgasm with a consenting other person.

So, within Sullivan's postulate, are any forms of sexuality inherently
problematic? I would say yes, that there are problems with anything that is
nonconsensual or coercive or seriously damaging to another person. One
example is what I call "invasive voyeurism." For most male voyeurs, at
least the ones who have sought treatment with me, the pleasure is not just
in seeing a woman naked; they require that she be seen naked against her
will. There is no thrill for a voyeur, for example, in going to a strip club,
since seeing the nakedness of a woman who wants to show off her body is
of no interest. The thrill is to see the woman against her will. Sometimes
it is without her knowledge, although there seems, for some voyeurs, to be
a special thrill for her to discover that she is being watched, and although
she wants to stop it, she cannot. It thus becomes a form of ocular rape.

I once worked with a man who had found a way to enjoy his voyeurism without getting in trouble with the law. He had an arsenal of cameras
with powerful telephoto lenses and infra-red lighting, which allowed him

to see close-ups of women many blocks away in their homes. New York City, with its huge number of high-rise apartments whose occupants leave their blinds open, was a paradise for him. The trouble was, he couldn't just remain satisfied with his long-distance looking. He started to obsess about one particular woman, whom he tracked down, and eventually started calling and harassing, which put him in legal danger. What started as an expression of long-distance aggression got intensified and mixed in with desires for love and intimacy, and he needed to analyze and disentangle those conflicting desires before he damaged both himself and her.

Sullivan's postulate has broader ramifications, beyond sexuality, for the basic principles of bioethics. The pressure in our society against queerness, against tolerance of the unusual, is very strong, and some leading medical ethicists argue that we can and should pathologize things that disgust us. Leon Kass (1997), who was the head of President Bush's commission on bioethics, argues for what he calls "the wisdom of repugnance." Kass believes that the disgust reaction has a primal wisdom and is reason to judge some things unethical. He has written: "In crucial cases, repugnance is the emotional expression of deep wisdom, beyond reason's power to fully articulate . . . we intuit and feel, immediately and without argument, the violation of things we rightfully hold dear . . ." (p. 20).

I think that Kass's argument is not only flawed but dangerous. A big problem with his statement is the word "we." "*We* intuit and feel, immediately and without argument, the violation of things *we* rightfully hold dear..." Whom does he mean by "we"? Statements that appeal to the common sense and wisdom of the majority have a long history of abusing the rights of innocent minorities based on strong feelings of disgust and contempt. In Nazi Germany, the majority "we" thought Jews were disgusting and inferior and should therefore be ostracized or killed. In traditional India, upper castes consider that the "untouchables" are disgusting and inferior and should have limited rights. Before the Civil War, many Americans thought Black people were disgusting and inferior, and therefore deserved to be slaves.

Unlike Kass, I would say that personal disgust is not a reliable guide to evaluate other people's behavior.* Recall Kass's statement: "*We* intuit and feel, immediately and without argument, the violation of things *we* rightfully hold dear..." I would say, on the contrary, that when you feel

---

* Martha Nussbaum (2004) argues strongly against Kass's position from a moral-legal standpoint. Modern neuroscience research has demonstrated that there is a common, often unconscious, disgust reaction to old people. Would Kass argue that therefore we should condemn people for being old?

a disgust reaction about someone else's behavior, immediately and without argument, you should pause. You should consider, *not* immediately and *not* without argument, but with delay and with rational argument, whether the person's seemingly disgusting behavior harms anyone. You should put yourself in that person's place and imagine being told that your innermost desire is immoral or forbidden or pathological. You should try to consider some way to empathize with that person's experience. That is a very hard thing to do and takes a concerted effort. It requires you to be in an open dialogue with the person about whom you feel disgust, and to be honest with yourself and others about your own practices that might disgust someone else.

The risks are enormous to allowing disgust reactions or old religious prejudices to pathologize the desire of a harmless minority and take away their rights. Sullivan's postulate shows a way for psychoanalysts to avoid these pitfalls. We can consider the value of each individual's desire on its own terms, whether it provides happiness, whether it is harmless to other people, and whether it can be integrated with interpersonal intimacy. With this approach, we can be more clinically effective at helping people create a life in which they can explore their desires and live them out with satisfaction and joy.

15

Erotic and Anti-Erotic Transference

Author's Introduction

The year 2007 marked the debut of the television series *In Treatment*, which tracked the work of a middle-aged, married psychoanalyst with four different patients. The series generated a great deal of public interest in psychoanalytic treatment and the principles behind it. The "Monday" patient, Laura, is passionately in love with her analyst, and he gradually admits to her that he is in love with her, too. This is the standard idea of an erotic transference and countertransference, and it generated a lot of discussion in the general public and the press, as well as among analysts. Many people were very judgmental about the behavior of the analyst; my colleagues reported squirming when they saw the analyst sitting on the couch with his patient or hugging her. In the end, he never actually had intercourse with her, although in the real world, many psychoanalysts and other psychotherapists do. It has been estimated that 12% of male therapists and 3% of female therapists have had sexual contact with their patients, which is alarmingly high, considering that it is unethical behavior that can lead to the loss of one's professional license (Pope, 1994).

In my view, there were aspects of erotic transference in all the cases portrayed by *In Treatment*, even if they were not so obvious. The "Tuesday" patient, Alex, a fighter pilot who felt guilty about having killed many citizens with a bomb, discusses a dream in which one pilot pursues another pilot from behind. Alex says he "wants to put a missile up his rear" and identifies this as a homosexual wish. The "Wednesday" patient, a teenage girl with her arm in a cast, asks the psychoanalyst to change her wet clothes, and later shows off her body as she does acrobatics on his couch. The "Thursday" patients are a heterosexual married couple, and the wife flirts brazenly with the analyst. These are all versions of erotic transference.

In 2008, there was a psychoanalytic conference on "Responding to the Erotic Transference" in New York, and I was invited to speak. I decided not to prepare a formal talk, but to see how the conference progressed. During the discussions during the day, many people in the audience asked "nuts and bolts" questions about how to handle erotic transference, how the analyst should behave, and how it can be made useful to the patient's treatment. In my talk, which I later developed into a formal paper, I tried to answer these questions as fully as possible. In thinking about these issues, I realized how much my own experience on the outskirts of standard sex and gender stereotypes affected the way I worked with erotic transference.

Erotic and Anti-Erotic Transference*

Everyone is interested in erotic transference, but many psychoanalysts are afraid of it. Several colleagues have told me that they had been taught little or nothing useful about erotic transference during their training. This was true of me, too; in fact, some of the things I was taught, I decided were wrong as I gained more experience. In this paper, I am going to address some basic questions about erotic transference and countertransference. I will start with the most basic question: What is erotic transference?

The popular view of erotic transference is that the patient "falls in love" with the analyst and may express the wish to have sex with the analyst, have an affair with, or marry him or her.† This is a very limited view of erotic transference. I would define erotic transference instead as any expression of erotic feelings toward the psychoanalyst. That can include all kinds of flirting and attention to the analyst's body, including how the analyst dresses, walks, sits, moves, breathes, smells, and how his voice sounds.

The Anti-Erotic Transference

I also think it is an aspect of erotic transference when the patient expresses a lack of attraction or even a physical repulsion toward the analyst. You could

---

* Portions of this chapter were first presented at the conference "Responding to the Erotic Transference," March 8, 2008, New York, NY. It was published in *Contemporary Psychoanalysis*, 2009, 45, 82–92.
† In this chapter, I will sometimes write only "he" or "she," but, unless otherwise specified, I always mean to imply "he or she."

call it "the anti-erotic transference"; it is just as significant erotically, only in the negative. I will give three examples of the anti-erotic transference.

Example 1

Sometimes in the erotic transference, a patient will focus on a particular aspect of the analyst's body as attractive or as unattractive. One day, I stood up to close the window in my office, and in doing so turned my back to my patient, a gay man named Mike. Mike got very quiet. I asked him what he was thinking, and he told me reluctantly that his thought was that my ass was too small. He liked a larger, fleshier ass. He then said he was afraid he had hurt me, and that I must be mortified. I wasn't really. I told him I knew that my ass was not very large, but fortunately, in this world, there were people who liked a smaller ass. Everybody has to accept the body that they have and make the best of it. Even if you do not fit a popular stereotype of attractiveness, it matters more if you can find someone who finds you attractive and not let your own inferiority feelings get in the way of being loved by that person. Mike felt relieved to hear me say this, and then associated to his obsessive concern that his penis was too small. One could say that he had projected his concern of bodily inferiority onto me.

By the way, a similar pattern can happen with a male patient and a female analyst; I once had a female supervisee whose male patient criticized her small breasts, and this led to a similar exploration of his concern about the size of his penis.

Example 2

Bonnie came to her first session with me, more than 30 years ago, carrying a large tree branch, which she waved menacingly all through the session. You might say, "That's not very erotic!" I did not think what she did was related to eroticism at the time either. It seemed mostly to be a gesture of terror and threat. Bonnie had good reason to defend herself physically; she had been thrown against a wall by her father when she was 2 years old, and she was raped by her brother when she was 11, so her eroticism and erotic transference were mixed up with a fear of violence and pain.

The treatment started during my psychology internship, and Bonnie was well known to the supervisors of the internship. The interns served there for one year. Each year they would leave, and Bonnie would start therapy over with someone new. When I started working with her, she had already been in treatment with eight different interns, always for only one year. She still had never had a romantic relationship, although she wanted one ardently, she said. It was one of her main goals in treatment.

I told Bonnie early on that I thought she had used the revolving door of the internship system to avoid having any relationship with a therapist that would go on too long. I thought she feared trusting anyone, and that she expected that in any relationship that went on long enough, she would be beaten, raped, or left, or all three. When my year of internship was over, after many such interpretations, she continued with me in my private practice for many years. By continuing with me in my practice, she was able to work through those fears rather than just relive them over and over.

There were many fascinating things about this treatment, but here I am going to focus on the erotics. Bonnie hated her father, who had abandoned the family when Bonnie was six, leaving the mother and five children to survive on welfare. Bonnie insisted that I not refer to him as her father, but only as "my mother's husband." She was always warning me and threatening me, and yet, she did not frighten me. She was direct and street smart, and the truth was, I loved working with her, although it was often difficult.

At the beginning of treatment, she looked like a frightened animal. Her eyes would glare at me with a mixture of fear and warning. But over the years of our work together, her look softened. One day, she came into session with pendant earrings, the first time I had ever seen her adorn herself like that. I commented on how attractive they looked. She had an enormous reaction to this. It brought back memories of her maternal grandfather (whom she had never spoken about) who once told her she looked pretty. I think that session launched a recovery of her sense of herself as potentially attractive, and she started to transform herself. She changed the way she dressed and groomed herself, and her face itself changed. She was beautiful, when she was not so terrified.

She started to bring in sexual material; the anti-erotic transference was transformed into an erotic transference. The moment I remember most clearly was when she brought in her own drawing. It showed a man standing in water up to his chest, and a woman was giving him oral sex under water. We spoke about it quite a lot. I looked into her fantasies about that, and managed, without really knowing what I was doing, to convey an interest in her sexuality without, I think, being prurient or inappropriately seductive. I think she was trying to do what most girls do with their fathers—find a way to be flirtatious without having sex with them, and then transferring that feeling of sexual acceptance to someone else with whom they could realize it.

By the end of treatment, she got married and had two children. I know that is a cliché of successful treatment; but in her case, it was something that she really wanted, and that she and my supervisors had thought would never be possible.

Example 3

Anthony, in his first session with me, expressed the fear that I might fall in love with him and that he would have to fend me off. I found his fear puzzling; it actually felt off-putting to me, since I do not generally gravitate toward people who collect admirers and reject them. As the treatment progressed, I heard about episodes in his childhood in which he felt intensely attracted to a friend of his father. The romance was not lived out; he doubted whether the man even noticed his attraction, although his mother did and was upset about it. I wondered if his fear that I would become attracted to him was a reaction against that early rejection. He used the defense of reversal: He would no longer be attracted to one who would fend him off; from now on, he would fend off those who were attracted to him.

However, later in the treatment, Anthony discovered that his mother, in her old age, was obsessed with a handsome movie star. She followed all the details of his life and spoke excitedly about his romantic entanglements and breakups. Anthony suspected that his mother had formed crushes like this throughout her life, and that when he was a young and handsome adolescent, he may well have been the object of her romantic interest. This has been identified as a common pattern in the families of gay men; their mothers may flirt with them, as they do with all their sons. Straight sons may flirt back, but gay sons may not reciprocate the flirting, and may indeed experience their mother's romantic interest as intrusive (Goldsmith, 1995, 2001).

Anthony thought that his fear of my becoming attracted to him and his having to fend me off might have been based on his experience with his mother, and I think he was right. I had assumed there was a transference based on my own gender, but he felt that a more powerful determinant was a cross-gender transference (male analyst as the mother figure). It is possible, too, that the psychodynamics identified by him and me co-determined the transference.

Technical Approaches to Erotic Transference

At its best, the expression of erotic transference in the treatment will lead the patient to learn important things about himself and his erotic life and get as comfortable as possible with his eroticism, so that he can enjoy eroticism better with other people in the world. Just as with any transference, the analyst should accept the patient's feelings, ideally without fear or defensiveness, but with a lot of curiosity and inquisitiveness. *It is more important to explore erotic transference than to interpret it.*

There are many examples reported in the literature of an analyst who panics when a patient expresses love for him and feels a wish to "interpret it away" (Gabbard, 1996b). A common maneuver is what I call "a transposition interpretation." The analyst says to the patient, "You don't really feel that way toward me. You are displacing feelings that you had to your mother (or father or nursemaid or whomever)." This is not so good. It probably is never good for one person to say to another, "You do not really feel what you think you feel." Nobody ought to tell another person such a thing. Our emotions are our most private and personal source of information; it is unnerving and insulting to be told "what you feel is not real." It is better to ask the patient more about their experience: What about the analyst does she love? How does she imagine the love would play out? The aim is to understand: What is your way of loving? The details are essential, and each person has a unique pattern of eroticism.

Lovemaps, Sexprints, and Core Erotic Themes

John Money (1986) coined the term "lovemap" to describe the very personal pattern of feeling sex and love; Ethel Person (1980) called it the "sexprint." Jack Morin (1995) called it the "core erotic theme." Whatever you call it, everyone has a very personal way of experiencing and expressing eroticism. How much did you learn about this in your own analysis? What is the particular mixture of emotions that most excites you? How much pleasure with how much anxiety? What other emotions add to your excitement or dampen it? Hostility? Teasing? Fear? Shame? Anger? What is the erotic script that you find most compelling to play out with your partner? Which sexual practices do you find most appealing or repellant? Which body parts turn you on or off?

Each person has such a complex pattern of sexuality, and probably no one is fully conscious of the patterns they are seeking. The erotic transference, when explored in analysis, can be a precise and vivid way to learn about your own lovemap; it can be the "royal road" to understanding and accepting your sexuality.

It helps if the analyst is aware of his own lovemap and how it interacts with other people's lovemaps—it gives the analyst a head start on countertransference analysis. If the analyst's lovemap matches the patient's, he will probably have the most empathy with the patient, but will also be most vulnerable to countertransference erotic reactions that feel overwhelming or dangerous.

If the analyst is truly curious about his patients, there is no shortage of surprise and variation in lovemaps that he will find. For example, one of my patients imagined she would wrestle me to the ground and force me to have sex with her. She also masturbated to fantasies of being bound and raped. The combination showed that, for her, eroticism always had an aspect of coercion, and that caused a lot of consternation among her would-be boyfriends.

The Gender and Sexual Orientation of the Patient and Analyst

How much is the erotic transference shaped by the analyst's and the patient's gender and sexual orientation? Ethel Person (2003) wrote:

> While the erotic transference and countertransference were first identified in the context of a male therapist and a female patient, there are four primary kinds of transference situations: heterosexual women in treatment with heterosexual male therapists, heterosexual men in treatment with heterosexual female therapists, homosexual men in treatment with homosexual male therapists and homosexual women with homosexual female therapists. The latter two constellations have only recently received attention. (p. 29)

I admired Person for including gay and lesbian analysts in her discussion, which was a relatively new development in the psychoanalytic literature. Nevertheless, I think her formulation was too limiting. There are many more constellations possible, and *the gender that the analyst is, male or female, is not necessarily the only gender the analyst can be in the erotic transference*—the analyst can be experienced by the patient as a different gender than the one he presents. This may sound confusing; I will give a few examples. A woman, Nora, started analysis with me, considering herself to be a lesbian. To her surprise, she started to fall in love with me, and imagined our getting married. However, she also told me that my office smelled like menstrual blood, which was an attractive smell to her. This and other details suggested that she was loving me, at least in part, as a woman.

In the transference, Nora was able to experience the full range of her (and my) bisexuality and worked out a way that she could experience bisexual passion with a single person. I thought she was beautiful, smart, and enormously talented. Was she loving me as a gay man, straight man, or as a woman (gay or straight)? At times, it seemed like she alternated among all four possibilities.

But gender and sexual orientation did not exist in isolation from other aspects of Nora's personality. It is a basic principle of psychoanalytic treatment that we study erotic feelings and character issues in tandem. Each affects the other, and neither is necessarily primary. Nora's lovemap was colored by her oppositionalism; her parents were strong-willed, and she often used her sexual preferences as a way to define herself as different from them. When she talked of imagining marrying me, I noted that although her parents might be pleased that she was with a man, they would be horrified that she married someone Jewish and who came from an unacceptable social-class background. Almost any choice she made was going to sharply displease someone, and since I was culturally so different from her parents, choices that would have pleased her parents might displease me. This helped her see how she juggled desire and conformity, and freed her to find her own way. She eventually married a man who was himself complex in his gender identity and gave a good fit to her lovemap. Her choice, though, inevitably enacted the transference. She knew that I was a gay man and that I was concerned about her entering a heterosexual marriage. So in marrying him, she could carry out her oppositionalism toward me, too.

In the example of Anthony that I discussed above, there also were complex interactions of gender and sexual orientation in the transference. He felt that he perceived me as his mother in the transference, a woman whose desires for him were unreciprocated and caused him guilt and anxiety. Although in reality I am a gay man, and Anthony knew this, in the transference I became a heterosexual female.

Another patient, Luke, also a gay man who knew I was a gay man, had a dream early in treatment that he was in my home with my wife and me. This set the stage for his experiencing me as a heterosexual married man. This evolved into a transference in which he presumed that I strongly disliked him. He imagined, when he rang my bell, that I felt revulsion at the thought of having to spend the next hour with him. He also tended to keep secret the range of his homosexual experiences, feeling shame about them and expecting that I would be put off by them, as well as by sexual fantasies that involved me. This was not my conscious experience of him, but his transference cast me, a gay man, as a heterosexual, married, homophobic man.

I think that the psychoanalyst can be perceived as gay or straight, male or female, and many other variations; the range of possibilities probably varies more if the analyst is open to thinking of himself in any of those identities. It also helps if the analyst can freely register his or her own emotions, erotic and otherwise, including a lack of sexual responsiveness. The analyst can experience anti-erotic countertransference just as much as the patient can experience anti-erotic transference. Sherby (2009) described a situation in which she felt no erotic feelings, despite consciously thinking that her patient was an attractive man. She used her experience as a clue to the way that the patient's sexuality was dissociated. He was very seductive, but only with "loose women."

Clarity about Sexual Enactment

I am often asked by students, "Should the analyst make clear that he will not have sex with his patient? Can saying that impede the expression of erotic transference? If you do not say it, are you leading the patient on?"

Thirty years ago, one of my supervisors told me that you should never tell a patient that sexual relations between you and him or her will not happen. The supervisor's rationale was that such a statement cuts off the expression of eroticism and prevents the analysis of the erotic transference. He mentioned to me a woman with whom he was then working who was ready to terminate, but who held onto the treatment with the hope that the analyst would still consummate their love.

His advice sounded wrong to me, although I could not spell out why at the time. Today, I think my supervisor was definitely enjoying being so desired by his younger female patient. All psychoanalysts can have such erotic countertransferences, but they seem most common among the middle-aged, when the body is declining and many people experience personal losses through death, divorce, or the "empty nest" (Dahlberg, 1970; Gabbard, 1996a). At the time, my supervisor was between his third and fourth marriages. I think he did not want to tell his female patient that her lust would never be consummated with him, because she might have stopped pining for him and channeled her sexuality into a relationship with someone else.

Stephen Mitchell referred to this psychoanalytic pattern as "The Revenge of the Nerds."* Mitchell discussed erotic transference as a triumph for a man who felt like a nerd when he was growing up. The pretty girls never

---

* I have not been able to find any publication in which Mitchell used this phrase, but several colleagues have reported hearing him speak about it. *Revenge of the Nerds* was a popular film that was released in 1984. Although the nerds in the film were all men, the concept of *Revenge of the Nerds* can apply to women as well as men.

wanted to go out with him as an adolescent. Now, as an adult psychoanalyst with a beautiful woman on his couch expressing erotic yearning for him, he thinks, consciously or not, "I can't believe how lucky I am." And while she talks about how hot he makes her, he is reluctant to have this experience end prematurely. One can see why such an analyst might like a theory that says, "Don't tell her it will never actually happen."

Therefore, every psychoanalyst should be clear, in his mind and with his patient, that actual sexual activity between him and his patient will never happen. He will not leave his wife for her. He will not hook up with her after the treatment is over. It will never happen. I tell patients that we can talk about any erotic feelings or fantasies they have, but that we will never act on them. It does not seem to stop the exploration of erotic feelings; in fact, I think it makes the exploration possible. Of course, tact, empathy, and timing are important in making such statements. If, for example, when the patient first tentatively expresses some erotic transference, the analyst were to immediately respond that actual sexual relations will not happen, the patient might well feel it as a reprimand and never express those feelings again.

Also, there are ethical and legal aspects to this question: I have a colleague who worked with a patient with a volatile mix of love and hatred of him. She thought he made a seductive comment to her, although it sounded quite innocuous to me. Nevertheless, she reported him to the American Psychological Association for an ethics violation, and in the hearing, he was asked, "Did you ever state outright to your patient that there was no possibility of sexual relations with her?" Since he had not made such a statement, he was found to be unethical and nearly lost his license. Hearing about an experience like that makes one cautious.

Evolution and Resolution of the Erotic
Transference and Countertransference

Psychoanalytic students often ask, "When patients say they want to run away with you and live happily ever after, do they really mean it?" This is an important question. It is not for the analyst to decide in advance what the patient will want, or how the transference will play out. We analysts are continually surprised by our patients, and that is a good thing.

For example, I once had a patient who was a gay man but felt it was terribly wrong to be gay, and he avoided all sexual relations. He also assumed (wrongly) that I was heterosexual, and that I shared his disgust with homosexuality. Yet he expressed intense love feelings for me. He invited me to join him on the couch, to embrace him, and to run away with him and live happily ever after. I did not do any of those things, but I did become increasingly uncomfortable with his presumption of my homophobia. And so one day in the analysis, perhaps later than it should have been, I told him that I was gay and that I did not share his contempt for gay people, including himself. What would you predict happening? Would you expect the expressions of erotic transference to get stronger or weaker? Now that he knew I could comfortably entertain homoerotic fantasies, would you expect him to put more pressure on me to join him on the couch? The truth was that he was profoundly moved by my revelation; yet from that moment on, he stopped pressuring me to have sex with him or spend my life with him. Instead, he eventually went out and found a male romantic partner.

Harold Searles (1959) wrote that whenever he has experienced a good treatment termination with a patient, he has had the feeling toward the end of the analysis that the patient, male or female, is someone toward whom he feels romantic and erotic desires, someone with whom he would like to spend the rest of his life. He felt that other psychoanalysts have such feelings near termination, but few admit it. This put an unusual spin on the erotic countertransference; it is not necessarily a problem. It may be a sign that you have done good work, and it is time for termination.

16

The Political Is Psychoanalytic
On Same-Sex Marriage

Author's Introduction

In February 2006, same-sex marriage had still not been made legal in my home state of New York, but my partner Chris and I decided to buy wedding rings at Tiffany's. The saleswoman was apparently quite experienced in dealing with gay couples, and in no time she had dissolved any differences between us about which ring to choose. We bought the simple platinum ring. I thought, "Perhaps it is only a symbol, but at least it will be a public display of the love we feel for one another."

I was astonished at the effect the rings had. Symbolism is powerful, and the rings instantly made many people take our relationship much more seriously, in ways we had not imagined. My mother said, "May I refer to Chris as my son-in-law now?" My sister offered to host our marriage ceremony, if same-sex marriage ever became legal in New York. We realized immediately the power of marriage in people's minds and the great yearning for socially sanctioned relationships among our families and friends. People, like my late psychoanalyst, do not know what to make of the terms that gay couples have used to designate their relationships—lover (too sexual), boyfriend (too flip), significant other (too clinical), partner (too businesslike)—but everyone feels that they know what "husband" means.

The Political Is Psychoanalytic: On Same-Sex Marriage*

> First they ignore you, then they laugh at you, then they fight you, then you win.
>
> Mahatma Gandhi

The political is psychoanalytic. A psychoanalyst cannot adequately address the mental health issues of stigmatized people without also taking a stand against discrimination and bigotry in society, as Harry Stack Sullivan showed us in word and deed (Perry, 1982; Blechner, 2005a; Wake, 2005, 2006, 2008). Some people argue that same-sex marriage is a legal, political, and economic issue, but not a topic for psychoanalysis. They are wrong on two points:

1. Psychoanalysis as a treatment is involved with optimizing mental health, and the ban on same-sex marriage has serious mental health ramifications for gay men, lesbians, and their children.
2. Psychoanalysis is the science of irrationality, and the arguments about same-sex marriage are filled with irrationality. It is within the purview of psychoanalysts to analyze this irrationality, to seek out its roots and causes.

The Mental Health of Gay and Lesbian Adults

We all grow up with certain values, life aims, and role models. In our culture, one of the main ones is marriage and family. Most children's fantasy life about the future includes the expectation of marriage and children, and most people try to actualize those fantasies during adulthood, with more or less success. However, when a person realizes that he or she is gay or lesbian, there is a disruption of this fantasy. The message is sent to a gay or lesbian person, "What society holds as a primary goal in life and source of satisfaction is unavailable to you. You are unfit for it." This causes a host of psychological problems or at least challenges: It may lead gay and lesbian youth to distrust the possibility of having a full relationship and, in despair, seek primarily sexual connections without love. It allows the "conversion therapists" to bolster their spurious message that you can be happier if you convert to heterosexuality. When a young person is contemplating a future of being denied basic rights, privileges, and social support,

---

* Originally published in *Studies in Gender and Sexuality*, 2008, 9, 146–154.

it may seem obvious, at least in theory, that heterosexuality is preferable. Those who follow such thinking can be seriously damaged by conversion therapy and eventually discover that sexuality is not malleable, and no amount of societal support will make up for a loss of genuine passion.

As adults, most gays and lesbians come to realize that they are as equipped as heterosexuals, emotionally and psychologically, to form lasting and meaningful relationships. Yet not being allowed to marry robs them of many kinds of security and support. You may have a wonderful relationship with your gay or lesbian partner, but when issues come up that involve the public and society, not being married will cause you enormous grief. In the eyes of the law, you and your partner are *strangers*—and this is not an exaggeration. When your partner gets sick and is hospitalized, the hospital may not let you in to see him. When your partner dies, if you were married, you could inherit his assets tax-free. Without marriage, the government will tax his estate as if you are a stranger, which may cost you more than 50% of his assets. If your partner fathers a child, and you raise the child together, and your partner dies suddenly, your partner's parents can sue to get custody of the child, and you may then not even be allowed to visit the child. All of these situations will be so stressful that they will surely affect your mental health.

In 2004, the United States Government Accountability Office identified a total of 1,138 federal statutory provisions in which marital status is a factor in determining or receiving rights, benefits, and protections (Shah, 2005). I cannot discuss here all the ways being denied these 1,138 rights can cause hardship for gay and lesbian couples, so I will describe just one case. A gay man, whom I will call Mr. X, had certain personality barriers that were interfering with his finding a long-term partner, which he ardently desired. He worked through those issues in psychoanalytic therapy. He then met a man from Brazil, Mr. Y, with whom he experienced great mutual love. But the combination of U.S. immigration law and the unavailability of same-sex marriage combined to turn Mr. X's life into a nightmare. When his partner went back to Brazil to renew his visa, the American government refused to allow him to return to the United States. Mr. X had to commute from New York to Brazil for a year and a half, until his multinational corporation allowed him to relocate to London, where his partner could join him. When Mr. X testified before Congress in 2006 about the injustice of U.S. immigration law, he said:

> At every turn, U.S. immigration law disqualifies lesbian and gay families like ours....I feel ashamed that my country has treated my partner this way and

furious that we cannot visit or live together in this great country. Despite the
fact that I am a tax-paying, law-abiding and voting citizen, I feel unfair discrimination from my government.

The Mental Health of Children

Perhaps the most vulnerable victims of the ban on same-sex marriage are
children. It is cruelly ironic that judicial decisions in the United States
denying the right to same-sex marriage cite the welfare of children, yet
those very decisions harm the welfare of the estimated one million children currently being raised by gay and lesbian couples. A report by the
American Academy of Pediatrics captures the irrational disjuncture
between the stated aim of United States policy on same-sex marriage and
its effect (Pawelski et al., 2006):

> Public policy designed to promote the family as the basic building block of soci-
> ety has at its core the protection of children's health and well-being. Children's
> well-being relies in large part on a complex blend of their own legal rights and
> the rights derived, under law, from their parents. Children of same-gender par-
> ents often experience economic, legal, and familial insecurity as a result of the
> absence of legal recognition of their bonds to their nonbiological parents. (pp.
> 251–252)

Several studies have now shown that the quality of gay and lesbian parenting is equivalent to that of heterosexual parents (Stacey & Biblarz, 2001).
Nevertheless, children of gay and lesbian parents are essentially punished
by our society, deprived of many legal, social, and financial benefits available to the children of heterosexual parents.

And what if same-sex couples turn out, in many instances, not only to be
just as good parents as heterosexuals, but better parents? There is one clear
reason this could occur: Many children of heterosexuals are unplanned,
either through the carelessness of a chance encounter, the failure of birth
control, or some other reason. Some unplanned children are loved by
their parents, but some remain unwanted and resented by their parents.
Unwanted children tend not to do well in development (Ferenczi, 1929).
The occurrence of unwanted children is likely to be lower in gay couples,
who must not only intend to have the child, but often have to go through
bureaucratic and legal hoops to get a child. So unwanted children may be
rarer among gay couples; unplanned children are almost nonexistent.

Irrationality

Psychoanalysis is the science of the irrational (Blechner, 2005b), and we ought to identify the irrationality about same-sex marriage and help understand its sources. Judge Robert Smith, in the 2006 New York ruling against same-sex marriage, said there was little scientific evidence to support one kind of parenting over another, but the idea that a mother and a father were the best parents was supported by "intuition" and "common sense." We know that when people argue that the facts show one thing but that intuition and common sense show another, they are blatantly disavowing rationality for prejudice. Were we to follow such reasoning, we would still believe that the sun revolved around the Earth. Such arguments are dangerous, but continue to be made.

Judge Smith's decision echoed a previous ruling by the Indiana Court of Appeals in *Morrison v. Sadler*. The Indiana court theorized that while same-sex couples can only have children as a result of deliberate intention through adoption or donor insemination, opposite-sex couples can have children through carelessness or accidents (broken condoms, orgies, etc.), and therefore the rights and benefits of marriage should be used as an incentive to corral those careless heterosexuals into more responsible behavior, through the bonds of matrimony. Yet the New York and Indiana courts utterly fail to explain why not letting same-sex couples marry advances the goal of getting opposite-sex couples to do so. As New York Chief Judge Judith Kaye wrote in her dissent, there are "enough marriage licenses to go around." Kenneth Choe, an attorney for the American Civil Liberties Union, has pointed out:

> It is not enough that there is reason for including the included class. There must also be a reason for excluding the excluded class. The state could not grant right-handed people but not left-handed people the right to marry simply by observing that marriage benefits right-handed people and their children. (*New York Times*, 2006, p. A20)

The analogy with handedness is telling; like gay people, left-handed people were once thought to be defective, and various measures were taken to help them (or force them) to become right-handed, to no avail.

What leads well-educated people to make spurious and irrational arguments? Some of it is simply the difficulty of abandoning attitudes with which one was raised. As Charles Rosen (1994) has said, "The name generally given to widely accepted error is *tradition*" (p. 11).

People born in the 1940s or earlier heard it said that homosexuality was evil, that most homosexuals had bad ethics and molested children—all falsehoods. Many mainstream older people, psychoanalysts among them, still cling to such prejudices. They lived through the 1950s, when such "common sense" was made the law of the land, when Eisenhower banned gay people from serving in government. The underlying idea is that gay people are bad and dangerous, or, to use the hoary shibboleth of religion-derived pseudoscience, *perverted*. We are loath to yield such early lessons, unless we are regularly faced with their untruth. Younger people today, on average, know many more openly gay people and recognize the irrationality of such prejudices.

In addition, many nominal heterosexuals have a dread of homosexuality in themselves. They may fear that if same-sex marriage is legal, their own heterosexuality will be tainted, through fears of contagion. This is totally illogical, but they are not operating in the realm of logic. They are operating in the realm of von Domarus logic (von Domarus, 1944; discussed in Chapter 11), in which things that are merely associated with one another are seen to have a causal relationship. For example, a schizophrenic may think, "If my mother's name is Mary, and Mary is the mother of God, then I am God." You may think that only schizophrenics think like this, but as Freud and Jung have shown us, when we are under great emotional pressure, we are all capable of reasoning like madmen. Thus a frightened heterosexual may unconsciously reason: If homosexuals are allowed to be married, and I am married, then I may be a homosexual. And if I make it impossible for homosexuals to marry, and I am married, then I will make it impossible for me to be a homosexual.

By fighting against same-sex marriage, some heterosexuals may unconsciously feel they are fending off any dreaded homosexual impulses in themselves. This idea is supported by the many films and books in which a person in homosexual panic marries to prove his heterosexuality (e.g., *Mambo Italiano*). If same-sex marriage is legalized, marriage may lose its status as an unconscious safe haven for the conflicted. Until then, we will have to watch endless repetitions of public figures most adamant against same-sex marriage and equal rights for gay people being exposed as closet homosexuals. As I write this, the most recent examples are

1. Robert Skolrood, the attorney whose legal arguments led Cincinnati to deprive gays and lesbians of legal rights in 1993, was arrested on charges of uttering obscenities and making sexual advances to a male policeman at a highway overlook (D. Martin, 2008).

2. Reverend Ted Haggard, married to a woman, who preached strong opposition to gay rights, yet was revealed to have monthly trysts for three years with a male prostitute, Mike Jones (Ireland, 2006).

3. Senator Larry Craig, married with three adopted children, a longtime supporter of anti-gay legislation, who was arrested in 2007 for soliciting sex in a men's room—but there have been many other examples in the past (e.g., Roy Cohn, J. Edgar Hoover, Terry Dolan), and there surely will be more in the future.

America is a religious country for the most part, and religious people cite the Bible to prove that God supports their bigotry, whether against Black people, gay people, or others. Jefferson Davis, president of the Confederacy, said: "Slavery was established by decree of Almighty God...it is sanctioned in the Bible, in both Testaments, from Genesis to Revelation." And he was right. In the Old Testament, we find unequivocal descriptions of slaves as property:

> However, you may purchase male or female slaves from among the foreigners who live among you. You may also purchase the children of such resident foreigners, including those who have been born in your land. You may treat them as your property, passing them on to your children as a permanent inheritance. (Leviticus 25: 44–46; see also the New Testament, Luke 12:47–48; 1 Timothy 6:1–2)

The Bible's prohibition against men lying with other men (Leviticus 18:22) has been similarly used to argue against same-sex marriage. Although the Supreme Court ruled in 2002 that homosexual relations are not a crime, religious people continue to consider such relations a sin. They say that their ideas are supported by God's own words in the Bible, and thus they feel safe from challenge when they oppose same-sex marriage.

Yet they cite selectively. Few people today would argue that because the Bible condones slavery, it is right for contemporary society. By means of selective inattention, those who claim religious authority to punish homosexuals do not also demand the death penalty for those who break the Sabbath or disobey their parents, as called for in the Bible. Some day, we will consider with astonishment that the Bible's ban on homosexuality was used to deny civil rights to gay people and their children, just as we are astonished that the Bible was once used to defend slavery.

Same-sex marriage has now been legal for some time in The Netherlands, Belgium, Spain, Canada, South Africa, and the states of Massachusetts, California, and Connecticut. The institution of marriage has shown no ill effects, nor have those societies reported being damaged in any way by same-sex marriage—on the contrary. The prime minister of Spain, Jose Luis Rodriguez Zapatero, put the situation clearly in his speech to the Spanish Parliament after they legalized same-sex marriage:

> Today, the Spanish society answers to a group of people who, during many years, have been humiliated, whose rights have been ignored, whose dignity has been offended, their identity denied, and their liberty oppressed. Today the Spanish society grants them the respect they deserve, recognizes their rights, restores their dignity, affirms their identity, and restores their liberty.... Honorable members, there is no damage to marriage or to the concept of family in allowing two people of the same sex to get married. To the contrary, what happens is this class of Spanish citizens get the potential to organize their lives with the rights and privileges of marriage and family. There is no danger to the institution of marriage, but precisely the opposite: this law enhances and respects marriage.

Afterword

None of us can escape from the confines of our era, no matter how hard we try. One of the thrills of living long enough is the chance to see how much can change in just four or five decades. Truths that were once seen as self-evident come to seem suspect or preposterous, and we may wipe our brows and wonder, how could we have thought that then?

I sometimes ask my colleagues and students to imagine the future: In 100 years, which of our current ideas will seem wrong, even ridiculous? The question challenges us to get perspective on our society and imagine very different premises for civilization. You may dismiss this question as a futile exercise in fortune-telling, but some science-fiction writers have anticipated the future quite well. In the 1940s, Dick Tracy used a watch that also functioned as a camera and telephone. At the time, such a device seemed a fantasy; today, it is a reality. Many developments in civilization start as dreams or fantasies.

In the future that I imagine, being gay, lesbian, or bisexual will seem as ordinary and innocuous as being tall. It will be just one more dimension that contributes to the grand tapestry of human nature. Students in schools will learn about the great contributions of gay men and lesbians to society, not as a special subject, but just as a matter of fact. They will appreciate that society has benefited enormously from the achievements of gay men and lesbians, such as the music of Aaron Copland, the plays of Tennessee Williams, the novels of E. M. Forster and Willa Cather, the paintings of Jasper Johns, the foundation of the computer by Alan Turing, the economic theories of John Maynard Keynes, the psychiatric vision of Harry Stack Sullivan, the great tennis-playing of Billie Jean King and Martina Navratilova, the consummate acting of John Gielgud, and the piano artistry of Vladimir Horowitz.

In the future, no one will have to endure the agony of "coming out" as gay. No teenagers will be disowned by their parents for being gay, thrown out of the house, and left to fend for themselves on the street. The fact of being gay will be heard as just one more fact about a person. Gay men and lesbians will have the same opportunity as straight people to form loving bonds, supported in society by marriage. Gay men and lesbians will also have the same opportunity as straight people to mess up their relationships and end up in divorce court. When sickness comes, hospitals will automatically let in a gay person's husband or wife to administer care and bring courage through love. And when death comes, the gay person's spouse will be entitled to all the protection of pensions, social security, and inheritance laws. Life as a gay person will be as safe, happy, and thrilling (or as dangerous, unhappy, and boring) as life as a straight person. Gay men and lesbians will have the same opportunities as straight people; women will have the same opportunities as men; and Black people will have the same opportunities as White people.

Sex will always change, but society will change, too. The enormous progress of the last 40 years will continue. Sometimes there will be jerky movements back and forth between progress and regression, but gradually society will move toward true equality for all people. That is my vision of the future. As Robert Browning wrote in his poem, *Andrea del Sarto*, "Ah, but a man's reach should exceed his grasp, or what's a heaven for?"

References

Adams, H., Wright, L., & Lohr, B. (1996). Is homophobia associated with homosexual arousal? *Journal of Abnormal Psychology, 105*, 440–445.

Alexander, F. (1948). *Fundamentals of psychoanalysis*. New York: Norton.

Al-Fatiha (2004). Homosexuality and same-sex acts in Islam. http://www.al-fatiha. net/pamphlet.html.

Allen, M. (1995). Sullivan's closet: A reappraisal of Harry Stack Sullivan's life and his pioneering role in American psychiatry. *Journal of Homosexuality, 29*, 1–18.

Andersen, D., & Seitz, F. (1969). Rorschach diagnosis of homosexuality: Schafer's content analysis. *Journal of Projective Techniques, 5*, 406–408.

Archuleta, M. (1998). Suicide statistics for lesbian and gay youth: A bibliography. http://isd.usc.edu/~retter/suicstats.html.

Armon, V. (1960). Some personality variables in overt female homosexuality. *Journal of Projective Techniques, 24*, 292–309.

Aronson, M. (1952). A study of the Freudian theory of paranoia by means of the Rorschach test. *Journal of Projective Techniques, 16*, 397–411.

Aronson, S. (1996). The bereavement process in children of parents with AIDS. *The Psychoanalytic Study of the Child, 51*, 422–435.

Bagemihl, B. (1999). *Biological exuberance: Animal homosexuality and natural diversity*. New York: St. Martin's Press.

Bartlett, F. (1934). *Remembering*. Cambridge: Cambridge University Press.

Bassi, F., &. Galli, P., eds. (2000). *L'Omosessualità nella psicoanalisi*. Torino, Italy: Piccola Biblioteca Einaudi.

Bayer, R. (1981). *Homosexuality and American psychiatry*. New York: Basic Books.

Belluck, P., & Cowan, A. (2007). Partner adopted by an heiress stakes her claim. *New York Times*, March 19, 2007, A1, 10.

Bem, S. (1993). *The lenses of gender: Transforming the debate on sexual inequality*. New Haven, CT: Yale University Press.

Bergler, E. (1956). *Homosexuality: Disease or Way of Life*. New York: Hill and Wang.

Bergman, S. J. (1996). Male relational dread. *Psychiatric Annals, 26*, 24–28.

Bergmann, M. (1945). Homosexuality on the Rorschach test. *Bulletin Menninger Clinic, 9*, 78–83.

——— (1987). *The anatomy of loving*. New York: Columbia University Press.

Bérubé, A. (1990). *Coming out under fire: The history of gay men and women in World War Two*. New York: Free Press.

Bieber, I., Dain, H., Dince, P., Dreilich, M., Grand, H., Gundlach, R., Kremer, M., Rifkin, A., Wilbur, C., & Bieber, T. (1962). *Homosexuality: A psychoanalytical study*. New York: Vintage.

Blechner, M. (1992a). *Psychoanalysis, homophobia, racism, and anti-Semitism: Introduction*. Presented at the conference of the William Alanson White Society, "The Experience of Hating and Being Hated," November 18, 1992, New York.

_____ (1992b). Working in the countertransference. *Psychoanalytic Dialogues, 2,* 161–179.

_____ (1993a). Homophobia in psychoanalytic writing and practice. *Psychoanalytic Dialogues, 3,* 627–637.

_____ (1993b). Psychoanalysis and HIV disease. *Contemporary Psychoanalysis, 29,* 61–80.

_____ (1994a). Review of Darlene Ehrenberg's *The Intimate Edge*. *Psychoanalytic Dialogues, 4,* 283–292.

_____ (1994b). Projective identification, countertransference, and the "maybe-me." *Contemporary Psychoanalysis, 30,* 619–630.

_____ (1995a). The patient's dreams and the countertransference. *Psychoanalytic Dialogues, 5,* 1–25.

_____ (1995b). Homosexuality, homophobia, and clinical psychoanalysis. Presented to the Graduate Faculty, New School for Social Research, March 9, 1995.

_____ (1995c). The shaping of psychoanalytic theory and practice by cultural and personal biases about sexuality. In T. Domenici & R. Lesser, (Eds.), *Disorienting sexuality* (pp. 265–288). New York: Routledge.

_____ (1995d). The interaction of societal prejudice with psychodiagnosis and treatment aims. *The Round Robin*, September, 10–14.

_____ (1995e). Schizophrenia. In: Lionells, M. et al., eds., *Handbook of Interpersonal Psychoanalysis*. Hillsdale, NJ: Analytic Press, 1995, pp. 375–396.

_____ (1996). Psychoanalysis in and out of the closet. In B. Gerson (Ed.), *The therapist as a person: Life crises, life choices, life experiences, and their effects on treatment* (pp. 223–239). Hillsdale, NJ: The Analytic Press.

_____ (1997). *Hope and mortality: Psychodynamic approaches to AIDS and HIV*. Hillsdale, NJ: The Analytic Press.

_____ (1998a). Maleness and masculinity. *Contemporary Psychoanalysis, 34,* 597–613.

_____ (1998b). On sexuality in the age of AIDS. *International Journal of Psycho-Analysis, 79,* 1007–1008.

_____ (1999). Psychoanalytic approaches to the AIDS epidemic. In H. Kaley, M. Eagle, & D. Wolitsky (Eds.), *Psychoanalytic therapy as health care* (pp. 199–220). Hillsdale, NJ: The Analytic Press.

_____ (2001). *The dream frontier.* Hillsdale, NJ: The Analytic Press.

_____ (2002). Intimacy, pleasure, risk, and safety. *Journal of Gay and Lesbian Psychotherapy, 6,* 27–33.

_____ (2005a). The gay Harry Stack Sullivan: Interactions between his life, clinical work, and theory. *Contemporary Psychoanalysis, 41,* 1–19.

_____ (2005b). Disgust, desire, and fascination: Psychoanalytic, cultural, historical, and neuroscientific perspectives. *Studies in Gender and Sexuality, 6,* 33–45.

_____ (2005c). Ways to stem AIDS. *New York Times,* February 22, 2005, F4.

_____ (2005d). The grammar of irrationality: What psychoanalytic dream study can tell us about the brain. *Contemporary Psychoanalysis, 41,* 203–221.

_____ (2006). Love, sex, romance, and psychoanalytic goals. *Psychoanalytic Dialogues, 16,* 779–791.

_____ (2007). Sexual facts and values. *Studies in Gender and Sexuality, 8,* 373–380.

Blechner, M., & Casden, S. (1994). Special considerations in the psychoanalytic psychotherapy of gay men. Presented to the Connecticut Society of Psychoanalytic Psychologists, December 3, 1994.

_____ (1995). Further considerations in the psychoanalytic psychotherapy of gay men and lesbians. Presented to the Connecticut Psychological Association, Hartford, November 3, 1995.

Bornstein, K. (1994). *Gender outlaw.* New York: Routledge.

_____ (1998). *My gender workbook.* New York: Routledge.

Bose, J. (1994). Hassen und gehasst werden (Hating and being hated). In J. Wiesse (Ed.), *Aggression am Ende des Jahrhunderts. Psychoanalytische Blätter,* Band 1 (pp. 33–42). Göttingen: Vandenhoeck & Ruprecht.

Boswell, J. (1980). *Christianity, social tolerance, and homosexuality.* Chicago: University of Chicago Press.

_____ (1990). Sexual and ethical categories in premodern Europe. In D. McWhirter, S. Sanders, & J. Reinisch (Eds.), *Homosexuality/heterosexuality: Concepts of sexual orientation* (pp. 15–31). New York: Oxford University Press.

_____ (1994). *Same-sex unions in premodern Europe.* New York: Random House.

Boyd, H. (2003). *My husband Betty: Love, sex, and life with a cross-dresser.* New York: Thunder's Mouth Press.

Brown, H. (1976). *Familiar faces, hidden lives.* New York: Harcourt Brace Jovanovich.

Butler, J. (1990). *Gender trouble.* New York: Routledge.

_____ (1991). Imitation and gender insubordination. In D. Fuss (Ed.), *Inside/out* (pp. 13–31). New York: Routledge.

_____ (1995). Melancholy gender—Refused identification. *Psychoanalytic Dialogues, 5,* 165–180.

Byne, W., Hamer, D., Isay, R., & Stein, T. (1995). Sexual orientation is primarily a biological phenomenon: A debate. Meeting of the American Psychiatric Association. Available from Mobiltape, Valencia, CA.

Califia, P. (1999). Gay men, lesbians, and sex: Doing it together. In: Gross, L. & Woods, J., eds., *The Columbia Reader on Lesbians and Gay Men in Media, Society, and Politics*. New York: Columbia University Press. Originally published in: *The Advocate*, July 7, 1983, pp. 24–27.

Cartwright, S. A. (1981). Report on the diseases and physical peculiarities of the Negro race. In A. L. Caplan et al. (Eds.), *Concepts of health and disease: Interdisciplinary perspectives* (pp. 305–326). Reading, MA: Addison-Wesley. (Originally published in 1851.)

Chapman, A., & Reese, D. (1953). Homosexual signs in Rorschachs of early schizophrenics. *Journal of Clinical Psychology, 9*, 30–32.

Chatelaine, K. (1981). *Harry Stack Sullivan: The formative years*. Washington, DC: University Press of America.

Chauncey, G. (1994). *Gay New York*. New York: Basic Books.

Chivers, M., Rieger, G., Latty, E., & Bailey, J. (2004). A sex difference in the specificity of sexual arousal. *Psychological Science, 15*, 736–744.

Chivers, M., Seto, M., & Blanchard, R. (2007). Gender and sexual orientation differences in sexual response to sexual activities versus gender of actors in sexual films. *Journal of Personality and Social Psychology, 93*, 1108–1121.

Chodorow, N. (1978). *The reproduction of mothering*. Berkeley: University of California Press.

Clark, S. (2002). Schubert, theory, and analysis. *Music Analysis, 21*, 209–244.

CNN (2003). http://www.cnn.com/2003/ALLPOLITICS/04/22/santorum.gays.

Cohler, B. (1969). Letter to the editor. *Journal of Projective Techniques, 33*, 399.

Cook, B. (1992). *Eleanor Roosevelt*. New York: Viking.

Corbett, K. (1993). The mystery of homosexuality. *Psychoanalytic Psychology, 10*, 345–358.

_____ (1996). Homosexual boyhood: Notes on girlyboys. *Gender and Psychoanalysis, 1*, 429–462.

Dahlberg, C. (1970). Sexual contact between patient and therapist. *Contemporary Psychoanalysis, 6*, 107–124.

Davids, A., Joelson, M., & McArthur, C. (1956). Rorschach and TAT indices of homosexuality in overt homosexuals, neurotics, and normal males. *Journal of Abnormal and Social Psychology, 53*, 161–172.

Diefendorff, A., & Dodge, R. (1908). An experimental study of the ocular reactions of the insane from photographic records. *Brain, 31*, 451–489.

Dimen, M. (1997). The engagement between psychoanalysis and feminism: A report from the front. *Contemporary Psychoanalysis, 33*, 527–548.

Dimen, M. (2005). Sexuality and suffering, or the Eew! factor. *Studies in Gender and Sexuality, 6*, 1–18.

Dominus, S. (2004). Growing up with mom and mom. *New York Times Magazine*, October 24.

Dommermuth-Costa, C. (1998). *Emily Dickinson: Singular Poet*. Breckenridge, CO: Twenty-First Century Books.

Doty, R., Ford, M., Preti, G., & Huggins, G. (1975). Changes in the intensity and pleasantness of human vaginal odors during the menstrual cycle. *Science, 190*, 1316–1318.

Doty, R., Preti, G., & Ford, M. (1976). Reply to Globus and Cohen. *Science, 192*, 96.

Drescher, J. (1992). Psychoanalysis, hatred, homosexuality. Presentation at the conference "The Experience of Hating and Being Hated," William Alanson White Society, New York, November 18, 1992.

_____ (1996). Psychoanalytic subjectivity and male homosexuality. In *The textbook of homosexuality and mental health* (pp. 173–189). Washington, DC: American Psychiatric Press.

_____ (1998). *Psychoanalytic therapy and the gay man.* Hillsdale, NJ: The Analytic Press.

Duberman, M. (1991). *Cures.* New York: Dutton.

Due, F., & Wright, M. (1949). The use of content analysis in Rorschach interpretation. *Rorschach Research Exchange, 13*, 127–140.

Eatwell, R. (1997). *Fascism: A History.* New York: Penguin.

Faber, D. (1980). *The Life of Lorena Hickok: E. R.'s Friend.* New York: W. Morrow.

Fausto-Sterling, A. (1985). *Myths of gender.* New York: Basic Books.

Fein, L. (1950). Rorschach signs of homosexuality in male college students. *Journal of Clinical Psychology, 6*, 248–253.

Feinman, S. (1981). Why is cross-sex-role behavior more approved for girls than for boys? A status characteristics approach. *Sex Roles, 7*, 289–300.

Fenichel, O. (1945). *The psychoanalytic theory of neurosis.* New York: Norton.

Ferenczi, S. (1902). Homosexualitas feminine. *Gyogyaszat, 11*, 167–168.

_____ (1924). *Versuch einer Genitaltheorie.* Leipzig: Internationale Psychoanalytische Verlag. English translation: *Thalassa: A Theory of Genitality* (H. Bunker, Trans.). London: Maresfield Library (Karnac), 1989.

_____ (1929). The unwelcome child and his death instinct. In M. Balint (Ed.), *Final contributions to the problems and methods of psychoanalysis* (pp. 102–107). London: Hogarth Press, 1955.

_____ (1932). *The clinical diary of Sándor Ferenczi* (J. Dupont, Ed.; M. Balint & N. Jackson, Trans.). Cambridge, MA: Harvard University Press, 1988.

_____ (1933). Confusion of tongues between adults and the child. In *Final contributions to the problems and methods of psychoanalysis* (pp. 156–167). New York: Brunner/Mazel.

Fernandez, A. (1998). *Castro's daughter.* New York: St. Martin's Press.

Ferracuti, F., & Rizzo, G. (1956). Analisi del valore discriminativo di alcuni segni di omosessualita rilevabili attraverso techniche proiettive. *Bolletino di Psicologia Applicata, 13*, 128–134.

Fiscalini, J. (2004). *Coparticipant psychoanalysis: Toward a new theory of clinical inquiry.* New York: Columbia University Press.

Franklin, R. (2006). The epilogue. Review of *Fear: Anti-Semitism in Poland after Auschwitz. The New Republic*, October 2, *235*(14), 36–41.

Freud, S. (1900). *The interpretation of dreams. Standard edition* (Vols. 4–5). London: Hogarth Press.

_____ (1901). *The psychopathology of everyday life. Standard edition* (Vol. 6). London: Hogarth Press.

_____ (1905a). *Three essays on the theory of sexuality. Standard edition* (Vol. 7). London: Hogarth Press.

_____ (1905b). *Jokes and their relation to the unconscious. Standard edition* (Vol. 8). London: Hogarth Press.

_____ (1916–1917). *Introductory lectures on psycho-analysis. Standard edition* (Vol. 16). London: Hogarth Press.

_____ (1920). On the psychogenesis of a case of female homosexuality. *International Journal of Psychoanalysis, 1*, 125–149.

_____ (1930). Address delivered in the Goethe House at Frankfurt. *Standard Edition* (Vol. 21, pp. 208–212). London: Hogarth Press.

Frommer, M. (1994). Homosexuality and psychoanalysis. *Psychoanalytic Dialogues, 4*, 215–233.

Fry, S. (2004). http://www.theofficialasexualsociety.com/productssimple1.html.

Furth, G., & Smith, R. (2000). *Apotemnophilia: Information, questions, answers and recommendations about self-demand amputation.* Bloomington, IN: 1stBooks Publishers.

Gabbard, G. (1996a). The analyst's contribution to the erotic transference. *Contemporary Psychoanalysis, 32*, 249–273.

_____ (1996b). *Love and hate in the analytic setting.* Northvale, NJ: Aronson.

Ganzfried, S. (1961). *The code of Jewish Law* (H. E. Goldin, Trans.). New York: Hebrew Publishing Company.

Garber, M. (1995). *Vice versa: Bisexuality and the eroticism of everyday life.* New York: Simon & Schuster.

Gartner, R. (1999). *Betrayed as boys: Psychodynamic treatment of sexually abused men.* New York: Guilford Press.

Gibson, P. (1989). Gay male and lesbian youth suicide. Report of the Secretary's Task Force on Youth Suicide, U.S. Department of Health and Human Services.

Glazer, D. (2001). Lesbian mothers: A foot in two worlds. In E. Gould & S. Kiersky (Eds.), *Moving violations: Psychoanalysis, culture, and lesbians* (pp. 247–257). Madison, CT: International Universities Press.

Globus, G., & Cohen, H. (1976). Human vaginal odors. *Science, 192*, 96.

Goldfried, M. (1966). On the diagnosis of homosexuality from the Rorschach. *Journal of Consulting Psychology, 30*, 338–349.

Goldner, V. (1991). Toward a critical relational theory of gender. *Psychoanalytic Dialogues, 1*, 249–272.

Goldsmith, S. (1995). Oedipus or Orestes? Aspects of gender identity development in homosexual men. *Psychoanalytic Inquiry, 15*, 112–124.

_____ (2001). Oedipus or Orestes? Homosexual men, their mothers, and other women revisited. *Journal of the American Psychoanalytic Association, 49*, 1269–1288.

Gonsiorek, J. (1977). Psychological adjustment and homosexuality. *Social and Behavioral Sciences Documents* (Manuscript #1478, Vol. 7), San Raphael, CA: Select Press.

_____ (1991). The empirical basis for the demise of the illness model of homosexuality. In J. Gonsiorek & J. Weinrich (Eds.), *Homosexuality: Research implications for public policy* (pp. 115–136). Newbury Park, CA: Sage Publications.

Graham, S. (1834). *A Lecture to Young Men on Chastity, Intended Also for the Serious Consideration of Parents and Guardians*. Boston: George W. Light.

Greenberg, J., & Mitchell, S. (1983). *Object relations in psychoanalytic theory*. Cambridge, MA: Harvard University Press.

Greenberg, S. (2004). *Wrestling with God and men: Homosexuality in the Jewish tradition*. Madison: University of Wisconsin Press.

Greenson, R. (1968). Dis-identifying from mother: Its special importance for the boy. *International Journal of Psycho-Analysis, 49*, 370–374.

Greer, G. (1971). *The female eunuch*. New York: McGraw-Hill.

Grotjahn, M. (1951). Historical notes: A letter from Freud. *International Journal of Psychoanalysis, 32*, 331.

Grünbaum, A. (1984). *The foundations of psychoanalysis: A philosophical critique*. Berkeley: University of California Press, pp. 216–239.

_____ (1993). *Validation in the clinical theory of psychoanalysis*. Madison, CT: International Universities Press.

Hamer, D., Hu, S., Magnuson, V., Hu, N., and Pattatucci, A. (1993). A linkage between DNA markers on the X chromosome and male sexual orientation. *Science, 261*, 320–326.

Hanna, E. (1992). False-self sensitivity to countertransference: Anatomy of a single session. *Psychoanalytic Dialogues, 2*, 369–388.

Harned, J. (1998). Harry Stack Sullivan and the gay psychoanalysis. *American Imago, 55*, 299–317.

Harris, A. (2000). Gender as a soft assembly: Tomboys' stories. *Studies in Gender and Sexuality, 1*, 223–250.

_____ (2005). Tomboy stories. In: *Gender as Soft Assembly*. Hillsdale, NJ: The Analytic Press, 131–154.

Harris, S. (2004). *The end of faith*. New York: Norton.

Hartmann, H. (1960). *Psychoanalysis and moral values*. New York: International Universities Press.

Hatterer, L. (1970). *Changing Homosexuality in the Male*. New York: McGraw Hill.

Hausman, K. (1993). Needle-exchange programs effective but controversial. *Psychiatric News*, September 3, 11.

Hegarty, P. (2004). Was he queer … or just Irish? Reading the life of Harry Stack Sullivan. *Lesbian and Gay Psychology Review, 5*, 103–108.

_____ (2005). Harry Stack Sullivan and his chums: Archive fever in American psychiatry. *History of the Human Sciences, 18*, 35–53.

Herdt, G. (1981). *Guardians of the flute*. New York: McGraw-Hill.

Heredia, C. (1966). *El psicodiagnostico de Rorschach como detector de la homosexualidad*. Mexico: Universidad Nacional Autonoma de Mexico.

Herek, G. (1986). On heterosexual masculinity: Some psychical consequences of the social construction of gender and sexuality. *American Behavioral Scientist, 29*, 563–577.

Herek, G., & Capitanio, J. (1993). Public reaction to AIDS in the United States: A second decade of stigma. *American Journal of Public Health, 83*, 574–577.

Herndon, W. (1889). *Life of Lincoln*. Chicago: Belford, Clarke, and Co.

Hirsch, E., Kett, J., & Trefil, J. (2002). *The new dictionary of cultural literacy* (3rd ed.). New York: Houghton Mifflin Company.

Hirsch, I. (1997). On men's preference for men. *Gender and Psychoanalysis, 2*, 469–486.

_____ (2007). Imperfect love, imperfect lives: Making love, making sex, making moral judgments. *Studies in Gender and Sexuality, 17*, 355–372.

Hirschfeld, M. (1914/2000). *The homosexuality of men and women* (M. Lombardi-Nash, Trans.). Amherst, NY: Prometheus Books.

HIV Center for Clinical and Behavioral Studies Report (Vol. 1). New York State Psychiatric Institute, May 1991.

Holzman, P. (1970). *Psychoanalysis and psychopathology*. New York: McGraw-Hill.

Holzman, P., Proctor, L., & Hughes, D. (1973). Eye tracking patterns in schizophrenia. *Science, 181*, 179–181.

Hooker, E. (1957). The adjustment of the male overt homosexual. *Journal of Projective Techniques, 21*, 18–31.

_____ (1958). Male homosexuality in the Rorschach. *Journal of Projective Techniques, 22*, 33–54.

_____ (1959). What is a criterion? *Journal of Projective Techniques, 23*, 278–281.

Hunt, G., & Hunt, M. (1977). Female-female pairing in western gulls (*Larus occidentalis*) in Southern California. *Science, 196*, 1466–1467.

Ireland, D. (2006). Ted Haggard: Victim of his own spiritual warfare. *Gay City News, 5*,1, 8, 9.

Isay, R. (1989). *Being homosexual*. New York: Farrar Straus Giroux.

_____ (1991). The homosexual analyst: Clinical considerations. *Psychoanalytic Study of the Child, 46*, 199–216.

_____ (1996). *Becoming gay: The journey to self-acceptance*. New York: Pantheon.

Johnston, R., & Zahorik, D. (1975). Taste aversions to sexual attractants. *Science, 189*, 893–894.

Jones, E. (1957). *Sigmund Freud: Life and Work. Vol 3: The Last Phase 1919–1939*. London: Hogarth Press.

Jones, W. (2006). *Grayson Perry: Portrait of the artist as a young girl*. London: Chatto & Windus.

Karel, R. (1993). Needle-exchange program yielding great success. *Psychiatric News*, January 1, 10–11.

Kass, L. (1997). The wisdom of repugnance. *The New Republic*, (June 2, 1997) 216: 17–26.

Kataguchi, Y. (1958). Rorschach homosexual indices (RHI). *Rorschachiana Japonica, 1,* 86–94.

Katz, J. N. (1978). *Gay American history.* New York: Avon.

_____ (1995). *The invention of heterosexuality.* New York: Dutton.

Kellogg, J. (1888). *Plain facts for old and young: Embracing the natural history and hygiene of organic life.* Burlington, IA: I. F. Segner. Reprinted 1974, New York: Arno Press.

Kernberg, O. (1957). Estudio de orientacion psicoanalitica del contenido del test de Rorschach en la homosexualidad masculina (Psychoanalytically-oriented content analysis of the Rorschach test of male homosexuals). *Revista de Psiquiatria, 21–22,* 45–57.

_____ (2002). Unresolved issues in the psychoanalytic theory of homosexuality and bisexuality. *Journal of Gay and Lesbian Psychotherapy, 6,* 9–27.

Kinsey, A., Pomeroy, W., & Martin, C. (1948). *Sexual behavior in the human male.* Philadelphia: W. B. Saunders.

Kite, M., & Whitley, B. (1998). Do heterosexual women and men differ in their attitudes toward homosexuality? A conceptual and methodological analysis. In G. Herek (Ed.), *Stigma and sexual orientation: Understanding prejudice against lesbians, gay men, and bisexuals* (pp. 39–61). Thousand Oaks, CA: Sage Publications.

Klein, P. (1962). *President James Buchanan.* University Park: Pennsylvania State University Press.

Kopay, D., & Young, P. (1977). *The David Kopay story.* New York: Arbor House.

Krafft-Ebing, R. von (1886). *Psychopathia Sexualis* (F. Klaf, Trans). New York: Stein & Day, 1965.

Kwawer, J. (1980). Transference and countertransference in homosexuality— Changing psychoanalytic views. *American Journal of Psychotherapy, 34,* 72–80.

Lakoff, G. (1987). *Women, fire, and dangerous things.* Chicago: University of Chicago Press.

Lakoff, G., & Johnson, M. (1980). *Metaphors we live by.* Chicago: University of Chicago Press.

Laumann, E., Gagnon, J., Michael, R., & Michaels, S. (1994). *The social organization of sexuality: Sexual practices in the United States.* Chicago: University of Chicago Press.

Laumann, E., & Paik, A. (2001). *Anal intercourse: Prevalence, subjective preferences, and sexual expression.* Paper read at the Workshop on Rectal Microbicides for the Prevention of HIV Transmission, NIAID, Baltimore, Maryland, June 7–8, 2001.

Lawrence, D. (2003). *Lady Chatterley's Lover.* New York: Signet. (Originally printed in 1928.)

Lesser, R. (1993). A reconsideration of homosexual themes. *Psychoanalytic Dialogues, 3,* 639–642.

Levay, S. (1993). *The Sexual Brain.* Cambridge, MA: MIT Press.

Levinger, L. (1969). Letter to the editor. *Journal of Projective Techniques, 33*, 480.

Lewes, K. (1988). *The psychoanalytic theory of male homosexuality.* New York: Simon and Schuster.

Lindner, R. L. (1946). Content analysis in Rorschach work. *Rorschach Research Exchange, 10*, 121–129.

Lorin, C. (1984), *Le jeune Ferenczi (The Young Ferenczi).* Paris: Aubier.

Luongo, M. (2008). Islamic war zones I have visited. *The Gay and Lesbian Review, 15*, 23–25.

MacIntosh, H. (1994). Attitudes and experiences of psychoanalysts in analyzing homosexual patients. *Journal of the American Psychoanalytic Association, 42*, 1183–1207.

Magee, M., & Miller, D. (1997). *Lesbian lives: Psychoanalytic narratives old and new.* Hillsdale, NJ: The Analytic Press.

Marisak, K. (1997). Psychotherapy of an AIDS patient with dementia. In: Blechner, M., ed., *Hope and Mortality: Psychodynamic Approaches to AIDS and HIV.* Hillsdale, NJ: The Analytic Press, pp. 133–142.

Marmor, J. (1942). The role of instinct in human behavior. *Psychiatry, 5*, 509–516.

_____ (1980). *Homosexual behavior: A modern reappraisal.* New York: Basic Books.

Maroda, K. (1997). Heterosexual displacements of homosexuality: Clinical implications. *Psychoanalytic Dialogues, 7*, 841–857.

Martin, D. (2008). Robert Skolrood obituary. *New York Times*, March 3, B7.

Martin, H. (1991). The coming-out process for homosexuals. *Hospital and Community Psychiatry, 42*, 158–162.

Mass, L. (1999). *Confessions of a Jewish Wagnerite: Being gay and Jewish in America.* London: Cassell.

McClary, S. (1993). Music and sexuality: On the Steblin/Solomon debate. *19th Century Music, 17*, 83–88.

_____ (1994). Constructions of subjectivity in Schubert's music. In P. Brett, E. Wood, & G. Thomas (Eds.), *Queering the pitch: The new gay and lesbian musicology.* New York: Routledge, pp. 205–233.

McDougall, J. (2001). Gender identity and creativity. *Journal of Gay and Lesbian Psychotherapy, 5*, 5–28.

Meketon, B., Griffith, R., Taylor, V., & Wiedman, J. (1962). Rorschach homosexual signs in paranoid schizophrenics. *Journal of Abnormal and Social Psychology, 65*, 280–284.

Mervis, C., & Rosch, E. (1981). Categorization of natural objects. *The Annual Review of Psychology, 32*, 89–115.

Miller, J. (1985). How Kohut actually worked. In A. Goldberg (Ed.), *Progress in self psychology* (Vol. 1, pp. 13–32). New York: Guilford.

Mitchell, S. (1978). Psychodynamics, homosexuality and the question of pathology. *Psychiatry, 41*, 254–263.

_____ (1981). The psychoanalytic treatment of homosexuality: Some technical considerations. *International Review of Psycho-Analysis, 8*, 63–80.

_____ (1992). Commentary of Trop and Stolorow's "Defense analysis in self psychology." *Psychoanalytic Dialogues, 2,* 443–453.

_____ (1996). Gender and sexual orientation in the age of postmodernism: The plight of the perplexed clinician. *Gender and Psychoanalysis, 1,* 45–73.

_____ (1997). Psychoanalysis and the degradation of romance, *Psychoanalytic Dialogues, 7,* 23–41.

_____ (2000). *Relationality: From attachment to intersubjectivity.* Hillsdale, NJ: The Analytic Press.

_____ (2002). *Can love last?* New York: Norton.

Monette, P. (1992). *Becoming a man.* New York: Harcourt Brace Jovanovich.

Money, J. (1986). *Lovemaps.* New York: Irvington.

_____ (1988). *Gay, straight, and in-between: The sexology of erotic orientation.* New York: Oxford University Press.

Money, J., & Ehrhardt, A. (1972). *Man and woman, boy and girl: The differentiation and dimorphism of gender identity from conception to maturity.* Baltimore, MD: Johns Hopkins University Press. Reprinted 1996, Northvale, NJ: Jason Aronson.

Money, J., Jobaris, R., & Furth, G. (1977). Apotemnophilia: Two cases of self-demand amputation as a paraphilia. *Journal of Sexual Research, 13,* 115–125.

Morin, J. (1995). *The erotic mind.* New York: Harper Collins.

_____ (1998). Clinical aspects of anal sexuality. Paper delivered to the joint conference of the Society for the Scientific Study of Sexuality and the American Association of Sex Educators, Counselors, and Therapists, Los Angeles, CA, November 11–15. Internet reference: http://www.sexuality.org/morin98.html.

Moss, D. (1992). Introductory thoughts: Hating in the first person plural: The example of homophobia. *American Imago, 49,* 277–291.

Mujica, E. (1997). When a patient becomes HIV-positive during psychotherapy. In M. Blechner (Ed.), *Hope and mortality* (pp. 193–207). Hillsdale, NJ: The Analytic Press.

Nagourney, A. (1995). Father doesn't know best. *Out,* February, 75–115.

New York Times (2006). For and against same-sex marriage at Maryland's highest court. December 5, A20.

Nussbaum, M. (2004). *Hiding from humanity: Disgust, shame, and the law.* Princeton, NJ: Princeton University Press.

Nyberg, K., & Alston, J. (1977). Homosexual labeling by university youths. *Adolescence, 12,* 541–546.

O'Leary, J. (1997). A heterosexual male therapist's journey of self discovery: Wearing a straight-jacket in a gay men's bereavement group. In M. Blechner (Ed.), *Hope and mortality* (pp. 209–220). Hillsdale, NJ: The Analytic Press.

Odets, W. (1995). *The shadow of the epidemic: Being negative in the age of AIDS.* Durham, NC: Duke University Press.

Orgel, S. (1996). *Impersonations: The performance of gender in Shakespeare's England.* Cambridge: Cambridge University Press.

Osborn, J. (1992). Interview with June Osborn. *The Advocate*, September 8, 40–43.

Otero, F., & Escardó, A. (1998). Sexuality in the age of AIDS. *International Journal of Psycho-Analysis. 79*, 136–139.

Ovesey, L. (1969). *Homosexuality and pseudohomosexuality*. New York: Science House.

Pawelski, J., Perrin, E., Foy, J., Allen, C., Crawford, J., DelMonte, M., Kaufman, M., Klein, J., Smith, K., Springer, S., Tanner, L., & Vickers, D. (2006). The effects of marriage, civil union, and domestic partnership laws on the health and well-being of children. *Pediatrics, 118*, 349–364.

Perry, H. (1982). *Psychiatrist of America: The life of Harry Stack Sullivan.* Cambridge, MA: Harvard University Press.

Person, E. (1980). Sexuality as the mainstay of identity: Psychoanalytic perspectives. *Signs: Journal of Women in Culture and Society, 5*, 605–630.

_____ (1988). *Dreams of love and fateful encounters: The power of romantic passion.* New York: Norton.

_____ (1995). *By force of fantasy*. New York: Basic Books.

_____ (2003). How to work through erotic transference. *Psychiatric Times, 20*, 29.

Petrucelli, J. (1997). "Playing with Fire": Transference-Countertransference configurations in the treatment of a sexually compulsive HIV-positive man. In M. Blechner (Ed.), *Hope and mortality* (pp. 143–161). Hillsdale, NJ: The Analytic Press,.

Pope, K. (1994). *Sexual involvement with therapists*. Washington, DC: American Psychological Association.

Quadland, M. (1985). Compulsive sexual behavior: Definition of a problem and an approach to treatment. *Journal of Sex and Marital Therapy*, 121–132.

Ramafedi, G., Farrow, J. A., & Delsher, R. W. (1989). Risk factors for attempted suicide in gay and bisexual youth. *Pediatrics, 87*, 869–875.

Randall, V. (2004). An early history—African American mental health. http://academic.udayton.edu/health/01status/mental01.htm

Raychauduri, M., & Mukerji, K. (1971). Rorschach differentials of homosexuality in male convicts: An examination of Wheeler and Schafer signs. *Journal of Personality Assessment, 35*, 22–26.

Read, C. (undated). "Harry Stack Sullivan: A Remembrance." Michael Allen Archive, p. 20.

Reitzell, J. (1945). A comparative study of hysterics, homosexuals, and alcoholics using content analysis of Rorschachs. *Rorschach Research Exchange, 9*, 169–177.

Richards, A. (1992). Commentary of Trop and Stolorow's "Defense analysis in self psychology." *Psychoanalytic Dialogues, 2*, 455–465.

Rosario, V. (2003). An interview with Judd Marmor, MD. *Journal of Gay and Lesbian Psychotherapy, 7*, 23–34.

Rosch, E. (1977). Human categorization. In N. Warren (Ed.), *Studies in cross-cultural psychology*. London: Academic.

Rosen, C. (1994). *The Frontiers of Meaning: Three Informal Lectures on Music.* New York: Hill and Wang.

Rothstein, E. (1992). Was Schubert gay? If he was, so what? Debate turns testy. *New York Times,* February 4, C11, C16.

Rowe, R. (1997). *Bert and Lori: Autobiography of a cross-dresser.* Amherst, NY: Prometheus Books.

Scasta, D. (2002). John E. Fryer, MD, and the Dr. H. Anonymous Episode. *Journal of Gay & Lesbian Psychotherapy. 6,* 73–84.

Schafer, R. (1954). *Psychoanalytic interpretation in Rorschach testing.* New York: Grune & Stratton.

_____ (1995). The evolution of my views on nonnormative sexual practices. In T. Domenici & R. Lesser (Eds.), *Disorienting sexuality* (pp. 187–202). New York: Routledge.

Schaffner, B. (1992). Recovering from the effects of hating and being hated. Presentation at the conference "The Experience of Hating and Being Hated," William Alanson White Psychoanalytic Society, November 18, 1992.

_____ (1995). The difficulty of being a gay psychoanalyst during the last 50 years. In T. Domenici & R. Lesser (Eds.), *Disorienting Sexuality* (pp. 243–254). New York: Routledge.

_____ (1948). *Fatherland: A study of authoritarianism in the German family.* New York: Columbia University Press.

Schwartz, D. (1993). Heterophilia—The love that dare not speak its aim. *Psychoanalytic Dialogues, 3,* 643–652.

Searles, H. (1959). Oedipal love in the countertransference. *International Journal of Psychoanalysis, 40,* 180–190.

Sedgwick, E. (1990). *Epistemology of the closet.* Berkeley: University of California Press.

Shah, D. (2005). US General Accounting Office. Defense of Marriage Act: update to prior (1997) report [letter to Bill Frist]. http://www.gao.gov/new.items/d04353r.pdf.

Shapiro, S. (1996). The embodied analyst in the Victorian consulting room. *Gender and Psychoanalysis, 1,* 297–322.

_____ (1997). There but for the Grace of …: Countertransference during the psychotherapy of a young HIV-positive woman. In M. Blechner (Ed.), *Hope and mortality* (pp. 115–131). Hillsdale, NJ: The Analytic Press.

Sheon, N., & Plant, A. (1997). Protease dis-inhibitors? The gay bareback phenomenon. ww.thebody.com/gay_men/txt/safer.html.

Sherby, L. (2009). Considerations on countertransference love. *Contemporary Psychoanalysis, 45*(1), 65–81.

Shore, K. (1998). Don't let them take your mind and spirit: On being called a "provider." Acceptance speech, Distinguished Psychologist of the Year, APA Division 42, February 7, La Jolla, CA.

Silverberg, W. (1938). The personal basis and social significance of passive homosexuality. *Psychiatry, 1,* 41–55.

Socarides, C. (1968). *The overt homosexual*. New York: Grune & Stratton.

Solomon, M. (1981). Franz Schubert's "My Dream." *American Imago, 38,* 137–154.

_____ (1989). Franz Schubert and the peacocks of Benvenuto Cellini. *19th Century Music, 12,* 193–206.

Stacey, J., & Biblarz, T. (2001). (How) Does the sexual orientation of parents matter? *American Sociological Review, 66,* 159–83.

Stoller, R. (1968). *Sex and gender: On the development of masculinity and femininity*. New York: Science House.

Stoller, R. (1979). *Sexual Excitement: Dynamics of Erotic Life*. New York: Pantheon Books.

Stolorow, D., and Trop, J. (1992). Reply to Richards and Mitchell. *Psychoanalytic Dialogues, 2,* 467–474.

Stone, L. (1954). On the principal obscene word of the English language (An inquiry, with hypothesis, regarding its origin and persistence). *International Journal of Psycho-Analysis, 35,* 30–56.

Streitmatter, R. (1998). *Empty without you: The intimate letters of Eleanor Roosevelt and Lorena Hickok*. New York: Free Press.

Sullivan, H. (1925). The oral complex. *Psychoanalytic Review, 12,* 31–38.

_____ (1926). Erogenous maturation. *Psychoanalytic Review, 13,* 1–15.

_____ (1927). Tentative criteria for malignancy in schizophrenia. *American Journal of Psychiatry, 84,* 759–782.

_____ (1938). Anti-Semitism. *Psychiatry, 1,* 593–598. Reprinted in: Sullivan, H. (1964). *The fusion of psychiatry and social science*. New York: Norton.

_____ (1940). *Conceptions of modern psychiatry*. New York: Norton.

_____ (1953). *The interpersonal theory of psychiatry*. New York: Norton.

_____ (1956). *Clinical studies in psychiatry*. New York: Norton.

_____ (1962). *Schizophrenia as a human process*. New York: Norton.

_____ (1964). The illusion of personal individuality. In *The fusion of psychiatry and social science*. New York: Norton.

_____ (1972). *Personal psychopathology*. New York: Norton.

Tabin, J. K. (1995). A note on homosexuality. *Round Robin*, September, 1.

Thompson, C. (1964). A study of the emotional climate of psychoanalytic institutes. In: Green, M., ed., *Interpersonal Psychoanalysis: The Selected Papers of Clara M. Thompson*. New York: Basic Books, 54–62.

Tripp, C. (1975). *The homosexual matrix*. New York: New American Library.

_____ (2005). *The intimate world of Abraham Lincoln*. New York: Free Press.

Troiden, R. (1988). Homosexual identity development. *Journal of Adolescent Health Care, 9,* 105–113.

Trop, J., & Stolorow, D. (1992). Defense analysis in self psychology: A developmental view. *Psychoanalytic Dialogues, 2,* 427–442.

Turnbull, D., & Brown, M. (1977). Attitudes toward homosexuality and male and female reactions to homosexual and heterosexual slides. *Canadian Journal of Behavioral Science, 9,* 68–80.

Ulett, G. (1950). *Rorschach introductory manual.* St. Louis, MO: Educational Publishers.

Verghese, A. (1994). *My own country.* New York: Simon & Schuster.

Voeller, B. (1991). AIDS and heterosexual anal intercourse. *Archives of Sexual Behavior, 20,* 233–276.

von Domarus, E. (1944). The specific laws of logic in schizophrenia. In J. S. Kasanin (Ed.), *Language and thought in schizophrenia* (pp. 104–114). New York: Norton.

von Hoffman, N. (1988). *Citizen Cohn.* New York: Doubleday.

Wagner, R. (1850). *Judaism in music.* In *Richard Wagner's Prose Works* (Vol. 3, W. Ellis, Trans.). Broude Brothers, 1966, pp. 75–122.

Wake, N. (2005). *Private practices: Harry Stack Sullivan, homosexuality, and the limits of psychiatric liberalism.* Ann Arbor, MI: ProQuest.

_____ (2006). The full story by no means all told: Harry Stack Sullivan at Sheppard-Pratt, 1922–1930. *History of Psychology, 9,* 325–358.

_____ (2008). On our memory of gay Sullivan: A hidden trajectory, *Journal of Homosexuality, 55,* 150–165.

Wakefield, J. (1992). The concept of mental disorder: On the boundary between biological facts and social values. *American Psychologist, 47,* 373–388.

Washington, R. A. (1995). The challenge for behavior science assisting AIDS service organizations to do HIV prevention work. *Psychology and AIDS Exchange,* Fall 1995, 3–4.

Weininger, O. (1903). *Sex and character.* London: Heinemann.

Wheeler, M. (1949). An analysis of Rorschach indices of male homosexuality. *Rorschach Research Exchange, 13,* 97–126.

White, K. (2002). Surviving hating and being hated: Some personal thoughts about racism from a psychoanalytic perspective. *Contemporary Psychoanalysis, 38,* 401–422.

Whitney, C. (1990). *Uncommon lives: Gay men and straight men.* New York: New American Library.

Wilson, D., & Davis, R. (Eds.), (1998). *Herndon's informants: Letters, interviews, and statements about Abraham Lincoln.* Chicago: University of Illinois Press.

Winston, R., ed. (1971). *Letters of Thomas Mann.* New York: Knopf.

Wittgenstein, L. (1953). *Philosophical investigations.* New York: Macmillan.

Wolstein, B. (1981). The psychic realism of psychoanalytic inquiry. *Contemporary Psychoanalysis, 17,* 399–412.

Wortis, J. (1954). *Fragments of an analysis with Freud.* New York: Simon & Schuster.

Yamahiro, R. & Griffith, R. (1960). Validity of two indices of sexual deviancy. *Journal of Clinical Psychology, 16,* 21–24.

Zhang, S.-D., & Odenwald, W. F. (1995). Misexpression of the white (w) gene triggers male-male courtship in *Drosophila. Proceedings of the National Academy of Sciences, USA, 92,* 5525–5529.

Zilbergeld, B. (1978). *Male sexuality.* New York: Bantam Books.

Index